*1998 Edition*

# Guide to Accreditation

*by the*
*National Association*
*for the Education*
*of Young Children*

*1998 Edition*

# Guide to Accreditation

*by the*
*National Association*
*for the Education*
*of Young Children*

Self-Study

Validation

Accreditation

National Association for the Education of Young Children
1509 16th Street, N.W., Washington, DC 20036-1426

*Photographs*
Cleo Photography, *127*
Bob Ebbesen Photography, 19
Jean-Claude Lejeune, *1, 7, 51, 99, 143*
Toni H. Liebman, *253*
Marilyn Nolt, *271*
Vme Edom Smith, *277*
Christina Tolomei, *295*

Design/production—Melanie Rose White

Copies of Guide to Accreditation by the National Association for the Education of Young Children are available from NAEYC, 1509 16th Street, N.W., Washington, DC 20036-1426.

Library of Congress Catalog Card Number: 85-60990
ISBN 0-935989-89-7
NAEYC #916

Printed in the United States of America.

# Contents

# *Welcome to accreditation . . .*

- The *Guide to Accreditation* is a compilation of all the self-study materials. It is designed to "guide" your program through the three-step process.

- Don't be alarmed by the size of this book. It contains copies of all the forms that are sent to the program separately in quantity. Fewer than 50 pages of this book are directions for conducting the self-study and completing the forms. The rest of this book is copies of the forms.

- Start by reading Sections 1 and 2 (pages 1 through 17). The task will seem much easier if you do.

- The Academy staff are available as a resource. Feel free to contact us if you need assistance by calling 800-424-2460 or 202-328-2601.

# *Foreword*

The National Association for the Education of Young Children's (NAEYC) accreditation system has been in operation since 1985. From its inception the accreditation system has been based on the concept of collaboration. The development of NAEYC's Criteria for High-Quality Early Childhood Programs reflects the collaboration of early childhood program administrators, teachers, parents, researchers, teacher educators, and policy makers from all 50 states and several foreign countries. In addition, the system has undergone two major revisions drawing on our experience administering the system and the input of thousands of early childhood professionals who continue to collaborate with the association to ensure that the standards reflect current research and practice in early childhood education.

This collaborative effort is further reflected in the accreditation process itself. The most important element in the accreditation system is the early childhood program's self-study, which is an opportunity for everyone in the program—the administrators, teachers, teacher assistants, parents, and even the children—to work togetjer to evaluate and improve the program. The next step is the on-site visit which is condubed by a validator—an early childhood professional whose role is to verify the program personnel's report of their own compliance with the Criteria. The system incorporates a self-study/valdiation process because NAEYC and the Academy believe that for real and lasting program improvement to result, it must be initiated from within the program, not be outside evaluators. The final step in the process, the accrediation decision, is another collaborative effort. The accreditation decision is not based on achieving a certain number of points. Accreditation decisions are made by a combination of internal and external Commission review, drawing on the diverse geographic, programmatic, and experiential backgrounds in applying professional judgment to the decision-making process.

The goal of the accreditation system is to improve the quality of care and education provided for young children in group programs. All children who participate in group programs must not only be safe and protected but must have the opportunity to experience an evnironment that enhances children's development. Achieving high-quality programs for all chidlren cannot be accomplished by inspecting centers, approving some and failing others. This goal of achieving high-quality programs can be met only by providing programs with an incentive to improve and by providing resources and referrals to facilitate this improvement. For the accreditation project to achieve its goals, the entire early childhood community must work in the spirit of collaboration on which the system is founded.

What does accreditation mean for the field of early childhood education? Accreditation assists families in making decisions about their children's care and education. Accreditation offers agencies, employers, and other program supporters a system for identifying high-quality programs. Accreditation provides program directors and teachers with guidelines for professional practice.

The existence of a national, voluntary accreditation system for early childhood programs is a major step toward the professionalization of the field of early childhood education. The standards for accreditation were developed by the early chilhdood profession. They represent the current consensus on what defines a high-quality program for young children. The accreditation system is the early childhood profession's definition of its standards for high-quality programs and its recognition of those programs that provide high-quality care and education for young children.

Just as the growth of a child is a gradual, developmental process, the implementation of a new concept or system needs fostering and time. The accreditation system of the National Association for the Education of Young Children is dynamic and will grow and develop over time. Just as families take great pride in the developmental strides of young children, the self-esteem and public perception of the early childhood profession is enhanced by the existence of the Academy's accreditation system for high-quality early childhood programs.

–Sue Bredekamp
*NAEYC Director of Professional Development*
*and Accreditation*

# Definitions

**Academy**—the department of the National Association for the Education of Young Children (NAEYC) that administers the accreditation system.

**Administrator**—person most responsible for the on-site, ongoing, daily supervision of the program and staff (for example, the administrator may be a principal in a public school or an education coordinator in a Head Start program). The terms *administrator* and *director* are used interchangeably throughout these materials.

**Chief administrative officer**—person legally responsible for the business operation of the program. This person may or may not be the same person who directs the daily implementation of the program including the supervision of staff and curriculum.

**Commissioners**—early childhood professionals who are appointed by the NAEYC Governing Board to join NAEYC staff in making accreditation decisions.

**Components**—aspects of an early childhood program that are evaluated. The Criteria address 10 components of an early childhood program: Interactions among Staff and Children, Curriculum, Relationships among Teachers and Families, Staff Qualifications and Professional Development, Administration, Staffing, Physical Environment, Health and Safety, Nutrition and Food Service, and Evaluation.

**Criteria**—standards by which the components of an early childhood program are judged. The complete list of NAEYC's Criteria for High Quality Early Childhood Programs with interpretations appears in the green book, *Accreditation Criteria & Procedures of the National Association for the Education of Young Children.*

**Criterion**—singular form of *criteria*.

**Director**—person who directs the daily implementation of the program including the supervision of staff and curriculum. See definition of *administrator*.

**Early childhood**—birth through 8 years of age.

**Early Childhood Classroom Observation**—observation form used by teachers, directors, and validators to determine how well each group or classroom meets the criteria that are assessed through observations.

**Group**—children assigned to a staff member or team of staff members occupying an individual classroom or well-defined physical space within a larger room.

**Indicators**—important points to look for in rating the quality of an early childhood classroom using the NAEYC's *Early Childhood Classroom Observation.*

**Infants***—children between the ages of birth and 12 months.

**Kindergartners**—children who are attending public or private kindergarten.

**NAEYC**—National Association for the Education of Young Children. The nation's largest early childhood professional membership association for early childhood educators.

**Parent/guardian**—legal custodian of the child in the program.

**Preschoolers***—children from 3 through 5 years of age.

**Program**—part-day and full-day group programs in schools and other facilities serving a minimum of 10 children from the age of birth through 5 years and/or school-age children before and/or after school. The terms *center* and *program* are used interchangeably through these materials.

**Program Description**—form programs use to report their compliance with the NAEYC's Criteria for validation and accreditation decisions.

**School-agers***—children attending first grade or beyond who are participating in a before- and/or after-school program.

**Teachers/teaching staff**—paid adults who have direct responsibilities for the care and education of the children.

**Toddlers***—children between the ages of 13 months and 35 months.

**Validator**—early childhood professional who conducts the on-site validation visit to verify the accuracy of the Program Description.

**Volunteer**—nonpaid individual who spends time in the classroom interacting with the children.

*When using these materials in programs serving children with special needs, it may be necessary to use developmental levels rather than chronological ages to assess the appropriateness of programming.

# Section 1

## Introduction to
## *Guide to Accreditation*

# Section 1

## Introduction to *Guide to Accreditation*

The purpose of the NAEYC accreditation system is to improve the quality of care and education provided for young children in group programs in the United States. The NAEYC accomplishes this purpose by developing training resources, by providing public information about the importance of high-quality early childhood programs, and by accrediting those programs that voluntarily demonstrate substantial compliance with the NAEYC's Criteria for High-Quality Early Childhood Programs.

**The accreditation process involves three steps:**

**Step 1**—Program personnel conduct a self-study to determine how well the program meets the NAEYC's Criteria, make needed improvements, and report the compliance with the Criteria in the Program Description.

**Step 2**—Validators make an on-site visit to verify the accuracy of the Program Description.

**Step 3**—Commissioners consider the validated Program Description and make the accreditation decision.

**How to use the *Guide to Accreditation***

This book is designed to help program personnel through the accreditation process. In this book you will find instructions and materials for conducting an in-depth self-study of an early childhood program, including sample copies of the

- Early Childhood Classroom Observation,
- Administrator Report,
- Teaching-Staff Questionnaire,
- Open-Ended Teaching-Staff Survey,
- Family Questionnaire,
- Open-Ended Family Survey, and
- Program Description.

These materials are used during the self-study and in reporting your results. Multiple copies of these materials are provided to programs along with the self-study materials. The Open-Ended Teaching-Staff Survey and Open-Ended Family Survey can be photocopied from the *Guide* for use during the self-study.

> The *Guide* is designed by sections to help you through the accreditation process. Each section contains a purpose, directions for use, and a sample document. The *Guide* is a workbook and may be photocopied for the purpose of self-study. A table of contents is provided for ease in locating sections.

This book is meant to be used with the green book, *Accreditation Criteria & Procedures of the National Association for the Education of Young Children*. In the green book you will find the complete list of the NAEYC's Criteria for High-Quality Early Childhood Programs with interpretations. The Criteria are the basis for the entire accreditation system. If at any time a criterion needs clarification, please use the green book as a reference. Criteria are always referred to by the same letter and number.

The Criteria address all components of a high-quality early childhood program:
- Interactions among Teachers and Children,
- Curriculum,
- Relationships among Teachers and Families,
- Staff Qualifications and Development,
- Administration,
- Staffing,
- Physical Environment,
- Health and Safety,
- Nutrition and Food Service, and
- Evaluation.

The children are a valuable resource as participants in the self-study. The primary purpose of the self-study is to examine the quality of life experienced by children in the program. Therefore, children are observed and, if old enough, should be consulted so that you gain an accurate understanding of what it is like to be a child in the program.

Early childhood personnel who choose to work toward accreditation for their programs demonstrate a professional commitment to self-evaluation and self-improvement. Programs accredited by the NAEYC achieve professional and public recognition as providers of high-quality care and education for young children. We commend you for your commitment and look forward to working with you through the accreditation process.

**Where do we begin?**

This guide is designed to help you through the self-study and validation. As with anything new, it may seem complicated at first, but it will become clearer with experience. Familiarize yourself with the tasks before presenting the concepts to staff members. Break down each task into parts and establish dates to serve as goals for completing each step. The chart on pages 15 to 17 will help.

Remember that although the Academy requires certain steps in the self-study, you should not be limited by those requirements. Depending on the unique features of your program, you may want to introduce other elements such as participation by board members who may be asked to evaluate the program using the Administrator Report.

Some programs are housed in or affiliated with religious institutions; these programs may wish to conduct a self-study of the relationship between the church/synagogue and the early childhood program. An excellent resource to assist this study is available from NAEYC and the Ecumenical Child Care Network of the National Council of *Churches—Congregations and Child Care: A Self-Study for Churches and Synagogues and Their Early Childhood Programs.* The process described in this book would also be helpful for examining the relationship between any early childhood program and the larger institution that governs it, such as in the case of programs related to colleges and universities, hospitals, or other employer-sponsored programs. The Bureau of Jewish Education of Greater Los Angeles has also published a resource—*Manual for Jewish School Accreditation*—specifically designed for Jewish Community Centers and accreditation. For more information, write to 5700 Wilshire Boulevard, Suite 2710, Los Angeles, CA 90036.

The potential benefits of the self-study/accreditation process will be achieved only if each program individualizes the process to its own needs and strengths. Be as creative as you like in examining your program and, if something works particularly well, share your ideas with the Academy so that other directors may benefit.

---

**Always keep sight of your goal—to provide the best quality program for young children and their families.**

# Section 2

## How to Do the Self-Study

# Section 2
## How to Do the Self-Study

**What is the self-study?**

The self-study is a comprehensive and internal evaluation of all aspects of the early childhood program.

**How is the self-study used?**

The self-study is used by program personnel to systematically evaluate their program and identify strengths and areas in need of improvement. After improvements are made, the results are reported to the Academy for use in validation and making accreditation decisions.

**What are the benefits of the self-study?**

Taking an objective look at the program as it operates today is the first step toward making the improvements you need. One way to take an honest look is through the self-study. The self-study helps program staff and administrators analyze the strengths and weaknesses of the program, focus attention on areas in need of improvement, and also congratulate themselves for achieving and maintaining those areas that are clearly strengths.

The self-study can have many benefits. The self-study process can be a unifying force for a staff. A "we're-all-in-this-together" feeling can result as long as the self-study process is applied to the roles and responsibilities of all staff members—including the administrators! Emphasizing the common goal of improving the quality of the program can create a feeling of professionalism among the staff that is very stimulating. Also, any improvements in operating procedures, although the changes take time and effort, undoubtedly will result in an improved service for children and families.

There are two ways to look at the self-study. It is similar to making a videotape of all things that happen in your program. It can be threatening. It can also be an exciting and revealing experience. Because it is a *self-study, you* are making the videotape and *you* are deciding who will see it and when it will be seen. Focusing on the potential for staff development, personal and professional growth, and an improved program for children and families will help the director and staff view self-study as an opportunity.

**How should the self-study be conducted?**

The self-study will be done by a variety of programs serving different populations and having different funding sources. As a result, the way in which the self-study is conducted will vary. Some programs have a large staff and many children, while others may serve fewer than 20 with a very small staff. This guide describes the steps required of all programs participating in the process. Staff can be as creative as possible in adding other dimensions. There is no one right way to do the self-study. However, programs find the process more beneficial when the following approach is taken.

**What is the most constructive way to conduct the self-study?**

- The director, staff, and board (if applicable) decide to undergo the accreditation process.
- Director delegates responsibilities and tasks and engages all staff in the process.
- Staff members give careful consideration and self-examination in evaluation.
- Staff members receive acknowledgment and praise for things they are doing well and receive constructive feedback and are part of the solution for criteria that can be improved.
- Parents are viewed as a valuable resource and encouraged to participate.
- Children are closely observed; measuring criteria from their experience.
- Adequate time is taken for the self-study process to reflect on and make necessary improvements.
- The process is viewed as an opportunity to collaborate with staff, grow professionally, and improve the quality of the program.

**Who does the self-study?**

The self-study is designed to involve all participants in an early childhood program—the administrators, teachers, assistants, parents, volunteers, and even the children themselves. The word *self* refers to each person's involvement in examining her or his own contribution to the program.

The person responsible for coordinating the self-study varies by setting. Throughout the *Guide* we refer to this person as "Director." The person responsible might be a principal, trainer, or early childhood coordinator.

**What resources are provided to assist you with the self-study?**

The *Guide* is designed to be comprehensive to assist you and your staff with the accreditation process. Academy staff can be contacted for assistance by e-mail at academy@naeyc.org or by calling NAEYC toll-free at **800-424-2460.** We recognize that the process may seem less overwhelming if you can talk to someone that has been through the process and achieved accreditation. Visit http://www.naeyc.org/accreditation/accred_index.htm for a list of accredited programs in your area. Many directors would be willing to share their experience with you and your staff. In addition, the Academy has trained NAEYC Liaisons to help facilitate the process. They are not consultants but are available to help you understand the three-step process and encourage your involvement. Finally, the Academy maintains a list of Networking Projects that includes supported accreditation projects throughout the country. You can contact the Academy to learn if there are any projects in your community that you may be eligible to be involved.

## How long will it take?

The self-study is designed to be self-directed, the program may take as much time as needed, but most programs average between 9 and 12 months to complete the self-study. If programs don't move ahead with the self-study process within one year, they will not likely complete the self-study . The length of time is determined by the program and the improvements that staff wish to make. A task and timeline chart is provided on pages 15 to 17.

> Regardless of how much time the staff take to get ready, **the information that is sent to the Academy in the Program Description must be current and should reflect the existing situation,** not what it was when the self-study began, nor what the staff plan to do in the future.

## What are the steps in the self-study?

These steps need to take place during the self-study. (See the NAEYC Accreditation Self-Study Flowchart on page 14.)

**Step 1—Introduce the concept to staff and families.** The self-study process is initiated and controlled by the administrator. Admittedly, the self-study involves a significant commitment of time and effort by the director. But it cannot be a solitary effort. For the self-study to be successful, it must involve all the people who are likely to be affected—the staff members and parents—as soon as possible. The initial presentation of the concept to the staff is particularly important. Whenever evaluation is implied, people can be threatened. Therefore, it is important for the director to let staff know how important work with young children is and commend them for their commitment to children and evaluation. Having their program accredited will help them get recognition for the high-quality program they provide. Of course, the self-study will also identify aspects of the program that they may wish to change or improve, but they will be active participants in the evaluation process.

**Step 2—Collect information about the program from various sources including at least**

a. Observations of each classroom or specific grouping in the program. Each classroom should be observed and rated using the **Early Childhood Classroom Observation** by the teachers, assistants, and the director (or appropriate person such as the education coordinator or a board member).

b. Evaluation of the administrative criteria by the director using the **Administrator Report.**

c. Evaluation of the program by the staff using the **Teaching-Staff Questionnaire.**

d. Evaluation of the program by parents using the **Family Questionnaire.**

Specific suggestions and directions for completing each of these parts of the self-study are presented in each section of the *Guide*.

**Step 3—Plan for improvement and make changes where needed.** If the self-study process is thorough, it will uncover both strengths and weaknesses of the program. Administrators and staff will identify aspects of the program where change is needed. It is likely that two different kinds of changes may be needed: (1) physical or technical changes, such as developing new procedures or rearranging classrooms, and (2) social or behavioral changes, such as implementing a more developmentally appropriate curriculum or developing better communication with families, more cooperative staff relations, or more positive and supportive relations with children. In some situations, both kinds of changes are involved. For instance, clearly written program policies will facilitate parent communication to some extent, but they cannot replace personal contact.

Because it is often easier to make physical or technical changes, those changes could be made first. For example, it is relatively easy to rearrange materials and furniture or to write clear personnel policies. If the technical changes can be implemented successfully, a positive foundation for improvement will be established. Then the potentially more difficult social or curricular changes can be undertaken.

Making improvements in your program can be a challenging process. Here are some pointers to help you overcome the most common obstacles to change in early childhood programs:

● **Recognize that change is stressful.**

Change can be a source of stress for people even when the change is a desirable one. But change is most stressful when the people involved do not control the change or do not participate in it. To minimize the stress, be sure to acknowledge the difficulties. Work together with the staff to establish priorities, suggest alternatives, try solutions, and agree on systems that work best in your program. Remember that for change to be real and lasting, the people who are most affected by the change must participate in it.

● **Recognize which change requires resources, and use limited resources wisely and carefully.**

Too often, early childhood program personnel say that they could provide a much better program if only they had more money. It is true that some change is financially impossible. For example, equipping a playground or expanding indoor space may be prohibitively expensive. However, many aspects of the program can be improved without additional expense. For instance, it does not cost more money to speak kindly to children and to treat them with respect than it does to be harsh and punitive. However, to bring about such change in staff behavior some additional staff training may be needed, for which funds may be limited. Do not overlook the many effective, low-cost training strategies now available. Many local NAEYC Affiliate Groups provide training and resources related to providing a high-quality early childhood program. Resource and referral agencies also maintain listings of resources that would be beneficial to you and your staff. Contact NAEYC's Membership Department if you need assistance locating your Affiliate Group or your local resource and referral agency.

● **Change the things you can.**

There will be aspects of the program that are easy to improve and some aspects that are difficult to change. For example, keeping better records of staff training is relatively easy to do and does not cost money, but correcting a problem playground may involve additional funding that is not available. **The important thing to remember is that the accreditation process does not require 100% compliance with all the Criteria.** Also, you will have the opportunity to indicate how you meet the Criteria a different way. For instance, you may develop alternative plans to provide a good outdoor play experience for children. Many of the Criteria can be met in different ways.

● **Decide whether to seek accreditation.**

Once you have made the improvements you wish to make and feel that you meet the Criteria as best you can, then you need to decide whether to go on and seek accreditation for the program. You are not committed to doing so and may decide that the self-study was sufficient to meet your personal goals for program evaluation and improvement. But don't try to be perfect; accreditation is awarded for substantial compliance with the Criteria. If you decide to seek accreditation, your next step is to use the information you learned during the self-study to complete the Program Description. See **How to Prepare Your Program Description** on page 143.

**Step 4—Prepare your Program Description for use in the validation and accreditation decision process.** After improvements are made, the results are reported to the Academy on the Program Description form. A sample copy of the Program Description appears in Section 7 of the *Guide.* A Program Description is sent with the self-study materials to complete and return to the Academy.

The Program Description form is designed to ensure uniformity in reporting and to facilitate use by validators and commissioners making accreditation decisions. The Program Description has three parts:

● Part 1 is the Center Profile that provides general information about how the program is staffed and organized.
● Part 2 presents the program's compliance with the criteria that are observed using the Classroom Observation.
● Part 3 presents the program's compliance with the administrative criteria that are assessed by the director. Some of the administrative criteria are also assessed by the staff and/or families on the questionnaires.

Specific directions for completing the Program Description appear in Section 7 of the *Guide.* The Academy recommends that you do not fill in the Program Description form that is sent to you with the self-study materials until the program is ready to request a validation visit. **The information on the Program Description must be current (within three months) to ensure an accurate validation.**

# NAEYC Accreditation Self-Study Flowchart

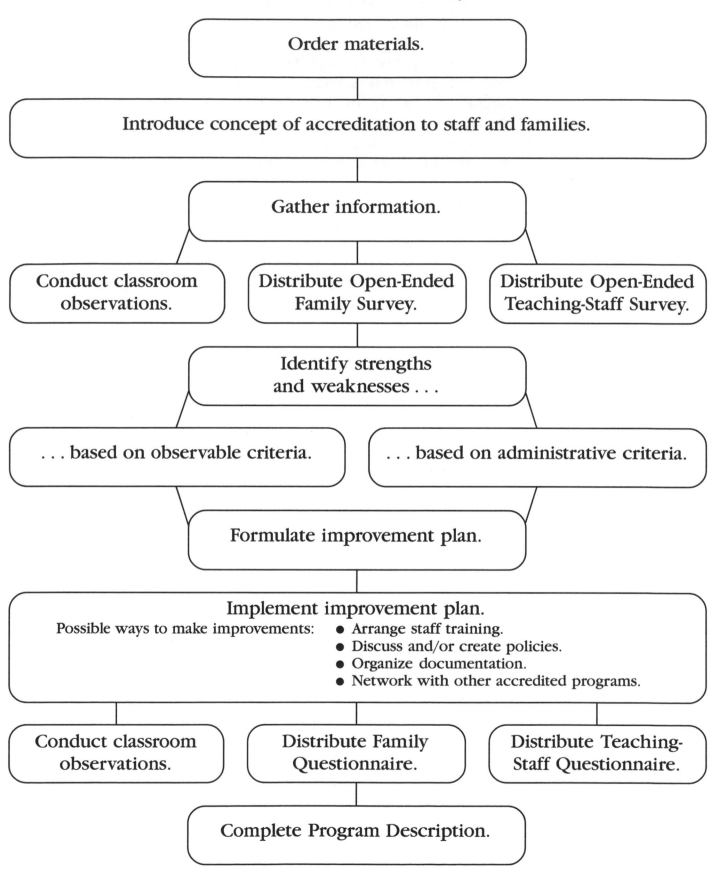

Order materials.

Introduce concept of accreditation to staff and families.

Gather information.

Conduct classroom observations.

Distribute Open-Ended Family Survey.

Distribute Open-Ended Teaching-Staff Survey.

Identify strengths and weaknesses . . .

. . . based on observable criteria.

. . . based on administrative criteria.

Formulate improvement plan.

Implement improvement plan.
Possible ways to make improvements:
- Arrange staff training.
- Discuss and/or create policies.
- Organize documentation.
- Network with other accredited programs.

Conduct classroom observations.

Distribute Family Questionnaire.

Distribute Teaching-Staff Questionnaire.

Complete Program Description.

# Task and Timeline Chart

The purpose of this chart is to help program directors develop their own individualized plan for completing all the self-study tasks. Fill in the names of the people responsible for each task, and also identify dates to serve as goals for completing each task.

| Tasks | Person(s) responsible | Goal dates |
|---|---|---|

**Orientation**
- Review the *Guide* and instructions.

  Director (or person responsible for coordinating the self-study)*

- Meet with staff to go over project and give instructions.

  Director*

**Self-study and program improvement**
- Observe and rate each classroom using Classroom Observation Form.

  Staff observe and rate their own classrooms.

- Observe and rate each classroom using Classroom Observation Form.

  Director* observes and rates each classroom

- Meet with individual staff to discuss results and plan for improvement.

  Director*

- Evaluate program using Administrator Report as your workbook.

  Director*

- Collect information on Staffing and Staff Qualifications to summarize on Center Profile.

  Director*

- Staff evaluate program using Teaching-Staff Questionnaire as a guide. (Use staff meetings, interviews, and Open-Ended Teaching-Staff Survey on pages 121 to 125 for discussion.)

  Director*

- Evaluate criteria related to parents using Family Questionnaire as a guide. (Use parent meetings, interviews, Open-Ended Family Survey on pages 139 to 142 for discussion.)

  Director*, staff member, and/or parent(s) assigned to this task.

*The person responsible for coordinating the self-study varies by setting and could be a trainer, principal, early childhood coordinator, or other qualified staff member.

- Other tasks you wish to add to study and improve your program.

_____    _____    _____

_____    _____    _____

_____    _____    _____

_____    _____    _____

_____    _____    _____

_____    _____    _____

## Program Description

- Meet with individual staff to decide on agreed-upon ratings on Observation form to be reported to Academy on Classroom Observation Summary Sheet. **(These ratings will take place after improvements have been made.)**

  Director*

- Tabulate results of Classroom Observation Summary Sheet and compute average ratings.

  Director*

- Distribute Teaching-Staff Questionnaire to staff.

  Director*

- Complete Teaching-Staff Questionnaire.

  Each staff member who works directly with children.

- Summarize Results of Teaching-Staff Questionnaire on Summary Sheet.

  Director*

- Distribute Family Questionnaire to parents. (Request return within three days or ask that the questionnaire be completed at the program. At least a 50% return rate is required for validation.

  Staff members

- Remind parents to return questionnaire. (Post notice or send home reminder.)

  Staff members

- Summarize results of Family Questionnaire on Summary Sheet.

  Director* or parent or staff member assigned to this task.

- Compile Program Description using Administrator Report and Center Profile and summary sheets of
  (1) Classroom Observation,
  (2) Teaching-Staff Questionnaire, and
  (3) Family Questionnaire.

  Director* _____   _____

- **Photocopy the completed Program Description.**

  Director* _____   _____

- **Mail Program Description, Classroom Observation Summary Sheet, and payment (check, money order, purchase order, VISA, or MasterCard) for validation fee to the Academy in envelope provided.** Do not send Family and Teaching-Staff Questionnaires or their Summary Sheets but keep those for the validation visit. **Use certified or registered mail.**

  Director* _____   _____

**Mail your Program Description in time to allow the Academy at least 40 working days (8 to 10 weeks) from the time we receive it to arrange your validation visit.**

# Section 3

## Early Childhood Classroom Observation

### Directions for use
### Sample Observation
### Sample summary sheet

# Section 3

## Early Childhood
## Classroom Observation

**What is the purpose
of the Early
Childhood
Classroom
Observation?**

Many of NAEYC's Criteria for High-Quality Early Childhood Programs relate to what happens to children in classrooms. **To determine how well a program meets those criteria, observations of individual classrooms (or groups) must be done.** The Early Childhood Classroom Observation includes only the criteria from the complete list that are to be observed in each classroom. The Observation form is a three-point rating scale. The letters and numbers of the items on the Observation form refer to the complete list of Criteria in the green book. Sometimes the exact wording of the item differs because the language has been changed to make the item more observable.

## Directions for use

**Who uses the Early
Childhood
Classroom
Observation?**

All staff that work directly with children use the form to observe and rate the quality of her or his own classroom (or clearly defined group of children). The director (or other appropriate person) observes and rates each classroom independently. A sample copy of the Early Childhood Classroom Observation begins on page 25 of the *Guide*. Multiple copies of the Observation form are sent with the self-study materials. Directions appear on the Observation form.

**When is the
Observation done?**

Teaching staff should take some time to become familiar with the Observation form before they begin to observe and rate their classroom. Because teachers cannot observe their own behavior, they will have to think about what they usually do before they can assign a rating. **(For example, "Do I speak to children at their level and call on children by their names?")** The Observation takes about an hour and a half to complete. **Teachers may use the Observation form numerous times throughout the self-study.**

The director (or other appropriate administrator) also observes and rates each classroom. Teachers may want to make improvements in their classrooms before they are observed by the director. The director's observation should be done during the peak period of activity while the children are present (usually the morning hours). In addition, the director should spend time observing throughout the day to obtain an understanding of the children's experience. For example, observe early morning to see arrival, transitions, snack and/or meals, rest times, and late afternoon departures. **In full-day programs, the director should return to the classroom in the afternoon to observe how the quality of interaction is maintained throughout the day.**

**How are the results used?**

- Teaching staff and the director should independently observe and rate the classroom.
- Teaching staff and director should compare their ratings, identify strengths and weaknesses, and develop a plan for making needed improvements.

The process of comparing ratings can be a positive, developmental experience or it can be threatening for teachers, depending on how it is handled. Write down the staff's and director's ratings for each item. There will probably be more agreements than disagreements. Begin by pointing out how many times you both agreed and by commenting on the aspects of the classroom that rated most highly. Where differences arise in ratings, the director begins by explaining why she rated the item as she did. For instance, "I gave it a 2 because during the time I observed I saw you interacting very positively with children, but your attention was taken up with Jamie and Anton." This type of communication, where the director describes what she saw from her own point of view is easier for the teacher to accept than a more accusing message that might make the teacher feel defensive. For example, compare the earlier statement with this one that is based on the same observation, "You obviously prefer Jamie and Anton to the other children because you spend all your time talking to Jamie and Anton while ignoring the rest of the group."

Sometimes ratings of teachers and directors will not be the same because a criterion is interpreted differently. When there is a difference in a rating, one way of resolving the situation is to refer to the green book which has the complete statement of the criterion and its interpretation, or refer to NAEYC's *Developmentally Appropriate Practice in Early Childhood Programs Serving Children From Birth Through Age 8 (Revised Edition),* edited by Sue Bredekamp and Carol Copple.

**How often can the classroom observations be completed?**

This process can be completed as many times as the program would like. Once staff have made the improvements they wish to make, the director and teachers agree on a rating for each criterion to report for that classroom on the Classroom Observation Summary Sheet. **The agreed upon rating for each criterion must be a whole number: a 3, 2, or 1.**

**How are the results reported on the Program Description?**

Observations provide a great deal of information about each classroom. However, the accreditation applies to the entire program, not the individual teachers. Therefore, the results of observations are averaged across classrooms and the average score is reported as the program rating for the criteria that are observed. For example, out of three classrooms in a program, two may have excellent materials rating a [3], and one may lack some variety, rating a [2]. The score on the materials criterion would be a 2.7 (3 + 3 + 2 = 8. 8 ÷ 3 = 2.7).

A summary sheet for the observation is provided to help the director tabulate the program's average ratings. Only the average ratings are reported by the director (or other qualified staff member) on Part 2 of the Program Description. A sample Summary Sheet appears on pages 49 and 50 of the *Guide*. A blank copy of the Classroom Observation Summary Sheet with space for reporting the consensus rating between the teacher and director for each group is sent with the self-study materials. For example, if the program has three groups, you should complete three rows—one for each group.

**How is the Classroom Observation Summary Sheet filled out?**

Copy the ratings for each classroom. These ratings will be the ratings agreed upon by the teacher and director after improvements are made. **They must be a whole number, either a 3, 2, or 1.** Total the ratings across all classrooms and record the sum total for each criterion. Divide the sum total by the number of observations to get the average rating across classrooms for each criterion. (Space is also provided to calculate an average total score for each classroom. However, this information is not needed by the Academy and is included for your use only.) **See the sample Summary Sheet on pages 49 and 50 of the *Guide.***

---

### Summary of Classroom Observation procedures

- Teaching staff and director independently rate the classroom.

- Teaching staff and director compare ratings and develop a plan for making needed improvements.

- Implement improvement plan.

- Teaching staff and director meet again to decide upon ratings to assign for each criterion.

- Classroom observation ratings are reported on Classroom Observation Summary Sheet.

- Center rating is completed by using the Classroom Observation Summary Sheet to determine average rating for each criterion.

- Classroom Observation Summary Sheet is mailed to the Academy along with the completed Program Description and validation fee when the program is ready for the validation visit.

---

Program ID Number

# Early Childhood Classroom Observation

Group or classroom being observed _____

Names of teaching staff _____

Number of children present _____ Number of paid staff present _____

Number of children enrolled _____ Ratio of paid staff to children _____

Number of children with diagnosed disabilities _____

Number of volunteers _____

Age range of children enrolled in group—youngest to oldest (in years/months) _____

Person observing    ❑ Teacher    ❑ Director    ❑ Validator _____
                                                                    (Name)

Observation date _____    Time began _____    Time completed _____

## Instructions

**What is the purpose of this form?**

This form is to help you observe and rate the level of quality of your early childhood program. Each item is related to NAEYC's Criteria for High-Quality Early Childhood Programs. The letters and numbers to the left of each item refer to a specific criterion that is found in *Accreditation Criteria & Procedures of the National Association for the Education of Young Children.*

**Who uses this form?**

All staff that work directly with children use the form to observe and rate the quality of her or his own classroom (or clearly defined group of children). The director (or other appropriate person) observes and rates each classroom independently. The teachers and director should discuss their ratings after each completes the form. After improvements are made the teachers and director agree on a rating to record on the Classroom Observation Summary Sheet. The validator also uses this form to observe during the validation visit.

**How do I use this form?**

Each boldface-numbered statement on the left side of the page is the criterion to be rated. Many criteria are followed by a list of indicators that *must* be considered in the rating. Indicators (important points to look for) are listed next to a box ❑.

Put a check mark in the box as you observe the indicator. Examples are sometimes provided to help define the Criteria. These specific examples do not have to be observed, but something similar should be seen. Rate each criterion using the following scale:

| [1]<br>Not met | [2]<br>Partially met | [3]<br>Fully met |
| --- | --- | --- |
| The criterion is not met.<br><br>There is **little evidence** that this statement accurately describes the program.<br><br>The behavior happens rarely or seldom. | The criterion is partially met.<br><br>There is **some evidence** that this statement accurately describes the program.<br><br>The behavior happens some of the time. | The criterion is completely met. There is a **great deal** of evidence that this statement accurately describes the program throughout the day.<br><br>The behavior happens most of the time.<br><br>For a criterion to rate a [3], all indicators (❑) related to the age group being observed must be present. (It is possible for all indicators to be present without rating the criterion a [3].) |

Rate each criterion by circling one of the numbers: [1] or [2] or [3]. **All criteria rated less than a [3] must have a written comment.** Explain your ratings under the "Comments" column in all of the following cases:
- The criterion is not met [1].
- The criterion is partially met [2].
- The criterion is met through an alternate means (explain how and why).
- The program exceeds the criterion.
  No explanation is needed if the criterion is fully met [3].

**What if I do not see evidence of an item during the observation time?**

Your ratings should be based on what happens typically in the program.
- A *teacher* who does not see evidence for an item during the observation should rate the item based on what happens typically. Please do not rate the item based on what you would like to have happen or plan to try in the future.
- A *director* or *validator* who does not see evidence for an item during the observation should interview the lead teacher following the observation and ask open-ended questions to obtain information about the item. An open-ended question does not suggest possible answers. For example, "What happens when the children arrive?" "What do you do when children hit each other?" are open-ended questions. It is important that directors not base their ratings on the policy of the program or what they believe ought to happen in

a classroom. When a rating is based on what a teacher says rather than what is observed, write an "R" for *report* on the Observation form.

In some cases, criteria (or indicators or examples) relate to specific age groups, such as infants, or specific kinds of programs. If you are not observing that age group or the criteria do not apply to the group, please check the box marked "not applicable."

**Suggestions for using this form**

1. Read over the entire Observation form before beginning to rate a classroom.

2. The director or outside observer should spend 10 to 15 minutes becoming familiar with the classroom before beginning to assign ratings.

3. The items on the form do not need to be completed in order. Some criteria are rated more easily than others and these can be done first. Start with the criteria observed most easily such as items for Physical Environment (G) and Health and Safety (H).

4. If children move among more than one teacher (between learning centers, for example), follow the children and base your rating on the quality of the children's overall experience.

5. When more than one teacher is observed with a group, base the ratings on all adults in the group who interact with the children. Rule of thumb: rate Criteria on the quality of the children's experience.

6. If there are no clearly defined groups in separate spaces, follow what is happening to a sample of an age group of children.

7. Do not feel pressured to rate a criterion too quickly. If you relax, observe, and gain a sense of what is happening, it is easier to make a rating decision.

## Definitions

In early childhood programs, children are grouped in a variety of ways—by chronological age, developmental age, or multiage grouping. These definitions are to simplify the use of this form, not to recommend a way of grouping children.

**Group**—the children assigned to a staff member or team of staff members occupying an individual classroom or well-defined physical space within a larger room.

**Indicators**—important points to look for in rating the quality of an early childhood classroom using NAEYC's *Early Childhood Classroom Observation*.

**Teaching staff**—adults who have direct responsibility for the care and education of the children.

**Infants\***—children between the ages of birth and 12 months.

**Toddlers\***—children between the ages of 13 months and 35 months.

**Young toddlers\***—children between the ages of 13 months to between 18 and 24 months.

**Older toddlers\***—children between the ages of 24 and 30 months to 35 months.

**Preschoolers\***—children from 3 through 5 years of age.

**Kindergartners**—children who are attending public or private kindergarten, usually 5-year-olds.

**School-agers\***—children attending first grade or beyond who are participating in a before- and/or after-school program. A majority of the school-agers in the program should be 8 years old or younger.

\*When observing in programs serving children with special needs, it may be necessary to use developmental levels rather than chronological age to assess the appropriateness of programming.

# A. Interactions among Teachers and Children

|  | Rating | | | Comments |
|---|---|---|---|---|
| **Criterion** | Not met | Partially met | Fully met | |

**A-1.** Teachers interact frequently with children showing affection, interest, and respect.

| 1 | 2 | 3 |

❑ Teachers interact nonverbally by smiling, touching, holding.
❑ Teachers speak with children at eye level, often, throughout the day.
❑ Teachers talk with and listen to individual children during activities and routines (arriving/departing, eating).
❑ Teachers actively seek meaningful conversations with children.
❑ Teachers give one-to-one attention to infants during feeding and diapering, allowing time for infants' responses.

**A-2.** Teachers are available and responsive to children.

| 1 | 2 | 3 |

❑ Quickly comfort infants in distress.
❑ Reassure crying toddlers.
❑ Listen to children with attention and respect.
❑ Respond to children's questions and requests.
❑ Teachers are aware of the activities of the entire group even when dealing with a smaller group; staff position themselves strategically and look up often from involvement.
❑ Teachers spend time observing each child without interrupting an actively involved child.

**A-3a.** Teachers speak with children in a friendly, positive, courteous manner.

| 1 | 2 | 3 |

❑ Speak with individual children often.
❑ Ask open-ended questions.
❑ Call children by name.
❑ Include child in conversations; describe actions, experiences, and events; listen and respond to children's comments and suggestions.

**A-3b.** Teachers talk with individual children, and encourage children of all ages to use language.

| 1 | 2 | 3 |

*For example,*
Repeat infants' sounds, talk about things toddlers see, help 2-year-olds name things, ask preschoolers open-ended questions, provide opportunities for school-agers to talk about their day. Talk positively to children about family members, family events, traditions, and routines.

## A.  Interactions among Teachers and Children *continued*

| | Rating | | | Comments |
|---|---|---|---|---|

**Criterion**

Not met · Partially met · Fully met

**A-4a.** Teachers treat children of all races, religions, family backgrounds, and cultures with equal respect and consideration.

[1] [2] [3]

*For example,*
Teachers initiate activities and discussions to build positive self-identity and teach the value of differences.

Teachers make it a firm rule that a person's identity (age, race, ethnicity, family life, physical appearance, and ability) is never used to tease or reject anyone.

Teachers talk positively about each child's physical characteristics and cultural heritage.

Teachers react to teasing or rejecting among children by intervening to discuss similarities and differences.

**A-4b.** Teachers provide children of both sexes with equal opportunities to take part in all activities.

[1] [2] [3]

*For example,*
Provide models, props, and visual images that counter traditional sex-role limitations (i.e., female firefighters, male nurses).

Value positive levels of noise and activity involving both girls and boys.

When acknowledging individual children, avoid gender stereotypes in language references (i.e., use words such as *strong, gentle, pretty, helpful* for both girls and boys).

**A-5.** Teachers encourage children's development of independent functioning, as appropriate. Teachers foster the development of age-appropriate self-help skills such as picking up toys, wiping spills, personal grooming (toileting, handwashing), obtaining and caring for materials, and other skills. (Cultural perspectives of family or community may influence expectations for independence.)

[1] [2] [3]

*For example,*
Infants: safe places for independent play

Older infants: finger feeding self

Toddlers: washing hands, selecting own toys

Three and fours: dressing, picking up toys

Kindergartners: doing responsible jobs within the school building, setting table, cleaning, acquiring self-help skills

School-agers: performing responsible jobs, participating in community activities

# A. Interactions among Teachers and Children *continued*

|  | Rating | | | Comments |
|---|---|---|---|---|
| **Criterion** | Not met | Partially met | Fully met |  |

**A-6a.** Teachers facilitate the development of responsibility, self-regulation, and self-control in children.

| 1 | 2 | 3 |

❑ Teachers set clear, consistent, fair limits for classroom behavior and in the case of older children, help them to set their own limits.

❑ Teachers use children's mistakes as learning opportunities, describing the situation and encouraging children's evaluation of the problem rather than imposing the solution.

❑ Teachers anticipate and eliminate potential problems, redirecting children to more acceptable behavior or activity.

❑ Teachers listen and acknowledge children's feelings and frustrations and respond with respect.

❑ Teachers guide children to resolve conflicts and model skills that help children to solve their own problems.

❑ Teachers encourage appropriate behavior, patiently reminding children of rules and their rationale as needed.

❑ Teachers apply logical or natural consequences in problem situations.

**A-6b.** Teachers do not use corporal punishment or other negative discipline methods that hurt, humiliate, or frighten children.

| 1 | 2 | 3 |

❑ Food or beverage is never withheld as a form of discipline.

❑ The environment is arranged so that a minimal number of "No's" are necessary, especially for young children.

**A-7.** Overall sound of group is pleasant most of the time.

| 1 | 2 | 3 |

*For example,*
Happy laughter, excitement, busy activity, pleasant conversation rather than harsh, stressful noise or enforced quiet

Adult voices do not predominate.

# A.   Interactions among Teachers and Children *continued*

| Criterion | Rating | | | Comments |
|---|---|---|---|---|
| | Not met | Partially met | Fully met | |

**A-8.** Teachers support children's emotional development, assisting them to be comfortable, relaxed, happy, and involved in play and other activities.

❑ Comfort and reassure children who are hurt, fearful, or otherwise upset.

❑ Help children deal with anger, frustration, or sadness by comforting, identifying, and reflecting feelings.

❑ Help children use various strategies to express emotions and solve social problems, as appropriate for age of child.

❑ Intervene quickly when children's responses to each other become physically aggressive, discuss the inappropriateness of such action, and help children to develop more positive strategies to solve conflicts.

❑ Encourage children to verbalize feelings and ideas, including both positive and negative emotions. For example, supply words for very young children to describe feelings; discuss alternative solutions with children 2 years and older.

Rating: 1   2   3

**A-9.** Teachers recognize and encourage prosocial behaviors among children, such as cooperation, helping taking turns, talking to solve problems, and concern for others. Expectations of children's social behavior are developmentally appropriate. Teachers support children's beginning friendships and provide opportunities for children to learn from each other as well as adults.

*For example,*
Infants interact (look, touch gently, vocalize) freely with one another as teachers observe, alert to respond and model safe interaction when necessary.

Two pieces of the same popular equipment are available so toddlers are not forced to share too often.

Preschoolers are encouraged to cooperate in small groups.

Kindergartners work with small, flexible groups on extended projects and participate in group problem-solving.

School-agers have opportunities to participate in group games or to work or play alone.

Rating: 1   2   3

## A. Interactions among Teachers and Children *continued*

| | Rating | | | Comments |
|---|---|---|---|---|
| **Criterion** | Not met | Partially met | Fully met | |

**A-10.** Teachers use a variety of teaching strategies to enhance children's learning and development throughout the day.

    ❑ Stimulate children's thinking and extend their learning using verbal methods such as posing problems, asking questions, and making comments and suggestions.

    ❑ Introduce children to new experiences, ideas, or challenges.

    ❑ Coach and/or directly guide children in the acquisition of specific skills as needed, being careful to challenge, but not frustrate any child.

Rating: 1   2   3

## B. Curriculum

**B-4.** The daily schedule provides a balance of activities in consideration of the child's total daily experience—what happens before, during, and after the program with attention to the following dimensions of scheduling:

**B-4a.** All age groups play outdoors daily, permitting conditions protect children's health and safety.

Rating: 1   2   3

**B-4b.** The schedule provides for alternating periods of quiet and active play.

Rating: 1   2   3

**B-4c.** A balance of large-muscle/small-muscle activities is provided in the daily schedule.

Rating: 1   2   3

**B-4d.** More than one option for grouping (such as individual, small group, or large group) is available to children most of the day. Infants and toddlers are not expected to function as a large group.

Rating: 1   2   3

# B. Curriculum *continued*

| | Rating | | |
|---|---|---|---|
| **Criterion** | Not met | Partially met | Fully met |

**B-4e.** A balance of child-initiated and teacher-initiated activity is provided. The amount of time spent in large-group, teacher-initiated activity is limited.

`1`  `2`  `3`

Comments

_____

_____

_____

**B-5a.** Materials and equipment appropriate to the age group (including books, dolls, toys, dress-up props, photos, pictures, music) that project diverse racial, gender, and age attributes are provided.

❑ Materials reflect the lives of the children and families served.
❑ Materials and equipment reflect the diversity found in society in general.

`1`  `2`  `3`

_____

_____

_____

_____

_____

_____

_____

**B-5b.** Developmentally appropriate materials and equipment are available for *infants*.

❑ Simple, lightweight, open-ended, easily washable toys such as containers, balls, pop-beads, nesting cups
❑ Rattles, squeak toys, action/reaction toys
❑ Cuddle toys
❑ Toys to mouth such as teethers, rings
❑ Pictures of real objects
❑ Crawling area with sturdy, stable furniture to pull up self

`1`  `2`  `3`

❑ **Not applicable**

_____

_____

_____

_____

_____

**B-5c.** Developmentally appropriate materials and equipment are available for *toddlers*.

❑ Push and pull toys
❑ Manipulatives such as stacking toys, large wooden spools/beads/cubes, pounding bench, simple puzzles
❑ Sturdy picture books, music
❑ Toys for pretending, such as play telephone, dolls
❑ Large paper, crayons
❑ Sturdy furniture to hold on to while walking
❑ Sand and water toys

`1`  `2`  `3`

❑ **Not applicable**

_____

_____

_____

_____

_____

_____

_____

_____

_____

_____

# B. Curriculum *continued*

| Criterion | Rating | Comments |
|---|---|---|
| | Not met / Partially met / Fully met | |

**B-5d.** Developmentally appropriate materials and equipment are available for *preschoolers.*

| 1 | 2 | 3 |

❑ **Not applicable**

- ❑ Active play equipment for climbing and balancing
- ❑ Unit blocks and accessories
- ❑ Puzzles, manipulative toys
- ❑ Picture books, audio recordings/tapes, musical instruments
- ❑ Art materials such as finger and tempera paints, crayons, safe scissors, and paste
- ❑ Dramatic play materials such as dolls, dress-up clothes and props, child-sized furniture, puppets
- ❑ Sand and water toys

**B-5e.** Developmentally appropriate materials and equipment are available for *kindergartners.*

| 1 | 2 | 3 |

❑ **Not applicable**

- ❑ Active play equipment for climbing and balancing
- ❑ Unit blocks and accessories such as figures, signs, cars, trees
- ❑ Construction materials
- ❑ Complex puzzles and manipulative toys for counting, sorting
- ❑ Picture books and early readers
- ❑ Audio recordings/tapes, musical instruments, computers with appropriate software
- ❑ Materials for writing and complex art projects
- ❑ A variety of dramatic play materials and props
- ❑ Board and card games

**B-5f.** Developmentally appropriate materials are available for *school-agers.*

| 1 | 2 | 3 |

❑ **Not applicable**

- ❑ Active play equipment and materials such as bats and balls for organized games
- ❑ Construction materials for woodworking, unit blocks, accessories for blocks
- ❑ Materials for hobby and art projects, science projects
- ❑ Materials for dramatics, cooking
- ❑ Books, audio recordings/tapes, musical instruments, computers with appropriate software
- ❑ Board and card games
- ❑ Complex manipulative toys (connecting or interlocking toys), jigsaw puzzles

# B. Curriculum *continued*

| | Rating | | Comments |

**Criterion**

|  | Not met | Partially met | Fully met |
| --- | --- | --- | --- |

**B-6a.** Active media that children can control, such as videotaping, cameras, audiotaping, and developmentally appropriate computer software may be used in the classroom as active learning materials, along with other materials that children can choose. If such technology is used, the program provides equal access for all children. Teachers help children use these media as independently as possible.

| 1 | 2 | 3 |

❏ **Not applicable**

*This criterion applies to children 3 years of age and older; it is not applicable to infants and toddlers. (Note: If no such media are used, score "Not applicable.")*

**B-6b.** The use of passive media, such as television, films, videotapes, and audiotapes is limited to developmentally appropriate programming.

| 1 | 2 | 3 |

❏ **Not applicable**

❏ Programs are previewed by adults prior to use.
❏ Another option for activity is always available.
❏ No child is required to view the program.
❏ Teachers discuss what is viewed with the children to develop critical viewing skills.
❏ Passive media are used only as infrequent events, rather than as regular, daily routines.

# B. Curriculum *continued*

## Criterion

**B-7.** Teachers provide a variety of developmentally appropriate activities and materials that are selected to emphasize concrete experiential learning and to achieve the following goals:

**B-7a.** Foster positive identity and sense of emotional well-being.

| Rating | | |
|---|---|---|
| Not met | Partially met | Fully met |
| 1 | 2 | 3 |

**Comments**

*For example,*
**Infants/ toddlers**
Hold and touch, make frequent eye contact, and communicate with babies especially during caregiving.

Talk and sing to babies.

Allow infants to achieve mastery of their bodies through self-initiated motor behavior such as rolling, sitting.

Allow toddlers to feed themselves and encourage their development of self-help skills when ready.

Encourage and support each toddler's developmental achievements such as pulling up self, walking, and climbing.

Listen and respond to toddler's emerging language.

**Preschoolers**
Allow time for children to talk about what they see, do, and like.

Use children's names frequently in songs, games.

Display children's work and photos of children and their families.

Encourage children to draw pictures and tell stories about self, family, and cultural practices.

Provide many opportunities for children to initiate activity, develop and demonstrate control of their bodies and self-help skills.

**Kindergartners**
Provide learning experiences that respond to children's individual differences in ability and interests.

Display children's unique products and work.

Engage children in experiences that demonstrate the explicit valuing of each child, such as sending a card to a sick classmate.

Provide learning experiences in which children can succeed most of the tme and yet be challenged to work on the edge of their developing capabilities.

**School-agers**
Provide opportunities to express growing independence/self-reliance such as the ability to make choices, initiate own activities.

Allow opportunities to work or play alone.

Provide ways to ensure privacy.

Plan cooperative rather than competitive activities.

Recognize preference for self-selected peer groups.

Encourage children to draw pictures and tell stories about self, family, and cultural practices.

Display children's work and photos of children and their families.

Provide opportunities to explore cultural heritage.

**B-7b.** Develop social skills.

| 1 | 2 | 3 |
|---|---|---|

*For example,*
**Infants/toddlers**
Hold, pat, and touch babies.

Talk to, sing to, and play with each baby on a one-to-one basis.

Respond to and expand on cues coming from child.

Interpret infants' actions to other children to help them get along in the group. ("Mary had it first.")

Assist toddlers in social interaction.

**Preschoolers**
Create space and time for small groups of children to build blocks together or enjoy dramatic play.

Coach children who have difficulty entering a play situation or making constructive use of child-chosen activity.

Provide opportunities for sharing, caring, and helping, such as making cards for a sick child or caring for pets.

Explore ways to respond to biased comments and behaviors.

**Kindergartners**
Use a variety of ways of flexibly grouping children.

Provide opportunities for children to collaborate and cooperate during play and projects.

Coach children in social problem-solving and conflict-resolution skills.

Engage children in setting and enforcing classroom rules.

Provide opportunities for sharing, caring, and helping, such as making cards for a sick child or caring for pets.

Provide opportunities to support children's beginning friendships.

**School-agers**
Arrange planned and spontaneous activities in team sports, group games, interest clubs, board and card games.

Allow time to sit and talk with friend or adult.

Focus on activities rather than outcomes (scores, winners).

# B. Curriculum *continued*

| Criterion | Rating | | | Comments |
|---|---|---|---|---|
| | Not met | Partially met | Fully met | |
| **B-7c.** Encourage children to think, reason, question, and experiment. | 1 | 2 | 3 | |

*For example,*

**Infants/toddlers**

Provide an appropriately challenging, safe environment for infants and toddlers to explore and manipulate.

Provide light colorful objects for babies to look at which they can reach for and grasp.

Play naming and hiding games such as peek-a-boo, pat-a-cake.

Provide simple toys that respond to infants' initiations so they may pay attention to cause and effect.

Provide large containers full of objects for toddlers to carry, dump, and refill.

Help toddlers develop awareness by reflecting their experiences. ("You're pointing to the street. Is it because you hear the garbage truck?")

Provide opportunities for making choices without interfering with selections.

Avoid interruptions of children's activities.

**Preschoolers**

Plan activities for labeling, classifying, sorting objects by shape, color, size.

Discuss daily and weekly routines in terms of time concepts, season of the year.

Extend children's thinking and learning during activities by adding new materials, asking open-ended questions, offering ideas or suggestions, joining in their play, and providing assistance in solving problems.

Observe natural events such as seeds growing, life cycle of pets.

Create opportunities to use numbers, counting objects.

Take walks around building or neighborhood.

Plan trips to provide new learning experiences for preschoolers.

Encourage water and sand play.

**Kindergartners**

Provide opportunities to learn basic science and math concepts through sand and water exploration, constructing with blocks and working with levers, pulleys, scales, and other simple machines.

Involve children in observing and investigating natural events and objects, sorting and classifying, searching for patterns, noting differences and similarities, and drawing and discussing what they see.

Engage children in sustained project work, seeking solutions to concrete problems; observe and record changes in the environment, work with tools.

Read for information and reference.

Engage children in representing their understanding in various ways, such as drawing, writing, speaking.

Plan trips to provide new learning experiences.

**School-agers**

Provide activities such as cooking, money-making projects, gardening, science experiments, trips in the community, interacting with visitors, multicultural experiences, computer projects.

Provide opportunities to complete homework if desired including peer or adult tutoring for children who request assistance.

# B. Curriculum *continued*

| Criterion | Rating | | | Comments |
|---|---|---|---|---|
| | Not met | Partially met | Fully met | |
| **B-7d.** Encourage language and literacy development | 1 | 2 | 3 | |

*For example,*

**Infants/toddlers**

Engage in many one-to-one, face-to-face interactions with infants.

Look at simple books and pictures.

Talk in a pleasant, calm voice, using simple language and frequent eye contact while being responsive to the infant's cues.

Verbally label objects and events within the infant's experience.

Respond to sounds infant makes, occasionally imitating infant's vocalization.

Describe children's and adult's actions and the events that occur in the child's environment.

Respond to toddlers' attempts at language in supportive ways, such as expanding their utterances and answering their questions, engaging in meaningful conversation about everyday experiences.

**Preschoolers**

Read books and poems, tell stories about experiences, talk about pictures, write down experience stories children dictate.

Provide time for conversation, ask child questions that require more than a one-word answer.

Answer children's questions.

Add more information to what a child says.

Label things in room, use written words with pictures and spoken language, provide a print-rich environment.

Use flannel board, puppets, songs, finger plays, rhyming games.

Encourage children's emerging interest in writing (scribbling, drawing, copying, and using invented spelling).

**Kindergartners**

Actively work to increase children's vocabulary every day.

Read books and poems, tell stories about experiences, talk about pictures, write down experience stories children dictate.

Help children develop book-handling skills and familiarity with the conventions of print (such as story/chapter titles, punctuation, and capital letters).

Help children develop the full range of strategies for reading, for instance, using letter-sound relationships, pictures, and their understanding of the text to figure out unknown words.

Provide many opportunities every day for children to write for reasons that make sense to them (such as making lists, labeling their work, and writing notes to their parents).

Give children frequent practice and help in composing, editing, and revising stories and other written products.

Observe and make plans to ensure each child's continual progress in oral language, reading, and writing.

**School-agers**

Provide opportunities to read books.

Write and produce plays, publish newspapers, write stories.

Share experiences with friends or adults.

Use audio-visual equipment such as tape recorders.

Make own filmstrips, recordings.

---

| **B-7e.** Enhance physical development and skills. | 1 | 2 | 3 | |
|---|---|---|---|---|

*For example,*

**Infants/toddlers**

Allow infants' self-initiated motor development such as rolling, sitting, walking at their own pace.

Provide open carpeted space as well as hard surfaces such as wood floors for crawling.

Provide low, sturdy furniture for child to pull up self or hold on to while walking.

Provide accessible outdoor activities for infants.

Provide simple objects infants may reach for and grasp.

Allow nonmobile infants to move and breathe comfortably, lying freely on their backs while looking about, kicking, reaching, practicing eye-hand coordination.

Provide toddlers objects for carrying, such as baskets, large empty plastic bottles, balls.

Provide toddlers simple puzzles, nesting toys, stacking toys, and pop-beads.

**Preschoolers**

Provide time and space for active play such as jumping, running, balancing, climbing, riding tricycles.

Provide creative movement activity using obstacle course or activity songs and records.

Provide fine-motor activities such as complex manipulatives toys, pegboards, puzzles, lacing cards and woodworking.

Provide art materials for drawing, modeling, writing.

**Kindergartners**

Provide equipment, time, and space for active play such as jumping rope, running, balancing, climbing, and playing group games.

Provide creative movement activity, music, songs and recordings.

Provide fine-motor activities such as jigsaw puzzles, sewing, woodworking, objects that can be taken apart and put back together, dolls and accessories.

Provide variety of art and writing materials and daily opportunities for drawing, painting, cutting and writing.

**School-agers**

Provide opportunities to get physical exercise and use variety of outdoor equipment.

Encourage participation in group games, individual and team sports.

Provide fine-motor activities and hobbies such as sewing, macramé, pottery, leatherwork, carpentry, computers.

# B. Curriculum *continued*

| | Rating | | | Comments |
|---|---|---|---|---|

**Criterion**

| | Not met | Partially met | Fully met |
|---|---|---|---|

**B-7f.** Encourage and demonstrate sound health, safety, and nutritional practices.

| 1 | 2 | 3 |
|---|---|---|

*For example,*

**All ages**

Cook and serve a variety of nutritious foods.

Discuss good nutrition.

Do activities to develop safety awareness in the center, home, and community.

Encourage health practices such as washing hands, brushing teeth, getting regular exercise and enough rest.

Talk about visiting doctor, dentist.

For infants/toddlers: Describe routine health activities as they are implemented.

For preschoolers, kindergartners, and school-agers: Study topics such as human body, nutrition, life skills.

**B-7g.** Encourage creative expression, representation, and appreciation for the arts.

| 1 | 2 | 3 |
|---|---|---|

*For example,*

**Infants/toddlers**

Occasionally use music for movement, singing, or listening.

Sing to baby, appreciate infants' vocalizations and sounds.

Display interesting things to look at.

Provide time and space for movement and play.

Encourage scribbling with crayons.

**Preschoolers**

Do creative art activities such as brush painting, drawing, collage, and playdough.

Provide time and space for dancing, movement activities, creative dramatics.

Do musical activities such as singing, listening to records, playing instruments.

Most art activities are offered as an exploratory process rather than to produce a product.

Adult-made models, patterns, and pre-drawn forms are used infrequently.

Provide materials representative of a variety of cultures.

**Kindergartners**

Provide opportunities for children to represent ideas and feelings and learn fundamental concepts and skills in the fine arts.

Do creative art projects, painting, drawing, collage, and modeling.

Provide time and space for dancing, movement activities, creative dramatics.

Do musical activities such as singing, listening to recordings, playing instruments.

Adult-made models, patterns, and pre-drawn forms are used infrequently.

Provide visits by artists, materials representative of a variety of cultures.

Develop appreciation for the arts by taking trips to galleries, concerts, cultural events.

**School-agers**

Provide planned and spontaneous activities in arts and crafts such as mural and easel painting, ceramics, carpentry, weaving.

Encourage dancing, creative dramatics, listening to recordings, singing, playing instruments.

Provide materials representative of a variety of cultures.

Provide visits by artists, materials representative of a variety of cultures.

Develop appreciation for the arts by taking trips to galleries, concerts, cultural events.

# B. Curriculum *continued*

| Criterion | Rating | | | Comments |
|---|---|---|---|---|
| | Not met | Partially met | Fully met | |

**B-7h.** Respect cultural diversity.     `1`   `2`   `3`

*For example,*
**All ages, as appropriate to age group**

Build sense of the group as a community, bringing each child's home culture and language into the shared culture of the school so each child feels accepted and gains a sense of belonging.

Provide books, materials, images, and experiences that reflect diverse cultures that children may not likely see, as well as those that represent their family life and cultural group.

Initiate discussions and activities to teach respect and appreciation for similarities and differences among people.

Talk positively about each child's physical characteristics, family, and cultural heritage.

Cook or serve foods from children's various contemporary cultures.

Avoid stereotyping any group through materials, objects, language.

Invite families' participation in all aspects of the program.

Take trips to museums, cultural resources of community.

Infuse all curriculum topics with diverse cultural perspectives, avoiding a "tourist" approach.

**B-8.** Teachers provide materials and time for children to select their own activities during the day.     `1`   `2`   `3`

❑ Infants and toddlers have objects and materials for free choice.

❑ Several alternative activities are available for children's choice.

❑ Teachers respect the child's right not to participate in some activities.

❑ Teachers pick up on activities that children start or interests that children show.

❑ Kindergartners and school-agers help prepare materials, plan and choose their own activities at times during the day.

**B-9.** Teachers conduct smooth and unregimented transitions between activities.     `1`   `2`   `3`

❑ Children are given advanced notice to prepare them for transitions ahead of time.

❑ Children are not always required to move as a group from one activity to another.

❑ The new activity is prepared before the transition from the completed activity to avoid prolonged waiting.

❑ School-age children help plan and participate in the change of activity, have time to adjust to change from school to program.

## B.    Curriculum *continued*

| Criterion | Rating | | | Comments |
|---|---|---|---|---|
| | Not met | Partially met | Fully met | |

**B-10.**   Teachers are flexible enough to change planned or routine activities.

[1]   [2]   [3]

*For example,*
Staff follow needs or interests of the children.

Staff adjust to changes in weather or other unexpected situations in a relaxed way without upsetting children.

**B-11.**   Routine tasks are incorporated into the program as a means of furthering children's learning, self-help, and social skills.

[1]   [2]   [3]

❑   For infants and toddlers, routines are used as a time for pleasant interaction and learning.
❑   Routines such as diapering or toileting, eating, dressing, and sleeping or resting are handled in a relaxed, reassuring, and individualized manner based on developmental needs.
❑   Teachers plan with families to make toileting, feeding, and the development of other self-regulation skills a positive experience for children.

*For example,*
Respect infants' individual sleeping schedules; provide alternatives to preschoolers who are early risers; offer kindergartners choices or permit preferences whenever possible; provide school-agers with a place to rest if they choose; respect school-agers' increasing interest in personal grooming.

## G.    Physical Environment

**G-1a.**   There is enough usable space indoors so children are not crowded.

[1]   [2]   [3]

**G-1b.**   There is enough usable space for outdoor play for each age group.

[1]   [2]   [3]

*For example,*
Age groups use different areas or are scheduled at different times.

# G. Physical Environment *continued*

| | Rating | | | Comments |
|---|---|---|---|---|

**Criterion**

| | Not met | Partially met | Fully met |
|---|---|---|---|

**G-2.** Space is arranged to accommodate children individually, in small groups, or in a large group.

☐ There are clear pathways for children to move from one area to another without disturbing activities.

☐ Areas are organized for easy supervision by staff.

Rating: 1 2 3

**G-3.** Space is arranged to facilitate a variety of activities for each age group.

☐ Nonwalkers (infants/younger toddlers) are provided open space for crawling/toddling and protected space for play, separating groups of nonmobile and mobile infants for safety.

☐ Older toddlers, preschoolers, and kindergartners have space arranged for a variety of individual and small group activities including block building, dramatic play, art, music, science, math, manipulatives, quiet book reading.

☐ Older toddlers, preschoolers, and kindergartners are occasionally offered sand and water play and woodworking.

☐ School-agers are provided separate space for their program including both active and quiet activities to permit sustained work on projects.

Rating: 1 2 3

**G-4.** A variety of age-appropriate materials and equipment are available for children indoors and outdoors.

☐ A sufficient quantity of materials and equipment is provided to avoid problems with sharing or waiting.

☐ Materials are durable and in good repair.

☐ Materials are organized consistently on low, open shelves to encourage independent use by children.

☐ Extra materials are accessible to staff to add variety to usual activities.

☐ Materials are rotated and adapted to maintain children's interest.

Rating: 1 2 3

**G-5.** Individual space is provided for each child's belongings.

☐ There is a place to hang or store clothing and places for storing other belongings such as artwork to be taken home.

Rating: 1 2 3

# G.   Physical Environment *continued*

|  | Rating | | | Comments |
|---|---|---|---|---|

**Criterion**

Not met / Partially met / Fully met

**G-6.**   Private areas where children can play or work alone or with a friend are available indoors and outdoors.

[1]  [2]  [3]

*For example,*
Book corners, tunnels, or playhouses that are easy for adults to supervise

**G-7.**   The environment includes soft elements.

[1]  [2]  [3]

*For example,*
Rugs, cushions, soft furniture, soft toys, comfortable chairs for adults to hold children in their laps

**G-8.**   Sound-absorbing materials such as ceiling tile and rugs are used to cut down noise.

[1]  [2]  [3]

**G-9a.**   A variety of activities can go on outdoors throughout the year.
☐ Balance of shade and sun
☐ Variety of surfaces such as hard area for wheel toys, grass, sand and soil, hills, flat sections
☐ Variety of age-appropriate equipment such as for crawling, pulling up to stand, riding, climbing, balancing, individual playing

[1]  [2]  [3]

**G-9b.**   The outdoor play area is protected from access to streets and other dangers by fences or by natural barriers.

[1]  [2]  [3]

*For example,*
Programs need to exercise professional judgment in situations where community conditions of violence or extreme weather threaten children's health or safety. If conditions for outdoor play are not safe, the program should provide regular, alternative activities to meet children's needs for fresh air and exercise.

# H. Health and Safety

| Criterion | Rating | | | Comments |
|---|---|---|---|---|
| | Not met | Partially met | Fully met | |

**H-7a.** Children are under adult supervision at all times.

☐ Infants and toddlers are never left unattended.
☐ Preschoolers are supervised by sight and sound.
☐ Kindergartners and school-agers may not be in sight, but staff know where children are and what they are doing.

Rating: 1 | 2 | 3

**H-12.** Children are dressed appropriately for active play indoors and outdoors.

☐ Extra clothing is kept on hand.
☐ Protective clothing such as smocks and mittens is kept on hand.

Rating: 1 | 2 | 3

**H-13a.** As children use the facility, staff and children keep areas reasonably clean.

☐ Tables are washed and floors are swept after meals.
☐ Toys are picked up after use.

Rating: 1 | 2 | 3

**H-13b.** Toileting and diapering areas are sanitary.

☐ Soiled diapers are disposed of or held for laundry in closed containers out of reach of children.
☐ Changing table is disinfected after each use.

Rating: 1 | 2 | 3

**H-14a.** Staff wash their hands with liquid soap and water at appropriate times:

☐ Upon arrival
☐ Before preparing or serving food
☐ Before feeding children
☐ After diapering or assisting children with toileting or nose wiping
☐ After handling pets or animals
☐ After contact with any potentially infectious materials, including bodily fluids

Rating: 1 | 2 | 3

**H-14b.** Staff follow proper procedures during handwashing.

☐ Wash with liquid soap and warm, running water for at least 10 seconds.
☐ Use single use or disposable towels.
☐ Avoid recontamination from faucets by turning off faucets with towel.

Rating: 1 | 2 | 3

**H-14c.** A sink with running water of comfortable temperature is very close to diapering and toileting areas. Signs are posted reminding staff of proper handwashing procedures.

Rating: 1 | 2 | 3

# H.   Health and Safety *continued*

|  | Rating | | | Comments |
|---|---|---|---|---|

**Criterion**

|  | Not met | Partially met | Fully met |  |
|---|---|---|---|---|

**H-15a.** The building, play yard, and all equipment are maintained in safe, clean condition and in good repair.

Rating: 1  2  3

- ❑ No sharp edges, splinters, protruding or rusty nails, or missing parts.
- ❑ Glass, trash is removed from children's play areas.
- ❑ Outdoor sandboxes are covered when not in use.
- ❑ The water play table is cleaned and sanitized with a bleach solution daily, when in use.

**H-15b.** Infants' and toddlers' toys are large enough to prevent swallowing or choking.

Rating: 1  2  3

❑ **Not applicable**

**H-16b.** Sides of infants' cribs are in a locked position when cribs are occupied. Young infants should be placed on their backs when sleeping.

Rating: 1  2  3

❑ **Not applicable**

**H-17a.** Toilets, drinking water, and handwashing facilities are easily accessible to children.

Rating: 1  2  3

*For example,*
Facilities are either child-sized or made accessible by nonslip stools, infants and toddlers have hands washed, infants and toddlers are offered drinking water or other beverages.

**H-17b.** Liquid soap and disposable towels are provided.

Rating: 1  2  3

**H-17c.** Children wash hands after toileting and before meals.

Rating: 1  2  3

- ❑ Staff assist infants and toddlers with face- and handwashing as needed.
- ❑ Children are educated by staff members concerning handwashing procedures: use of running water, soap, rubbing, and single use or disposable towels.

# H.  Health and Safety *continued*

| Criterion | Rating | | | Comments |
|---|---|---|---|---|
| | Not met | Partially met | Fully met | |

**H-18a.** Areas used by children are well-lighted and ventilated and kept at a comfortable temperature.

Rating: 1  2  3

**H-18b.** Electrical outlets are covered with protective caps. (NA for rooms used by school-agers only.)

Rating: 1  2  3

❑ **Not applicable**

**H-18c.** Floor coverings do not cause tripping hazards.

Rating: 1  2  3

*For example,*
Floor coverings are attached to the floor or backed with nonslip coverings, held down with furniture.

❑ **Not applicable**

**H-19a.** All pieces of playground equipment are surrounded by a resilient surface (fine, loose sand; wood chips; wood mulch; fine gravel) that extends at least 4 feet beyond the fall zone.

Rating: 1  2  3

**H-19b.** Climbing equipment, swings, and large pieces of furniture are securely anchored. (Program submits verification if anchoring cannot be easily observed.)

Rating: 1  2  3

*For example,*
Permanent equipment outdoors, tall storage shelves indoors. Heavy pieces of furniture such as video monitors are secured so they cannot be tipped over by children.

**H-20a.** All chemicals and potentially dangerous products such as medicines or cleaning supplies are stored in original, labeled containers in locked cabinets inaccessible to children (does not apply to diluted bleach solution which must be inaccessible, but not locked).

Rating: 1  2  3

## H.   Health and Safety *continued*

| Criterion | Rating | | | Comments |
|---|---|---|---|---|
| | Not met | Partially met | Fully met | |
| **H-21b.** Written emergency-evacuation procedures are posted in conspicuous places. | 1 | 2 | 3 | |

## I.   Nutrition and Food Service

**I-3.**   Mealtime is a pleasant social and learning experience for children.

☐ Mealtimes promote good nutrition habits.
☐ Infants are held in an inclined position while bottle fed so social interaction can occur.
☐ At least one adult sits with children during meals to provide a good role model and encourage conversation.
☐ Toddlers, preschoolers, and kindergartners are encouraged to serve and feed themselves and assist with clean-up.
☐ Chairs, tables, and eating utensils are suitable for the size and developmental levels of the children.

Rating: 1  2  3

# Classroom Observation Summary Sheet

| Program ID Number | | | | | | | | | | | | | | | | | | | Sum of scores | Number of ratings | Average rating |

| Room | 1 | 2 | 3 | 4 | 5 | 6 | 7 | 8 | 9 | 10 | 11 | 12 | 13 | 14 | 15 | 16 | 17 | 18 | Sum of scores | Number of ratings | Average rating |
|---|---|---|---|---|---|---|---|---|---|---|---|---|---|---|---|---|---|---|---|---|---|
| Group name | DC Inf. | DT Tod. | EW ½PS | WL FDPS | MA 3s | EW AS | | | | | | | | | | | | | | | |
| Lead teacher | DC | DT | EW HP | WL | MA | EW HP | | | | | | | | | | | | | | | |
| **Criterion** | | | | | | | | | | Rating | | | | | | | | | | | |
| A-1 | 2 | 3 | 3 | 3 | 3 | 3 | | | | | | | | | | | | | 17 | 6 | 2.83 |
| A-2 | 3 | 3 | 3 | 3 | 3 | 3 | | | | | | | | | | | | | 18 | 6 | 3.0 |
| A-3a | 3 | 3 | 3 | 3 | 3 | 3 | | | | | | | | | | | | | 18 | 6 | 3.0 |
| A-3b | 2 | 3 | 3 | 3 | 3 | 3 | | | | | | | | | | | | | 17 | 6 | 2.83 |
| A-4a | 3 | 3 | 3 | 3 | 3 | 3 | | | | | | | | | | | | | 18 | 6 | 3.0 |
| A-4b | 3 | 3 | 2 | 3 | 3 | 3 | | | | | | | | | | | | | 17 | 6 | 2.83 |
| A-5 | 3 | 3 | 3 | 3 | 3 | 3 | | | | | | | | | | | | | 18 | 6 | 3.0 |
| A-6a | 3 | 3 | 3 | 3 | 2 | 3 | | | | | | | | | | | | | 17 | 6 | 2.83 |
| A-6b | 3 | 3 | 3 | 3 | 3 | 3 | | | | | | | | | | | | | 18 | 6 | 3.0 |
| A-7 | 2 | 3 | 3 | 3 | 3 | 3 | | | | | | | | | | | | | 17 | 6 | 3.0 |
| A-8 | 3 | 3 | 3 | 3 | 3 | 3 | | | | | | | | | | | | | 18 | 6 | 3.0 |
| A-9 | 3 | 3 | 3 | 3 | 3 | 3 | | | | | | | | | | | | | 18 | 6 | 3.0 |
| A-10 | 3 | 2 | 3 | 3 | 3 | 3 | | | | | | | | | | | | | 17 | 6 | 2.83 |
| B-4a | 2 | 3 | 3 | 3 | 3 | 3 | | | | | | | | | | | | | 17 | 6 | 2.83 |
| B-4b | 3 | 3 | 3 | 3 | 3 | 3 | | | | | | | | | | | | | 18 | 6 | 3.0 |
| B-4c | 3 | 3 | 3 | 3 | 3 | 3 | | | | | | | | | | | | | 18 | 6 | 3.0 |
| B-4d | 3 | 3 | 3 | 3 | 3 | 3 | | | | | | | | | | | | | 18 | 6 | 3.0 |
| B-4e | 3 | 3 | 3 | 3 | 3 | 3 | | | | | | | | | | | | | 18 | 6 | 3.0 |
| B-5a | 3 | 3 | 3 | 3 | 3 | 3 | | | | | | | | | | | | | 18 | 6 | 3.0 |
| B-5b | 3 | — | — | — | — | — | | | | | | | | | | | | | 3 | 1 | 3.0 |
| B-5c | — | 3 | — | — | — | — | | | | | | | | | | | | | 3 | 1 | 3.0 |
| B-5d | — | — | 3 | 3 | 3 | — | | | | | | | | | | | | | 9 | 3 | 3.0 |
| B-5e | — | — | — | — | — | 3 | | | | | | | | | | | | | 3 | 1 | 3.0 |
| B-5f | — | — | — | — | — | 3 | | | | | | | | | | | | | 3 | 1 | 3.0 |
| B-6a | NA | NA | NA | NA | NA | 3 | | | | | | | | | | | | | 3 | 1 | 3.0 |
| B-6b | NA | NA | NA | NA | NA | 3 | | | | | | | | | | | | | 3 | 1 | 3.0 |
| B-7a | 3 | 3 | 3 | 3 | 3 | 3 | | | | | | | | | | | | | 18 | 6 | 3.0 |
| B-7b | 3 | 3 | 3 | 3 | 3 | 3 | | | | | | | | | | | | | 18 | 6 | 3.0 |
| B-7c | 3 | 3 | 3 | 3 | 3 | 3 | | | | | | | | | | | | | 18 | 6 | 3.0 |
| B-7d | 3 | 3 | 3 | 3 | 3 | 3 | | | | | | | | | | | | | 18 | 6 | 3.0 |
| B-7e | 3 | 3 | 3 | 3 | 3 | 3 | | | | | | | | | | | | | 18 | 6 | 3.0 |
| B-7f | 3 | 3 | 3 | 3 | 3 | 3 | | | | | | | | | | | | | 18 | 6 | 3.0 |
| B-7g | 2 | 3 | 3 | 3 | 3 | 3 | | | | | | | | | | | | | 17 | 6 | 2.83 |
| B-7h | 3 | 3 | 3 | 3 | 3 | 3 | | | | | | | | | | | | | 18 | 6 | 3.0 |

| Criterion | Rating | | | | | | | | | | | | | | | | | | Sum of scores | Number of ratings | Average rating |
|---|---|---|---|---|---|---|---|---|---|---|---|---|---|---|---|---|---|---|---|---|---|
| | 1 | 2 | 3 | 4 | 5 | 6 | 7 | 8 | 9 | 10 | 11 | 12 | 13 | 14 | 15 | 16 | 17 | 18 | | | |
| B-8 | 3 | 3 | 3 | 3 | 3 | 3 | | | | | | | | | | | | | 18 | 6 | 3.0 |
| B-9 | 3 | 3 | 2 | 3 | 3 | 3 | | | | | | | | | | | | | 17 | 6 | 2.83 |
| B-10 | 3 | 3 | 2 | 3 | 3 | 3 | | | | | | | | | | | | | 17 | 6 | 2.83 |
| B-11 | 3 | 3 | 3 | 3 | 3 | 3 | | | | | | | | | | | | | 18 | 6 | 3.0 |
| G-1a | 3 | 3 | 3 | 3 | 3 | 3 | | | | | | | | | | | | | 18 | 6 | 3.0 |
| G-1b | 3 | 3 | 3 | 3 | 3 | 3 | | | | | | | | | | | | | 18 | 6 | 3.0 |
| G-2 | 3 | 3 | 3 | 3 | 3 | 3 | | | | | | | | | | | | | 18 | 6 | 3.0 |
| G-3 | 3 | 3 | 3 | 3 | 3 | 3 | | | | | | | | | | | | | 18 | 6 | 3.0 |
| G-4 | 3 | 3 | 3 | 3 | 3 | 3 | | | | | | | | | | | | | 18 | 6 | 3.0 |
| G-5 | 3 | 3 | 3 | 3 | 3 | 3 | | | | | | | | | | | | | 18 | 6 | 3.0 |
| G-6 | 2 | 3 | 3 | 3 | 3 | 3 | | | | | | | | | | | | | 17 | 6 | 2.83 |
| G-7 | 3 | 3 | 3 | 3 | 3 | 3 | | | | | | | | | | | | | 18 | 6 | 3.0 |
| G-8 | 3 | 3 | 3 | 3 | 3 | 3 | | | | | | | | | | | | | 18 | 6 | 3.0 |
| G-9a | 3 | 3 | 3 | 3 | 3 | 3 | | | | | | | | | | | | | 18 | 6 | 3.0 |
| G-9b | 3 | 3 | 3 | 3 | 3 | 3 | | | | | | | | | | | | | 18 | 6 | 3.0 |
| H-7a | 3 | 3 | 3 | 3 | 3 | 3 | | | | | | | | | | | | | 18 | 6 | 3.0 |
| H-12 | 3 | 3 | 3 | 3 | 3 | 3 | | | | | | | | | | | | | 18 | 6 | 3.0 |
| H-13a | 3 | 3 | 2 | 3 | 3 | 3 | | | | | | | | | | | | | 17 | 6 | 2.83 |
| H-13b | 3 | 3 | 3 | 3 | 3 | 3 | | | | | | | | | | | | | 18 | 6 | 3.0 |
| H-14a | 3 | 3 | 3 | 3 | 3 | 2 | | | | | | | | | | | | | 17 | 6 | 2.83 |
| H-14b | 3 | 3 | 3 | 3 | 3 | 2 | | | | | | | | | | | | | 17 | 6 | 2.83 |
| H-14c | 3 | 3 | 3 | 3 | 3 | 3 | | | | | | | | | | | | | 18 | 6 | 3.0 |
| H-15a | 3 | 3 | 3 | 3 | 3 | 3 | | | | | | | | | | | | | 18 | 6 | 3.0 |
| H-15b | 3 | 3 | — | — | — | — | | | | | | | | | | | | | 6 | 2 | 3.0 |
| H-16b | 3 | — | — | — | — | — | | | | | | | | | | | | | 3 | 1 | 3.0 |
| H-17a | 3 | 3 | 3 | 3 | 3 | 3 | | | | | | | | | | | | | 18 | 6 | 3.0 |
| H-17b | 3 | 3 | 3 | 3 | 3 | 3 | | | | | | | | | | | | | 18 | 6 | 3.0 |
| H-17c | 3 | 3 | 3 | 3 | 3 | 3 | | | | | | | | | | | | | 18 | 6 | 3.0 |
| H-18a | 3 | 3 | 3 | 3 | 3 | 3 | | | | | | | | | | | | | 18 | 6 | 3.0 |
| H-18b | 3 | 3 | 3 | 3 | 3 | 3 | | | | | | | | | | | | | 18 | 6 | 3.0 |
| H-18c | 3 | 3 | 3 | 3 | 3 | 3 | | | | | | | | | | | | | 18 | 6 | 3.0 |
| H-19a | 3 | 3 | 2 | 2 | 2 | 2 | | | | | | | | | | | | | 14 | 6 | 2.33 |
| H-19b | 3 | 3 | 3 | 3 | 3 | 3 | | | | | | | | | | | | | 18 | 6 | 3.0 |
| H-20a | 3 | 3 | 3 | 3 | 3 | 3 | | | | | | | | | | | | | 18 | 6 | 3.0 |
| H-21b | 3 | 3 | 3 | 3 | 3 | 3 | | | | | | | | | | | | | 18 | 6 | 3.0 |
| I-3 | 3 | 3 | 3 | 3 | 3 | 3 | | | | | | | | | | | | | 18 | 6 | 3.0 |
| Total score (optional) | 186 | 188 | 181 | 185 | 184 | 192 | | | | | | | | | | | | | | | 204.29 |
| Number of items rated | 64 | 63 | 62 | 62 | 62 | 65 | | | | | | | | | | | | | | | 70 |
| Average rating | 2.90 | 2.98 | 2.91 | 2.98 | 2.96 | 2.95 | | | | | | | | | | | | | | | 2.91 |

NAEYC #932

# Section 4

## Administrator Report and Center Profile

Directions for use
Sample Administrator Report
Sample Center Profile
List of Documents
Worksheet on Staff Qualifications

# Section 4

## Administrator Report and Center Profile

**What is the purpose of the Administrator Report and Center Profile?**

Many of NAEYC's Criteria for High-Quality Early Childhood Programs address policies and procedures that are established for the entire program. This section includes

a. an **Administrator Report** where the director rates the criteria that relate to the administration of the entire program. The Administrator Report uses the same three-point rating scale that is used on the Observation form and the Teaching-Staff Questionnaire; and

b. a **Center Profile** where the director reports factual information about the program such as staff qualifications, ages and numbers of children enrolled, and the number of staff to children. Some of this information is related to specific criteria, but for validators and commissioners to understand the program, it is necessary to report it in some detail.

The Administrator Report is used by the director (and other administrators if appropriate) as a workbook during the self-study to evaluate the program and identify needed improvements. It is really a self-evaluation for the director. The Center Profile is part of the Program Description that is completed if the program seeks accreditation.

**What documents are required for validation?**

This section of the *Guide* also includes a List of Documents (pages 94 to 96) that are necessary to verify the program's compliance with the Criteria. If you wish to pursue accreditation, these documents should be collected in a central location or the location should be noted on pages 94 to 96 to assist the validator during the visit.

> **If the information is not available on-site, the director provides written certification by an authorized agency or individual of the documents' existence and location and level of compliance with the Criteria.**

53

# Directions for use

**Who completes the Administrator Report and Center Profile?**

The Administrator Report and Center Profile are completed by the program administrator who is most responsible for the on-site, ongoing daily supervision of the program.

**How is the Administrator Report prepared?**

The Administrator Report includes those criteria that are evaluated by the director for the entire program. A sample copy of the Administrator Report begins on page 57 of the *Guide.* A blank copy of the Administrator Report (on green paper) is sent with the self-study materials. Because one person completes this report, there is no need for a summary sheet. The ratings from the Administrator Report will be transferred onto the Program Description when the program pursues accreditation.

**How is the Center Profile prepared?**

The Center Profile asks some specific questions about the hours of operations, funding sources, licensing, and other general information about the program that should be easily answered by the director. The Center Profile also includes two charts that summarize a great deal of information about the program. One chart reports the Staffing Pattern (#10) and the other chart reports Staff Qualifications (#11). Because these charts may seem a little complicated, samples are provided on pages 84 to 88 and 89 to 93 of the *Guide* to show how the charts should be completed.

The **Staffing Pattern** chart is designed to present information about enrollment, grouping, staff-child ratios, and the hours of staff members throughout the day. If your program operates longer than 6:00 a.m. to 7:00 p.m., you will need to adjust this chart.

The **Staff Qualifications** chart is used to describe the education and experience of the administrators and all staff who work directly with children. To help the director collect information about staff qualifications, a sample worksheet (page 97) is provided in this section of the *Guide* that can be duplicated and distributed to staff members. Then the information from the worksheets can easily be transferred to the Staff Qualifications chart. Staff training in early childhood education/child development is reported in units with one unit equal to 16 classroom hours or 1 credit hour of study. Staff should be sure to report all forms of training they have experienced, including workshops, conferences, and in-service training, not just formal courses. To determine units for staff members, total the number of hours of professional development and divide by 16. For example, 100 clock hours of in-service training ÷ 16 (1 unit) = 6 units in ECE/CD.

**How are the results reported in the Program Description?**

Part 1 of the Program Description is the Center Profile. It is completed by the director and includes the following:

- Information about the program (#1 to #9)
- Staffing Pattern Chart (#10)
- Staff Qualifications Chart (#11)

The criteria that are rated by the director on the Administrator Report are reported on Part 3 of the Program Description in the column marked "Director ratings and comments." The director should rate these criteria based on the situation after improvements have been made. Comments should be recorded when the director rates a criterion a "**2**" or "**1.**"

# Administrator Report

Many of NAEYC's Criteria for High-Quality Early Childhood Programs require written documents or procedures that are established by the administrator for the entire program. This report includes the criteria that should be rated by the administrator. The letters and numbers next to each statement refer to the complete list of Criteria. This is why the letters and numbers may not be in consecutive order. (Refer to the green book, *Accreditation Criteria & Procedures of the National Association for the Education of Young Children,* for more detailed information on each criterion.)

## Instructions

Evaluate the early childhood program that you administer by rating the degree to which each criterion in the report describes your program.

| [1]<br>Not met | [2]<br>Partially met | [3]<br>Fully met |
| --- | --- | --- |
| The criterion is not met. | The criterion is partially met. | The criterion is completely met. |
| There is **little evidence** that this statement accurately describes the program. | There is **some evidence** that this statement accurately describes the program. | There is a **great deal** of evidence that this statement accurately describes the program throughout the day. |

Rate each criterion by circling one of the numbers: [1] or [2] or [3]. **All criteria rated less than a [3] must have a written comment.** Explain your ratings under the "Comments" column in all of the following cases:

- The criterion is not met [1].
- The criterion is partially met [2].
- The criterion is met through an alternate means (explain how and why).
- The program exceeds the criterion.

  No explanation is needed if the criterion is fully met [3].

  **This report is for your use only during the self-study. If you decide to pursue accreditation, you will report how your program meets these criteria, following improvements, on Part 3 of the Program Description in the column marked, "Director's Rating."**

Directors should make their ratings on the Administrator Report independent of the results from the Teaching-Staff Questionnaire and the Family Questionnaire.

# B.  Curriculum

|  |  | Rating | | | Comments |
|---|---|---|---|---|---|

| Criterion | | Not met | Partially met | Fully met | |
|---|---|---|---|---|---|

**B-1.** The program has a written statement of its philosophy and goals for children that is available to staff and families.

Rating: [1] [2] [3]

**B-2a.** The program has written curriculum plans, based on knowledge of child development and assessment of individual needs and interests.

Rating: [1] [2] [3]

**B-2b.** The learning environment and activities for children reflect the program's philosophy and goals.

Rating: [1] [2] [3]

**B-3a.** Teachers have clearly defined goals for individual children that guide curriculum planning.

Rating: [1] [2] [3]

❑ Accurately assess the skills and progress of each child in the program (through the use of observations, assessment tools, activity records).

❑ Adapt curriculum plans to meet the wide range of individual needs and interests of all children in the group.

❑ Identify children who have difficulties in behavior or development and form a plan to help them acquire the necessary skills.

❑ Prepare to meet the individual special needs of each child, including children with disabilities.

## B. Curriculum *continued*

| | Rating | | | Comments |
|---|---|---|---|---|

**Criterion**

| | | Not met | Partially met | Fully met |
|---|---|---|---|---|

**B-3b.** The program is designed to be inclusive of all children, including those with identified disabilities and special learning and developmental needs.

☐ Modifications are made in the environment and staffing patterns for children with special needs.

☐ Staff are aware of the identified/diagnosed special needs of individual children and trained to follow through on specific intervention plans.

☐ Therapy is developed appropriately and incorporated within classroom activities as much as possible rather than removing the child from the classroom.

☐ Staff make appropriate professional referrals when necessary.

☐ Family members are involved in development and use of Individualized Education Plans.

☐ Staff address the priorities and concerns of families of children with special needs.

[Rating: 1  2  3]

**B-11.** Teachers plan with families to make toileting, feeding, and the development of other self-regulation skills a positive experience for children.

[Rating: 1  2  3]

## C. Relationships among Teachers and Families

**C-1a.** A written description of the program's philosophy is available to families.

[Rating: 1  2  3]

**C-1b.** Written operating policies and procedures are available to families.

[Rating: 1  2  3]

## C. Relationships among Teachers and Families *continued*

|  | Rating | | | Comments |
|---|---|---|---|---|

| Criterion | Not met | Partially met | Fully met | Comments |
|---|---|---|---|---|
| **C-1c.** Families have opportunities to have input regarding policies and procedures and plans for meeting children's individual needs. | 1 | 2 | 3 | _____ _____ |
| **C-1d.** Programs with non-English speaking families provide materials in the family's native language or arrange for translation. ☐ **Not applicable** | 1 | 2 | 3 | _____ _____ _____ |
| **C-2.** A process has been developed for orienting children and families to the program that may include a pre-enrollment visit, family orientation meeting, or gradual introduction of children to the program that also supports children and families through the separation process. | 1 | 2 | 3 | _____ _____ _____ _____ |
| **C-3a.** Teachers work in collaborative partnerships with families, establishing and maintaining regular, ongoing, two-way communication with children's parents to build trust and mutual understanding and to ensure that children's learning and developmental needs are met. | 1 | 2 | 3 | _____ _____ _____ _____ |
| **C-3b.** Teachers listen to parents, seek to understand their goals and preferences for their children, and respect cultural and family differences. When staff are not of the linguistic and cultural background of the children/families, increased efforts are made to ensure communication with families, such as regular conferences with a translator present. | 1 | 2 | 3 | _____ _____ _____ _____ |
| **C-4a.** Family members are welcome visitors in the program at all times (for example, to observe, eat lunch with a child, or volunteer in the classroom). | 1 | 2 | 3 | _____ _____ |

## C. Relationships among Teachers and Families *continued*

| Criterion | | Rating | | Comments |
|---|---|---|---|---|
| | Not met | Partially met | Fully met | |

**C-4b.** Parents and other family members are encouraged to be involved in the program in various ways, taking into consideration working parents and those with little spare time.

⬜ 1  ⬜ 2  ⬜ 3

**C-5a.** A verbal and/or written system is established for sharing among both staff and parents the day-to-day happenings that affect children. (For example, information is exchanged between teachers at shift changes and passed on to parents at pick-up time.)

⬜ 1  ⬜ 2  ⬜ 3

**C-5b.** Changes in a child's physical or emotional state are reported to parents regularly.

⬜ 1  ⬜ 2  ⬜ 3

**C-6a.** Teachers and parents work together to make decisions about how to best support children's development and learning or to handle problems or differences of opinion as they arise.

⬜ 1  ⬜ 2  ⬜ 3

**C-6b.** Conferences are held at least once a year and at other times, as needed, to discuss children's progress, accomplishments, and difficulties at home and at the program.

⬜ 1  ⬜ 2  ⬜ 3

**C-6c.** Teachers solicit and incorporate parents' knowledge about their children into ongoing assessment and planning.

⬜ 1  ⬜ 2  ⬜ 3

**C-7.** Families are informed about the program and the curriculum and about policy or regulatory changes and other critical issues that could potentially affect the program and/or the early childhood profession through newsletters, bulletin boards, and other appropriate means.

⬜ 1  ⬜ 2  ⬜ 3

## C.   Interactions among Teachers and Families *continued*

| Criterion | Rating | | | Comments |
|---|---|---|---|---|
| | Not met | Partially met | Fully met | |
| **C-8a.** Teachers and families communicate to ensure that children experience smooth transitions from home to the program or from one program to another during the day. | 1 | 2 | 3 | |
| **C-8b.** Teachers and families communicate to ensure that the programs *(or classrooms)* from which children come and to which they go from one year to the next provide continuity over time. | 1 | 2 | 3 | |
| **C-9a.** Communication between staff and families conveys trust and respect. | 1 | 2 | 3 | |
| **C-9b.** Communication among teachers and families is frequent. (For example, teachers greet parents when they arrive and depart. Frequent friendly notes/telephone calls are used to communicate if parents do not bring their children to the program.) | 1 | 2 | 3 | |
| **C-9c.** Staff show sensitivity in their interactions with families. (For example, show sensitivity in interactions with families who are experiencing difficulties; include child in conversation when a child must be discussed in the child's presence; maintain privacy when discussions are held between parents and staff about problems and concerns regarding specific children.) | 1 | 2 | 3 | |
| **C-9d.** Teachers show acceptance of various family structures and cultural perspectives. (For example, teachers speak positively about families to the children and among themselves.) | 1 | 2 | 3 | |
| **C-9e.** Major changes that affect children, such as changes in room or teacher and use of special services, are discussed with parents before decisions are made. | 1 | 2 | 3 | |

## C. Relationships among Teachers and Families *continued*

| Criterion | Rating | | | Comments |
|---|---|---|---|---|
| | Not met | Partially met | Fully met | |

**C-9f.** Teachers seek parents' specific ideas for dealing with the child when at the program.

[ 1 ] [ 2 ] [ 3 ]

**C-10a.** Administrators and teachers are familiar with and make appropriate use of community resources including social services; mental and physical health agencies; and educational programs such as museums, libraries, and neighborhood centers.

[ 1 ] [ 2 ] [ 3 ]

**C-10b.** Program personnel connect families with needed resources and comprehensive services based on the needs and interests observed by staff or expressed by families.

[ 1 ] [ 2 ] [ 3 ]

**C-11.** Policies ensure that staff and parents have an effective way of negotiating difficulties and differences that arise in their interactions. The program has a variety of known and accepted techniques to handle differences, such as a parent policy council, an appeals committee, special conferences, or individual meetings.

[ 1 ] [ 2 ] [ 3 ]

## D. Staff Qualifications and Development

**D-1a.** Staff who work directly with children are 18 years of age or older and demonstrate the appropriate personal characteristics for working with children as exemplified in the criteria for Interactions among Teachers and Children and Curriculum.

[ 1 ] [ 2 ] [ 3 ]

**D-1b.** Early Childhood Teacher Assistants (staff who implement program activities under direct supervision) are high school graduates or the equivalent, have been trained in early childhood education/child development, and/or participate in ongoing professional development programs.

[ 1 ] [ 2 ] [ 3 ]

# D.  Staff Qualifications and Development *continued*

| Criterion | Rating | | | Comments |
|---|---|---|---|---|
| | **Not met** | **Partially met** | **Fully met** | |

**D-1c.** Early Childhood Teachers (staff who are responsible for the care and education of a group of children from birth through age 5) have at least a CDA Credential or an A.A. degree in early childhood/child development or equivalent, preferably teachers have baccalaureate degrees in early childhood education/child development.

Rating: [1] [2] [3]

**D-1d.** Staff working with school-age children have professional preparation in child development, early childhood education, elementary education, recreation, or a related field.

Rating: [1] [2] [3]

☐ **Not applicable**

**D-1e.** Volunteers receive orientation and ongoing professionals development and only work with children under supervision of qualified staff members.

Rating: [1] [2] [3]

**D-2a.** The administrator has expertise (acquired through formal education and experience) in both early childhood education/child development and administration such as human resource and financial management.

Rating: [1] [2] [3]

**D-2b.** In programs serving infants, toddlers, preschoolers, and/or kindergartners, an Early Childhood Specialist (an individual with a bachelor's degree in early childhood education/child development and at least three years of full-time teaching experience with young children and/or a graduate degree in ECE/CD) is employed to direct the educational program (may be the director or other appropriate person). In public schools, the individual who provides support to prekindergarten and kindergarten teachers and/or who is responsible for program development is a qualified Early Childhood Specialist.

Rating: [1] [2] [3]

# D. Staff Qualifications and Development *continued*

**Criterion**

**Rating**

| Not met | Partially met | Fully met |
|:---:|:---:|:---:|

**Comments**

**D-2c.** In programs serving only school-age children, the educational program is directed by a school-age specialist with a bachelor's degree in elementary education, recreation, or related field and at least three years of experience working with school-age children.

| 1 | 2 | 3 |
|:---:|:---:|:---:|

❑ **Not applicable**

**D-3.** New staff, volunteers, and substitutes are adequately oriented about the goals and philosophy of the program, emergency health and safety procedures, individual needs of children assigned to the staff member's care, guidance and classroom management techniques, child abuse and neglect reporting procedures, planned daily activities of the program, and expectations for ethical conduct.

| 1 | 2 | 3 |
|:---:|:---:|:---:|

**D-4a.** The program provides regular opportunities for staff to participate in ongoing professional development to improve skills in working with children and families or to prepare them to assume more responsible positions.

| 1 | 2 | 3 |
|:---:|:---:|:---:|

**D-4b.** Ongoing professional development provides continuing education and other opportunities for staff to keep abreast of the latest developments in the field, including new programs and practices and pending policy, legislation, or regulatory changes. The amount and kind of continuing education provided varies, depending on the needs of the program, the preservice qualifications of the staff, and the number of staff pursuing higher education while employed.

| 1 | 2 | 3 |
|:---:|:---:|:---:|

Administrator Report

# E.  Administration

| Criterion | | Rating | | | Comments |
|---|---|---|---|---|---|
| | | Not met | Partially met | Fully met | |

**E-1a.** At least annually, the director and staff conduct an assessment to identify strengths and weaknesses of the program and to set program goals for the year.

1 □   2 □   3 □

**E-1b.** The annual program evaluation examines the adequacy of staff compensation and benefits and rate of staff turnover, and a plan is developed to increase salaries and benefits to ensure recruitment and retention of qualified staff and continuity of relationships.

1 □   2 □   3 □

**E-2a.** The program has written policies and procedures for operating, including hours, fees, illness, holidays, refund information, and termination of enrollment. Child enrollment and termination policies protect children's rights as outlined in the Americans with Disabilities Act.

1 □   2 □   3 □

**E-2b.** The program has a child abuse and neglect policy that includes reporting requirements for staff as well as procedures to be followed should a staff member be accused of abuse or neglect.

1 □   2 □   3 □

**E-3a.** The program has written personnel policies, including job descriptions, salary scales with increments based on professional qualification, length of employment, and performance; benefits; resignation and termination; and grievance procedures.

1 □   2 □   3 □

**E-3b.** Hiring practices are nondiscriminatory. *(Present copy of advertised position or other evidence of equal opportunity employment.)*

1 □   2 □   3 □

**E-3c.** Every effort is made to hire staff who reflect diverse cultural, racial, and linguistic characteristics as needed to communicate with the children and families served.

1 □   2 □   3 □

# E. Administration *continued*

**Rating**        **Comments**

**Criterion**

Not met / Partially met / Fully met

**E-4.** Benefits packages for full-time staff include paid leave (annual, sick, and personal), medical insurance, and retirement. Other benefits such as subsidized child care or continued education may be negotiated as unique to the situation. Benefits for part-time staff who are employed at least half-time are available on a prorated basis.

☐ 1 ☐ 2 ☐ 3

**E-5a.** Attendance records of staff and children are kept.

☐ 1 ☐ 2 ☐ 3

**E-5b.** Confidential personnel files are kept including résumés with record of experience, transcripts of education, documentation of ongoing professional development, and results of performance evaluation. (See criterion **J-1**.)

☐ 1 ☐ 2 ☐ 3

**E-6a.** In cases where the program is governed by a board of directors, the program has written policies defining roles and responsibilities of board members and staff.

☐ 1 ☐ 2 ☐ 3   ☐ Not applicable

**E-6b.** Board members and other administrators such as school principals are informed about the elements and methods involved in implementing a high-quality, developmentally appropriate program.

☐ 1 ☐ 2 ☐ 3   ☐ Not applicable

**E-6c.** Records of board meetings (minutes) are kept.

☐ 1 ☐ 2 ☐ 3   ☐ Not applicable

# E.   Administration *continued*

| Criterion | Rating | | | Comments |
|---|---|---|---|---|
| | Not met | Partially met | Fully met | |

**E-7.** Fiscal records are kept with evidence of long-range budgeting and sound financial planning (projections of at least one year are needed). Operating budgets are prepared annually, and there is a quarterly reconciliation of expenses to budget.

Rating: ☐ 1   ☐ 2   ☐ 3

Comments: _____

**E-8a.** Accident protection and liability insurance coverage is maintained for children and adults. (*Present policy and/or most recent canceled check or receipt for payment.*)

Rating: ☐ 1   ☐ 2   ☐ 3

Comments: _____

**E-8b.** Vehicle insurance is maintained on any vehicle owned or leased by the facility and used to transport children.

Rating: ☐ 1   ☐ 2   ☐ 3

☐ Not applicable

Comments: _____

**E-9a.** Staff interactions reflect mutual trust, respect, and support for each other.

Rating: ☐ 1   ☐ 2   ☐ 3

Comments: _____

**E-9b.** Staff members seek out and acknowledge each other's ideas and opinions. Staff give positive recognition to each other's skills and accomplishments.

Rating: ☐ 1   ☐ 2   ☐ 3

Comments: _____

**E-9c.** Staff provide appropriate supports for each other when dealing with stress.

Rating: ☐ 1   ☐ 2   ☐ 3

Comments: _____

**E-9d.** Staff respect each other's rights to confidentiality.

Rating: ☐ 1   ☐ 2   ☐ 3

Comments: _____

# E. Administration *continued*

| Criterion | Rating | | | Comments |
|---|---|---|---|---|
| | Not met | Partially met | Fully met | |

**E-9e.** Staff communicate with each other to ensure smooth operations.

Rating: 1 | 2 | 3

**E-10a.** Staff and administrators plan and consult together frequently about the program, children, and families.

Rating: 1 | 2 | 3

**E-10b.** Staff plan and consult together.

Rating: 1 | 2 | 3

**E-10c.** Regular staff meetings are held for staff to consult on program planning, to plan for implementing and attaining goals, to plan for individual children, and to discuss program and working conditions (may be meetings of small group of or full staff).

Rating: 1 | 2 | 3

**E-10d.** Teachers are provided weekly paid planning time, away from responsibility for children.

Rating: 1 | 2 | 3

**E-11.** Staff are provided space and time away from children during the day. (When staff work directly with children for more than four hours, staff are provided breaks of at least 15 minutes in each four-hour period.)

Rating: 1 | 2 | 3

**E-12.** Staff keep information about children, families, and associates confidential. Staff refrain from commenting about children or families in the presence of other adults or children.

Rating: 1 | 2 | 3

**E-13.** An appropriate person on-site is designated to assume authority and to take action in an emergency, in the event of the director's absence.

Rating: 1 | 2 | 3

# F.    Staffing

**F-1 and F-2. Recommended staff-child ratios within group size***

|                                    |     |     |     |     |     | Group size |     |     |     |     |     |
| --- | --- | --- | --- | --- | --- | --- | --- | --- | --- | --- | --- |
| **Age of children**               | 6   | 8   | 10  | 12  | 14  | 16  | 18  | 20  | 22  | 24  | 30  |
| Infants (birth to 12 months)       | 1:3 | 1:4 |     |     |     |     |     |     |     |     |     |
| Toddlers (12 to 24 months)         | 1:3 | 1:4 | 1:5 | 1:4 |     |     |     |     |     |     |     |
| 2-year-olds (24 to 30 months)      |     | 1:4 | 1:5 | 1:6 |     |     |     |     |     |     |     |
| 2½-year-olds (30 to 36 months)     |     |     | 1:5 | 1:6 | 1:7 |     |     |     |     |     |     |
| 3-year-olds                        |     |     |     |     | 1:7 | 1:8 | 1:9 | 1:10 |     |     |     |
| 4-year-olds                        |     |     |     |     |     | 1:8 | 1:9 | 1:10 |     |     |     |
| 5-year-olds                        |     |     |     |     |     | 1:8 | 1:9 | 1:10 |     |     |     |
| Kindergartners                     |     |     |     |     |     |     |     | 1:10 | 1:11 | 1:12 |     |
| 6- to 8-year-olds                  |     |     |     |     |     |     |     | 1:10 | 1:11 | 1:12 | 1:15 |
| 9- to 12-year-olds                 |     |     |     |     |     |     |     |     | 1:12 | 1:15 |     |

*Smaller group sizes and lower staff-child rations have been found to be strong predictors of compliance with indiciators of quality such as positive interactions among staff and children and developmentally appropriate curriculum. Variations in group sizes and ratios are acceptable in cases where the program demonstrates a very high level of compliance with criteria for interactions (A), curriculum (B), staff qualifications (D), health and safety (H), and physical environment (G).

|                |                                                                 | **Rating** |             |             | **Comments** |
| --- | --- | --- | --- | --- | --- |
| **Criterion**  |                                                                 | Not met | Partially met | Fully met |             |
| F-1.           | The number of children in a group is limited in accordance with NAEYC Criteria to facilitate adult-child interaction and constructive activity among children. Groups of children may be age-determined or multiage. (A group is the number of children assigned to a staff member or a team of staff members occupying an individual classroom or well-defined space, with clear physical boundaries that prevent intermingling of children, within a larger room.) *(Using the chart on this page, determine which groups meet or exceed the required group sizes.)* <br><br> Out of _____ groups, <br> (total number of) <br><br> _____ groups meet NAEYC's group-size requirements. | **1** | **2** | **3** |             |

# F. Staffing *continued*

|  | Rating | | | Comments |
|---|---|---|---|---|
| **Criterion** | Not met | Partially met | Fully met | |

**F-2a.** Sufficient staff with primary responsibility for working with children are available to provide frequent personal contact, meaningful learning activities, and supervision and to offer immediate care as needed. *(Using the chart on the previous page, determine which groups meet or exceed the required staff-child ratios.)*

Rating: `1` `2` `3`

Out of _____ groups,
(total number of)

_____ groups meet NAEYC's staff-child ratio requirements.

**F-2b.** Substitutes are provided to maintain staff-child ratios when regular staff are absent. Substitutes for infants and toddlers are familiar with the children and oriented to children's schedules and individual differences in a systematic way before assignment. Volunteers who work with children complete a pre-assignment orientation and participate in ongoing training.

Rating: `1` `2` `3`

**F-3a.** Each staff member has primary responsibility for and develops a deeper attachment to an identified group of children.

Rating: `1` `2` `3`

**F-3b.** Every attempt is made to have continuity of adults who work with children within each day and over extended periods of time (several years of the child's enrollment), particularly infants and toddlers.

Rating: `1` `2` `3`

**F-3c.** Infants and toddlers spend the majority of the time interacting with the same person each day.

Rating: `1` `2` `3`

❏ **Not applicable**

## F.   Staffing *continued*

| Criterion | Rating | | | Comments |
|---|---|---|---|---|
| | Not met | Partially met | Fully met | |

**F-3d.**  The program is organized and staffed to minimize the number of group transitions an individual child experiences during the time the child is enrolled in the program. Every attempt is made to maintain continuity of relationships between teachers and children and among groups of children.

Rating: [1] [2] [3]

**F-4.**  A majority of the child's day is spent in activities utilizing recommended staff-child ratios and group-size limitations while minimizing the number of transitions or regroupings children experience and maintaining relationships among groups of children as much as possible.

Rating: [1] [2] [3]

## G.   Physical Environment

**G-1a.**  There is a minimum of 35 square feet (preferably 50 square feet) of usable playroom floor space per child indoors.

Provide actual square feet if less than 35 square feet _____.

Rating: [1] [2] [3]

**G-1b.**  There is a minimum of 75 square feet (preferably 100 square feet) of play space outdoors per child (when space is in use).

Provide actual square feet if less than 75 square feet _____.

Rating: [1] [2] [3]

**G-10a.**  The work environment for staff, including classrooms and staff rooms, is comfortable, well-organized, and in good repair.

Rating: [1] [2] [3]

**G-10b.**  The environment includes a place for adults to take a break or work away from children, an adult-sized bathroom, a secure place for staff to store their personal belongings, and an administrative area that is separated from the children's areas for planning or preparing materials.

Rating: [1] [2] [3]

# H. Health and Safety

| | Rating | | | Comments |
|---|---|---|---|---|
| **Criterion** | Not met | Partially met | Fully met | |

**H-1.** The program presents valid certification that it is in compliance with all legal requirements for protection of the health and safety of children in group settings, such as building codes, sanitation, water quality, and fire protection. The program is licensed or accredited to operate by the appropriate state/ local agencies. The program maintains a high level of compliance with licensing standards, free of a record of repeated serious violations. If exempt from licensing, the program demonstrates compliance with its own state or local community's regulations (building, sanitation, and licensing codes) for early childhood programs/child care centers subject to licensing.

Rating: [ 1 ] [ 2 ] [ 3 ]

**H-2a.** Staff health records include results of pre-employment tuberculosis test and evaluation of any infection and evidence of tuberculosis test every two years thereafter and emergency contact information.

Rating: [ 1 ] [ 2 ] [ 3 ]

**H-2b.** Hiring practices include careful checking of personal references of all potential employees and volunteers.

Rating: [ 1 ] [ 2 ] [ 3 ]

**H-2c.** New staff members serve a probationary employment period during which the director or other qualified person makes a professional judgment as to their physical and psychological competence for working with children.

Rating: [ 1 ] [ 2 ] [ 3 ]

**H-3.** Child health records include
- ❑ results of recent health examination,
- ❑ up-to-date record of immunizations,
- ❑ emergency contact information,
- ❑ names of people authorized to call for the child, and
- ❑ important health history (such as allergies, chronic illness).

Rating: [ 1 ] [ 2 ] [ 3 ]

# H. Health and Safety *continued*

| Criterion | Rating | | | Comments |
|---|---|---|---|---|
| | Not met | Partially met | Fully met | |

**H-4a.** The program has a written policy given to all families specifying the conditions under which sick children are excluded, included but isolated, or included in the regular classroom, in accordance with local licensing and public health regulations.

Rating: 1 2 3

**H-4b.** When sick children are permitted to attend, the decision is based on the comfort of ill children, the protection of well children and staff, the resources available to the program to meet any special care that is required, and the needs of families.

Rating: 1 2 3

**H-5.** Provisions are made for safe arrival and departure of all children that also allow for parent-staff interaction. A system exists for ensuring that children are released only to authorized people. A procedure for accountability when a child fails to show for the program is in place and followed. A system exists to ensure the safety of older school-age children whose parents have agreed to allow their children to leave the program on their own. The system includes written agreements between parents and the program and consistent sign-out procedures for released children.

Rating: 1 2 3

**H-6.** If transportation is provided for children by the program, vehicles are equipped with age-appropriate restraint devices, and appropriate safety precautions are taken. The program presents certification that vehicles used in transporting children are appropriately licensed, inspected, and maintained.

Rating: 1 2 3

☐ Not applicable

**H-7b.** There is specific accountability for each child by one staff member. Systems are in place for accounting for children's whereabouts at regular intervals, especially during periods of transition.

Rating: 1 2 3

# H. Health and Safety *continued*

|  | Rating | | | Comments |
|---|---|---|---|---|
| **Criterion** | Not met | Partially met | Fully met | |

**H-7c.** Families are informed about procedures and policies for field trips. Families are notified of all activities outside the center. Field trips are accompanied by parents and other volunteers to ensure adequate supervision. Field trips are preplanned and emergency procedures are prepared. Transportation meets requirements (see **H-6**).

| 1 | 2 | 3 |

**H-8.** Staff are alert to the health of each child. Individual medical problems and accidents are recorded and reported to staff and families, and a written record is kept of such incidents.

| 1 | 2 | 3 |

**H-9a.** Staff know procedures for reporting suspected incidents of child abuse and/or neglect.

| 1 | 2 | 3 |

**H-9b.** Suspected incidents of child abuse and/or neglect by families, staff, volunteers, or others are reported to the appropriate local agencies.

| 1 | 2 | 3 |

**H-10.** At least once staff member who has certification in emergency pediatric first-aid treatment, including CPR for infants and children and emergency management of choking, from a licensed health professional is always present. Current certificates are kept on file.

| 1 | 2 | 3 |

**H-11a.** Adequate first-aid supplies are readily available.

| 1 | 2 | 3 |

**H-11b.** A plan exists for dealing with medical emergencies that includes a source of emergency care, written parental consent forms, and transportation arrangements.

| 1 | 2 | 3 |

Administrator Report

# H. Health and Safety *continued*

| Criterion | Rating | | | Comments |
|---|---|---|---|---|
| | Not met | Partially met | Fully met | |

**H-13a.** The facility is cleaned daily, including disinfecting bathroom fixtures and removing trash.

[1] [2] [3]

_____
_____
_____
_____

**H-13b.** Infants' equipment is washed and disinfected at least twice a week. Toys that are mouthed are washed daily.

[1] [2] [3]

❑ **Not applicable**

_____
_____
_____
_____

**H-14b.** Staff and volunteers know and follow proper procedures during handwashing, including washing with soap and warm, running water for at least 10 seconds; using single use or disposable towels; and avoiding recontamination from faucets by turning off faucets with towel.

[1] [2] [3]

_____
_____
_____
_____
_____
_____

**H-14d.** Staff and volunteers follow universal precautions to prevent transmission of blood-borne diseases.

[1] [2] [3]

_____
_____
_____
_____

**H-16a.** Individual bedding is washed at least once a week and used by only one child between washings. Individual cribs, cots, and mats are washed if soiled.

[1] [2] [3]

❑ **Not applicable**

_____
_____
_____
_____

**H-17.** Hot water does not exceed 120°F (43°C) at faucets used by children.

[1] [2] [3]

_____
_____
_____
_____

**H-18d.** Program provides certification that nontoxic building materials, no lead paint or asbestos, are used in the facility (or lead abatement procedures are in place for older facilities).

[1] [2] [3]

_____
_____
_____
_____
_____

# H. Health and Safety *continued*

| | Rating | | |
|---|---|---|---|
| **Criterion** | Not met | Partially met | Fully met |

**H-18e.** Stairways are well-lighted and equipped with handrails.

| 1 | 2 | 3 |
|---|---|---|

❑ **Not applicable**

**Comments**

**H-20b.** Medication is administered to children only when a written order is submitted by a parent and the medication is administered by a consistently designated staff member. Written records are kept of medication given to children.

| 1 | 2 | 3 |
|---|---|---|

**H-21a.** Staff and volunteers are familiar with primary and secondary evacuation routes and practice evacuation procedures monthly with children.

| 1 | 2 | 3 |
|---|---|---|

**H-22a.** Staff and volunteers are familiar with emergency procedures and procedures for severe storm warnings.

| 1 | 2 | 3 |
|---|---|---|

**H-22b.** Smoke detectors and fire extinguishers are provided and periodically checked.

| 1 | 2 | 3 |
|---|---|---|

**H-22c.** Emergency telephone numbers including police, fire, rescue, and poison control services are posted by telephones.

| 1 | 2 | 3 |
|---|---|---|

Administrator Report

# I. Nutrition and Food Service

| | Rating | | | Comments |

| Criterion | Not met | Partially met | Fully met | |

**I-1.** Meals and/or snacks are planned to meet the child's nutritional requirements in proportion to the amount of time the child is in the program each day, as recommended by the Child Care Food Program of the U.S. Department of Agriculture. Amount of food served is adjusted according to the age of the children because infants and toddlers require smaller amounts of food served more frequently and school-age children require much more food than preschoolers.

〔1〕 〔2〕 〔3〕

**I-2a.** Written menus are provided for families.

〔1〕 〔2〕 〔3〕

**I-2b.** Feeding times and food consumption information is provided to families of infants and toddlers at the end of each day.

〔1〕 〔2〕 〔3〕

❑ **Not applicable**

**I-3.** Foods indicative of children's cultural backgrounds are served periodically.

〔1〕 〔2〕 〔3〕

**I-4.** If the program does not provide food, families are educated regarding well-balanced meals that may be brought from home. Food brought from home is stored appropriately until consumed.

〔1〕 〔2〕 〔3〕

❑ **Not applicable**

**I-5.** Where food is prepared on the premises, the program is in compliance with legal requirements for food preparation and service. Food may be prepared at an approved facility and transported to the program in appropriate sanitary containers and at appropriate temperatures.

〔1〕 〔2〕 〔3〕

# J. Evaluation

| Criterion | Rating | | | Comments |
|---|---|---|---|---|
| | Not met | Partially met | Fully met | |

**J-1a.** All staff, including the program administrator, are evaluated at least annually by the director or other appropriate supervisor.

1   2   3

**J-1b.** Results of staff evaluation are written and confidential. They are discussed privately with the staff member.

1   2   3

**J-1c.** Staff evaluations include classroom observation. Evaluation is based on the employees's job description and previously established goals for improvement.

1   2   3

**J-1d.** Staff are informed of evaluation criteria in advance.

1   2   3

**J-1e.** Staff have an opportunity to evaluate their own performance.

1   2   3

**J-1f.** A plan for staff training is generated from the staff-evaluation process.

1   2   3

**J-2a.** At least annually, administrators, families, staff, school-age children, and other routinely participating adults are involved in evaluating the program's effectiveness in meeting the needs of children and families.

1   2   3

# J.   Evaluation *continued*

| Criterion | Rating | | | Comments |
|---|---|---|---|---|
| | Not met | Partially met | Fully met | |
| **J-2b.** The program regularly establishes goals for continuous improvement and innovation. | 1 | 2 | 3 | |
| **J-3.** Individual descriptions of children's development and learning are written and compiled as a basis for planning appropriate learning activities, as a means of facilitating optimal development of each child, as a means of identifying children who may be in need of more systematic diagnosis of a learning or developmental problem, and as records for use in communications with families. | 1 | 2 | 3 | |

Program ID Number

# Early Childhood Program Description
## *Part 1–Center Profile*

**Program identification—This page is removed before the Commission considers the Program Description.**

Name of program ___Everywhere Child Development Center___

Name and title of person completing this form ___Jane Doe, Director___

Name and title of person legally responsible for administration of program (if different from above)
___Jane and John Doe, Owners___

**Location(s) of program** (overseas programs should provide mailing address)

(1)　Street ___1234 Main Street___

　　　City ___Everywhere___　State ___MD___　ZIP code ___20785___

　　　Telephone ( ___301___ ) ___555-1212___

　　　Program FAX ( ___301___ ) ___555-1213___

　　　Program e-mail ___jjdoe@sample.org___

**For multisite applications:**
**No more than three sites may apply under one Program Description.**

(2)　Street _____

　　　City _____　State _____　ZIP code _____

　　　Telephone ( 　　 ) _____

(2)　Street _____

　　　City _____　State _____　ZIP code _____

　　　Telephone ( 　　 ) _____

Number of sites applying for accreditation under this Program Description _____. Sites must be within 15 minutes from one another; additional sites cannot serve more than 60 children per site.

Program ID Number

# Early Childhood Program Description

## *Part 1—Center Profile*

1.  How long has the program been in operation? ___5 / 6___
    (years/months)

    If applicable, at site 2? _____
    (years/months)

    If applicable, at site 3? _____
    (years/months)

2.  Does the program currently meet local licensing regulations?

    If yes, by what agencies is the program licensed/accredited? _State health department_
    _____

    If no, explain. _____
    _____

3.  What are your program's hours of operation? _7:00 a.m. to 5:00 p.m._

    Days per week _Monday — Friday_ Months per year _12_

    Does your program change during summer? _yes_

    If yes, what is the last day of the regular school year? _June 2_

    In what way does the program change for the summer? _school-age children attend_
    _full-time_

4.  What funding sources support the program? Please provide the estimated percentage of funding received from each source.

    _100 %_ Parent tuition                    _____ Public funds (federal/state)

    _____ Community funds (United Way, etc.)   _____ Church contributions

    _____ Employer contributions              _____ Other (please specify below)

5.  If the program has a governing board or policy or advisory group, describe the composition of the group and its functions.

Group of nine parents function as advisory group

6.  What is the purpose of the program? (Describe the type of program, for example, a full-day child care center, half-day preschool, public school kindergarten, parent cooperative, Head Start, or Montessori School.)

Full-day child care center with half-day preschool and afterschool care

7.  What is the philosophy of the program? (Provide a brief description of the program's goals and objectives for children. Use the space below or attach additional sheets if necessary.)

(Individual to each program)

8.  What is the total number of children enrolled in the program? ___101___

    Daily enrollment (if different from total above) __101__ Monday    __81__ Tuesday    __101__ Wednesday
    __81__ Thursday    __101__ Friday    _____ Saturday    _____ Sunday

9.  Provide the number of children enrolled by developmental level.
    __8__ Infants (birth through 12 months)
    __12__ Toddlers (13 months to 35 months)
    __53__ Preschoolers (3- through 5-year-olds)
    __10__ Kindergarteners (attending public or private kindergarten program)
    __18__ School-agers (6-year-olds and older)

10.  Staffing Pattern—use the following chart to describe how the program is staffed. For each hour of the day indicate the number of children enrolled in the group, the number of staff members assigned to the group (use first name and last initial only), and the hours worked by the staff members. A *group* is the number of children assigned to a staff member or team of staff members occupying an individual classroom or well-defined space within a larger room. Each group should be listed separately on the Staffing Pattern. **If your program is not organized into self-contained classrooms but employs an open-space organizational structure, please attach clear information about the arrangements of the environment (a floor plan) and how the children are grouped within it.** Clarify how the staffing criteria (group size and staff-child ratio) are met in this environment throughout the day.

## Staffing Pattern

| Group of children | Staffing Pattern | | | | | | | | | | | | | | |
|---|---|---|---|---|---|---|---|---|---|---|---|---|---|---|---|

**Group name**
Infants
6 wks. - 12 mo.

| AM | | Number of children enrolled each hour | | | | | | | | | | | PM |
|---|---|---|---|---|---|---|---|---|---|---|---|---|---|
| 6:00 | 7:00 | 8:00 | 9:00 | 10:00 | 11:00 | 12:00 | 1:00 | 2:00 | 3:00 | 4:00 | 5:00 | 6:00 | 7:00 |
| | 3/5 | 8 | 8 | 8 | 8 | 8 | 8 | 8 | 8 | 6 | 3 | | |

Number of staff in attendance each hour

| 1/2 | 2 | 2 | 2 | 2 | 2 | 2 | 2 | 2 | 2 | 1 | | |

**Age range      Number**
Infants      8
Toddlers      ___
Preschoolers      ___
Kindergartners      ___
School-agers      ___

Hours of each staff member
7:00 ——— Joan B. (11:30 - 12:30 break) ——— 4:00
   7:30 ——— Donna C. (12:30 - 1:30 break) ——— 5:00
      11:30 ——— 12:30 Sara C.
         12:30 ——— 1:30 Holly P.

**Group name**
Toddlers
15 mo. - 30 mo.

| AM | | Number of children enrolled each hour | | | | | | | | | | | PM |
|---|---|---|---|---|---|---|---|---|---|---|---|---|---|
| 6:00 | 7:00 | 8:00 | 9:00 | 10:00 | 11:00 | 12:00 | 1:00 | 2:00 | 3:00 | 4:00 | 5:00 | 6:00 | 7:00 |
| | 4 | 8/12 | 12 | 12 | 12 | 12 | 12 | 12 | 12 | 8 | 4 | | |

Number of staff in attendance each hour

| | 1 | 2 | 2 | 2 | 2 | 2 | 2 | 2 | 2 | 2 | 1 | | |

**Age range      Number**
Infants      ___
Toddlers      12
Preschoolers      ___
Kindergartners      ___
School-agers      ___

Hours of each staff member
7:00 ——— Susan H. (12:00 - 1:00 break) ——— 4:00
   7:30 ——— Debbie T. (1:00 - 2:00 break) ——— 5:00
         12:00 ——— 2:00 Jennifer G.

**Group name**
Half-day
preschool
M - W - F

| AM | | Number of children enrolled each hour | | | | | | | | | | | PM |
|---|---|---|---|---|---|---|---|---|---|---|---|---|---|
| 6:00 | 7:00 | 8:00 | 9:00 | 10:00 | 11:00 | 12:00 | 1:00 | 2:00 | 3:00 | 4:00 | 5:00 | 6:00 | 7:00 |
| | | 20 | 20 | 20 | 20 | 20 | | | | | | | |

Number of staff in attendance each hour

| | | 2 | 2 | 2 | 2 | 2 | | | | | | | |

**Age range      Number**
Infants      ___
Toddlers      ___
Preschoolers      20
Kindergartners      ___
School-agers      ___

Hours of each staff member
8:00 ——— Emily W. ——— 12:30
   8:00 ——— Holly P. ——— 12:30

## Staffing Pattern *continued*

| Group of children | Staffing Pattern | | | | | | | | | | | | | |
|---|---|---|---|---|---|---|---|---|---|---|---|---|---|---|

**Group name: Full-day preschool (4-5 yrs.)**

| AM | | | | Number of children enrolled each hour | | | | | | | | | PM |
|---|---|---|---|---|---|---|---|---|---|---|---|---|---|
| 6:00 | 7:00 | 8:00 | 9:00 | 10:00 | 11:00 | 12:00 | 1:00 | 2:00 | 3:00 | 4:00 | 5:00 | 6:00 | 7:00 |
| 3/8 | 15/20 | 20 | 20 | 20 | 20 | 20 | 20 | 20 | 15 | 8/5 | | | |

Number of staff in attendance each hour

| 1 | 2 | 2 | 2 | 2 | 2 | 2 | 3 | 3 | 2 | 2 | | | |

| Age range | Number |
|---|---|
| Infants | |
| Toddlers | |
| Preschoolers | 20 |
| Kindergartners | |
| School-agers | |

Hours of each staff member

7:00 ____ Kim K. (12:00 - 1:00 break) ____ 4:00
8:00 ____ Melinda L. (1:00 - 2:00 break) ____ 5:00
12:00 ____ Jeff R. ____ 5:30

**Group name: Threes**

| AM | | | | Number of children enrolled each hour | | | | | | | | | PM |
|---|---|---|---|---|---|---|---|---|---|---|---|---|---|
| 6:00 | 7:00 | 8:00 | 9:00 | 10:00 | 11:00 | 12:00 | 1:00 | 2:00 | 3:00 | 4:00 | 5:00 | 6:00 | 7:00 |
| 5/8 | 13 | 13 | 13 | 13 | 13 | 13 | 13 | 13 | 8/5 | 3 | | | |

Number of staff in attendance each hour

| 1/2 | 2 | 2 | 2 | 2 | 2 | 2 | 2 | 2 | 2 | 1 | | | |

| Age range | Number |
|---|---|
| Infants | |
| Toddlers | |
| Preschoolers | 13 |
| Kindergartners | |
| School-agers | |

Hours of each staff member

7:00 ____ Amanda S. (12:00 - 1:00 break) 4:00
7:30 ____ Molly A. (1:00 - 2:00 break) ____ 4:30
11:30 ____ Amy T. ____ 1:30      4:00 ____ Amy T. 5:30

**Group name: Afterschool**

| AM | | | | Number of children enrolled each hour | | | | | | | | | PM |
|---|---|---|---|---|---|---|---|---|---|---|---|---|---|
| 6:00 | 7:00 | 8:00 | 9:00 | 10:00 | 11:00 | 12:00 | 1:00 | 2:00 | 3:00 | 4:00 | 5:00 | 6:00 | 7:00 |
| | | | | | | | | 10 | 10/28 | 18 | 7 | | |

Number of staff in attendance each hour

| | | | | | | | | 1 | | | | | |

| Age range | Number |
|---|---|
| Infants | |
| Toddlers | |
| Preschoolers | |
| Kindergartners | 28 |
| School-agers | |

Hours of each staff member

2:00 ____ Emily W. ____ 5:30
3:00 ____ Holly P. ____ 5:30
3:00 ____ Amy T. 4:00

**Group name:**

| AM | | | | Number of children enrolled each hour | | | | | | | | | PM |
|---|---|---|---|---|---|---|---|---|---|---|---|---|---|
| 6:00 | 7:00 | 8:00 | 9:00 | 10:00 | 11:00 | 12:00 | 1:00 | 2:00 | 3:00 | 4:00 | 5:00 | 6:00 | 7:00 |
| | | | | | | | | | | | | | |

Number of staff in attendance each hour

| | | | | | | | | | | | | | |

| Age range | Number |
|---|---|
| Infants | |
| Toddlers | |
| Preschoolers | |
| Kindergartners | |
| School-agers | |

Hours of each staff member

*Center Profile*

# Staffing Pattern *continued*

| Group of children | Staffing Pattern | | | | | | | | | | | | | | |
|---|---|---|---|---|---|---|---|---|---|---|---|---|---|---|---|
| **Group name** | **AM** | **Number of children enrolled each hour** | | | | | | | | | | | | | **PM** |
| | 6:00 | 7:00 | 8:00 | 9:00 | 10:00 | 11:00 | 12:00 | 1:00 | 2:00 | 3:00 | 4:00 | 5:00 | 6:00 | 7:00 |
| | | | | | | | | | | | | | | |
| | **Number of staff in attendance each hour** | | | | | | | | | | | | | | |
| **Age range   Number** | | | | | | | | | | | | | | | |
| Infants _____ | Hours of each staff member | | | | | | | | | | | | | | |
| Toddlers _____ | | | | | | | | | | | | | | | |
| Preschoolers _____ | | | | | | | | | | | | | | | |
| Kindergartners _____ | | | | | | | | | | | | | | | |
| School-agers _____ | | | | | | | | | | | | | | | |
| **Group name** | **AM** | **Number of children enrolled each hour** | | | | | | | | | | | | | **PM** |
| | 6:00 | 7:00 | 8:00 | 9:00 | 10:00 | 11:00 | 12:00 | 1:00 | 2:00 | 3:00 | 4:00 | 5:00 | 6:00 | 7:00 |
| | | | | | | | | | | | | | | |
| | **Number of staff in attendance each hour** | | | | | | | | | | | | | | |
| **Age range   Number** | | | | | | | | | | | | | | | |
| Infants _____ | Hours of each staff member | | | | | | | | | | | | | | |
| Toddlers _____ | | | | | | | | | | | | | | | |
| Preschoolers _____ | | | | | | | | | | | | | | | |
| Kindergartners _____ | | | | | | | | | | | | | | | |
| School-agers _____ | | | | | | | | | | | | | | | |
| **Group name** | **AM** | **Number of children enrolled each hour** | | | | | | | | | | | | | **PM** |
| | 6:00 | 7:00 | 8:00 | 9:00 | 10:00 | 11:00 | 12:00 | 1:00 | 2:00 | 3:00 | 4:00 | 5:00 | 6:00 | 7:00 |
| | | | | | | | | | | | | | | |
| | **Number of staff in attendance each hour** | | | | | | | | | | | | | | |
| **Age range   Number** | | | | | | | | | | | | | | | |
| Infants _____ | Hours of each staff member | | | | | | | | | | | | | | |
| Toddlers _____ | | | | | | | | | | | | | | | |
| Preschoolers _____ | | | | | | | | | | | | | | | |
| Kindergartners _____ | | | | | | | | | | | | | | | |
| School-agers _____ | | | | | | | | | | | | | | | |
| **Group name** | **AM** | **Number of children enrolled each hour** | | | | | | | | | | | | | **PM** |
| | 6:00 | 7:00 | 8:00 | 9:00 | 10:00 | 11:00 | 12:00 | 1:00 | 2:00 | 3:00 | 4:00 | 5:00 | 6:00 | 7:00 |
| | | | | | | | | | | | | | | |
| | **Number of staff in attendance each hour** | | | | | | | | | | | | | | |
| **Age range   Number** | | | | | | | | | | | | | | | |
| Infants _____ | Hours of each staff member | | | | | | | | | | | | | | |
| Toddlers _____ | | | | | | | | | | | | | | | |
| Preschoolers _____ | | | | | | | | | | | | | | | |
| Kindergartners _____ | | | | | | | | | | | | | | | |
| School-agers _____ | | | | | | | | | | | | | | | |

## Staffing Pattern *continued*

| Group of children | Staffing Pattern | | | | | | | | | | | | | | |
|---|---|---|---|---|---|---|---|---|---|---|---|---|---|---|---|

**Group name**

| AM | Number of children enrolled each hour | | | | | | | | | | | | | PM |
|---|---|---|---|---|---|---|---|---|---|---|---|---|---|---|
| 6:00 | 7:00 | 8:00 | 9:00 | 10:00 | 11:00 | 12:00 | 1:00 | 2:00 | 3:00 | 4:00 | 5:00 | 6:00 | | 7:00 |
| | | | | | | | | | | | | | | |

Number of staff in attendance each hour

| | | | | | | | | | | | | | | |
|---|---|---|---|---|---|---|---|---|---|---|---|---|---|---|

**Age range    Number**

Infants _____
Toddlers _____
Preschoolers _____
Kindergartners _____
School-agers _____

Hours of each staff member

---

**Group name**

| AM | Number of children enrolled each hour | | | | | | | | | | | | | PM |
|---|---|---|---|---|---|---|---|---|---|---|---|---|---|---|
| 6:00 | 7:00 | 8:00 | 9:00 | 10:00 | 11:00 | 12:00 | 1:00 | 2:00 | 3:00 | 4:00 | 5:00 | 6:00 | | 7:00 |
| | | | | | | | | | | | | | | |

Number of staff in attendance each hour

| | | | | | | | | | | | | | | |
|---|---|---|---|---|---|---|---|---|---|---|---|---|---|---|

**Age range    Number**

Infants _____
Toddlers _____
Preschoolers _____
Kindergartners _____
School-agers _____

Hours of each staff member

---

**Group name**

| AM | Number of children enrolled each hour | | | | | | | | | | | | | PM |
|---|---|---|---|---|---|---|---|---|---|---|---|---|---|---|
| 6:00 | 7:00 | 8:00 | 9:00 | 10:00 | 11:00 | 12:00 | 1:00 | 2:00 | 3:00 | 4:00 | 5:00 | 6:00 | | 7:00 |
| | | | | | | | | | | | | | | |

Number of staff in attendance each hour

| | | | | | | | | | | | | | | |
|---|---|---|---|---|---|---|---|---|---|---|---|---|---|---|

**Age range    Number**

Infants _____
Toddlers _____
Preschoolers _____
Kindergartners _____
School-agers _____

Hours of each staff member

---

**Group name**

| AM | Number of children enrolled each hour | | | | | | | | | | | | | PM |
|---|---|---|---|---|---|---|---|---|---|---|---|---|---|---|
| 6:00 | 7:00 | 8:00 | 9:00 | 10:00 | 11:00 | 12:00 | 1:00 | 2:00 | 3:00 | 4:00 | 5:00 | 6:00 | | 7:00 |
| | | | | | | | | | | | | | | |

Number of staff in attendance each hour

| | | | | | | | | | | | | | | |
|---|---|---|---|---|---|---|---|---|---|---|---|---|---|---|

**Age range    Number**

Infants _____
Toddlers _____
Preschoolers _____
Kindergartners _____
School-agers _____

Hours of each staff member

Center Profile

## Staffing Pattern *continued*

| Group of children | Staffing Pattern | | | | | | | | | | | | | |
|---|---|---|---|---|---|---|---|---|---|---|---|---|---|---|

**Group name**

| AM | Number of children enrolled each hour | | | | | | | | | | | | PM |
|---|---|---|---|---|---|---|---|---|---|---|---|---|---|
| 6:00 | 7:00 | 8:00 | 9:00 | 10:00 | 11:00 | 12:00 | 1:00 | 2:00 | 3:00 | 4:00 | 5:00 | 6:00 | 7:00 |
| | | | | | | | | | | | | | |

Number of staff in attendance each hour

| | | | | | | | | | | | | | |
|---|---|---|---|---|---|---|---|---|---|---|---|---|---|

| **Age range** | **Number** |
|---|---|
| Infants | _____ |
| Toddlers | _____ |
| Preschoolers | _____ |
| Kindergartners | _____ |
| School-agers | _____ |

Hours of each staff member

---

**Group name**

| AM | Number of children enrolled each hour | | | | | | | | | | | | PM |
|---|---|---|---|---|---|---|---|---|---|---|---|---|---|
| 6:00 | 7:00 | 8:00 | 9:00 | 10:00 | 11:00 | 12:00 | 1:00 | 2:00 | 3:00 | 4:00 | 5:00 | 6:00 | 7:00 |
| | | | | | | | | | | | | | |

Number of staff in attendance each hour

| **Age range** | **Number** |
|---|---|
| Infants | _____ |
| Toddlers | _____ |
| Preschoolers | _____ |
| Kindergartners | _____ |
| School-agers | _____ |

Hours of each staff member

---

**Group name**

| AM | Number of children enrolled each hour | | | | | | | | | | | | PM |
|---|---|---|---|---|---|---|---|---|---|---|---|---|---|
| 6:00 | 7:00 | 8:00 | 9:00 | 10:00 | 11:00 | 12:00 | 1:00 | 2:00 | 3:00 | 4:00 | 5:00 | 6:00 | 7:00 |
| | | | | | | | | | | | | | |

Number of staff in attendance each hour

| **Age range** | **Number** |
|---|---|
| Infants | _____ |
| Toddlers | _____ |
| Preschoolers | _____ |
| Kindergartners | _____ |
| School-agers | _____ |

Hours of each staff member

---

**Group name**

| AM | Number of children enrolled each hour | | | | | | | | | | | | PM |
|---|---|---|---|---|---|---|---|---|---|---|---|---|---|
| 6:00 | 7:00 | 8:00 | 9:00 | 10:00 | 11:00 | 12:00 | 1:00 | 2:00 | 3:00 | 4:00 | 5:00 | 6:00 | 7:00 |
| | | | | | | | | | | | | | |

Number of staff in attendance each hour

| **Age range** | **Number** |
|---|---|
| Infants | _____ |
| Toddlers | _____ |
| Preschoolers | _____ |
| Kindergartners | _____ |
| School-agers | _____ |

Hours of each staff member

11. Staff Qualifications—complete the chart below for each administrator and staff member who works directly with children. Check the highest level achieved in formal education and early childhood/child development training. Check all credentials completed. An ECE/CD unit = 16 classroom hours or 1 credit hour of study in early childhood education or child development. ECE/CD units may be earned through college level courses, vocational-technical courses, or other forms of ongoing professional development. Be sure to identify all staff members in this chart and on the Staffing Pattern using the same first name and last initials.

## Administrative Staff Qualifications

| | Staff members | | | | | |
|---|---|---|---|---|---|---|
| Staff member (use first name and last initial only) | Jane D. | John D. | | | | |
| Job title | Co-owner/ Director | Co-owner/ Manager | | | | |
| Years of relevant experience | 15 | 10 | | | | |
| Date of employment in this program | 1992 | 1992 | | | | |
| Formal education completed  Some high school | | | | | | |
| High school graduate | | | | | | |
| Some college | | | | | | |
| College graduate (specify major) | | Business Management | | | | |
| Early childhood training completed  1–6 units in ECE/CD | | | | | | |
| 7–12 units in ECE/CD | | | | | | |
| 13 or more units in ECE/CD (specify number) | | | | | | |
| A.A. degree in ECE/CD | | | | | | |
| B.A./B.S. degree in ECE/CD | ✓ | | | | | |
| Graduate work in ECE/CD (specify units) | 12 | | | | | |
| Master's degree in ECE/CD | | | | | | |
| Doctorate degree in ECE/CD | | | | | | |
| Administrative training completed (Specify the credential or comprehensive training program and the number of administrative units required.)  Administrative credential  Administrative training | | | | | | |

Center Profile

## Teaching Staff Qualifications

| | **Teaching staff members** | | | | | |
|---|---|---|---|---|---|---|
| Staff member (use first name and last initial only) | Joan B. | Donna C. | Susan H. | Debbie T. | Emily W. | Holly P. |
| Job title | Asst. Teacher | Lead Teacher | Asst. Teacher | Lead Teacher | Co-Teacher | Co-Teacher |
| Years of relevant experience | 3 | 5 | 1 | 10 | 2 | 4 |
| Date of employment in this program | 1997 | 1995 | 1997 | 1994 | 1997 | 1998 |
| Formal education completed   Some high school | | | | | | |
|   High school graduate | ✓ | | ✓ | | ✓ | |
|   Some college | ✓ | | | ✓ | ✓ | |
| College graduate (specify major) | | | | | | |
| Early childhood training completed   1–6 units in ECE/CD | | | ✓ | | | |
|   7–12 units in ECE/CD | ✓ | | | | | |
|   13 or more units in ECE/CD (specify number) | | | | 15 | | ✓ |
|   A.A. degree in ECE/CD | | | | | | |
|   B.A./B.S. degree in ECE/CD | | ✓ | | | | |
|   Graduate work in ECE/CD (specify units) | | | | | | |
|   Master's degree in ECE/CD | | | | | | |
|   Doctorate degree in ECE/CD | | | | | | |
| Credentials/certificates   CDA (year received) | | | | 1996 | 1996 | |
|   State certificate in early childhood education | | | | | | |
|   State certificate in elementary education | | | | | | |
| Other (specify the credential or comprehensive training program and the number of ECE/CD units required) | | | | | | |

## Teaching Staff Qualifications

| | Teaching staff members | | | | | |
|---|---|---|---|---|---|---|
| Staff member (use first name and last initial only) | Kim K. | Melinda L. | Jeff R. | Amanda S. | Molly A. | Amy T. |
| Job title | Asst. Teacher | Lead Teacher | Asst. Teacher | Asst. Teacher | Lead Teacher | Asst. Teacher |
| Years of relevant experience | 1 | 3 | 1 | 10 | 5 | 2 |
| Date of employment in this program | 1997 | 1995 | 1998 | 1994 | 1993 | 1996 |
| Formal education completed Some high school | | | | | | |
| High school graduate | ✓ | | | ✓ | | |
| Some college | | | | | ✓ | |
| College graduate (specify major) | | Elem. Educ. | Psychology | | | |
| Early childhood training completed 1-6 units in ECE/CD | ✓ | | | | | |
| 7-12 units in ECE/CD | | | ✓ | | | |
| 13 or more units in ECE/CD (specify number) | | 30 | | 24 | | |
| A.A. degree in ECE/CD | | | | | | ✓ |
| B.A./B.S. degree in ECE/CD | | | | | | |
| Graduate work in ECE/CD (specify units) | | | | | | |
| Master's degree in ECE/CD | | | | | | |
| Doctorate degree in ECE/CD | | | | | | |
| Credentials/certificates CDA (year received) | | | | | 1996 | |
| State certificate in early childhood education | | ✓ | | | | |
| State certificate in elementary education | | ✓ | | | | |
| Other (specify the credential or comprehensive training program and the number of ECE/CD units required) | | | | | | |

## Teaching Staff Qualifications

| | Teaching staff members | | | | | |
|---|---|---|---|---|---|---|
| Staff member (use first name and last initial only) | | | | | | |
| Job title | | | | | | |
| Years of relevant experience | | | | | | |
| Date of employment in this program | | | | | | |
| Formal education completed<br>    Some high school | | | | | | |
| High school graduate | | | | | | |
| Some college | | | | | | |
| College graduate (specify major) | | | | | | |
| Early childhood training completed<br>    1–6 units in ECE/CD | | | | | | |
| 7–12 units in ECE/CD | | | | | | |
| 13 or more units in ECE/CD (specify number) | | | | | | |
| A.A. degree in ECE/CD | | | | | | |
| B.A./B.S. degree in ECE/CD | | | | | | |
| Graduate work in ECE/CD (specify units) | | | | | | |
| Master's degree in ECE/CD | | | | | | |
| Doctorate degree in ECE/CD | | | | | | |
| Credentials/certificates<br>    CDA (year received) | | | | | | |
| State certificate in early childhood education | | | | | | |
| State certificate in elementary education | | | | | | |
| Other (specify the credential or comprehensive training program and the number of ECE/CD units required) | | | | | | |

## Teaching Staff Qualifications

| | Teaching staff members | | | | |
|---|---|---|---|---|---|
| Staff member (use first name and last initial only) | | | | | |
| Job title | | | | | |
| Years of relevant experience | | | | | |
| Date of employment in this program | | | | | |
| Formal education completed<br>   Some high school | | | | | |
|    High school graduate | | | | | |
|    Some college | | | | | |
| College graduate (specify major) | | | | | |
| Early childhood training completed<br>   1–6 units in ECE/CD | | | | | |
|    7–12 units in ECE/CD | | | | | |
|    13 or more units in ECE/CD<br>   (specify number) | | | | | |
|    A.A. degree in ECE/CD | | | | | |
|    B.A./B.S. degree in ECE/CD | | | | | |
|    Graduate work in ECE/CD<br>   (specify units) | | | | | |
|    Master's degree in ECE/CD | | | | | |
|    Doctorate degree in ECE/CD | | | | | |
| Credentials/certificates<br>   CDA (year received) | | | | | |
|    State certificate in early child-<br>   hood education | | | | | |
|    State certificate in elementary<br>   education | | | | | |
| Other (specify the credential or comprehensive training program and the number of ECE/CD units required) | | | | | |

There are _____ lead teachers; _____ of the leads were employed here 12 months ago.
     (total number of)          (number of)

There are _____ Assistant Teachers; _____ of the Assistant Teachers were employed here 12 months ago.
     (total number of)          (number of)

Comment on the turnover data. (Add additional pages if necessary.)

# List of Documents Required by the Criteria

Below is a list of the written documents that are required by the Criteria with the appropriate criterion reference numbers. This list is provided to help the director evaluate those criteria and also to organize for the validation visit. Because these documents will need to be available for the validators to see, the documents either should be collected in a central place or their location should be noted in the space provided. **If the information is not available on-site for the validator(s), the director provides written certification by an authorized agency or individual of the documents' existence, location, and level of compliance with the Criteria.**

| Criterion | Document(s) | Location |
|---|---|---|
| B-1 | Statement of philosophy<br>Goals for children | _____ |
| B-2 | Curriculum plans for individual groups | _____ |
| B-3 | Individual goals and assessments for children<br>Individualized Education Plans (IEPs)<br>for children with special needs | _____ |
| B-4 | Written daily schedule | _____ |
| C-1a | See **B-1** | _____ |
| C-1b | Operating procedures | _____ |
| C-1d | If applicable, materials in family's native language | _____ |
| C-5a | Written notification form for sharing day-to-day<br>happenings | _____ |
| C-11 | Grievance procedures | _____ |
| D-1a–e | Staff personnel files<br>Educational qualifications<br>Volunteer orientation and training plans | _____ |
| D-2a–c | Educational qualifications | _____ |
| D-3 | Staff training and orientation | _____ |
| D-4a; D-4b | Individual training plans for staff | _____ |
| E-1a | Annual program assessment and goals | _____ |
| E-1b | Staff turnover<br>Recruitment and retention plan | _____ |
| E-2a | Written operating procedures: hours and holidays,<br>fees and refunds, termination of employment<br>Statement of inclusion | _____ |
| E-2b | Child abuse and neglect policy | _____ |

| | | |
|---|---|---|
| **E-3a** | Written personnel policies; job descriptions, salary scales, benefits, resignation and termination, grievance procedures | _____ |
| **E-3b** | Statement of nondiscriminatory hiring practices | _____ |
| **E-5a** | Attendance records for staff and children | _____ |
| **E-5b** | Personnel files including résumés, transcripts, documentation of ongoing professional development, and performance evaluations | _____ |
| **E-6a** | Written responsibilities and roles for Governing Board | _____ |
| **E-6c** | Records of board meetings | _____ |
| **E-7** | Fiscal records<br>Long-range budget | _____ |
| **E-8a** | Accident protection and liability insurance | _____ |
| **E-8b** | Vehicle insurance | _____ |
| **F-1** | Staffing Pattern (group size) | _____ |
| **F-2a** | Staffing Pattern (ratios) | _____ |
| **F-3a–d** | Staffing Pattern | _____ |
| **F-4** | Staffing Pattern | _____ |
| **H-1** | Certification of legal requirements, including license or accreditation certificate, from appropriate state or local agencies, results of recent licensing inspections | _____ |
| **H-2a** | Health records of staff including results of pre-employment tuberculosis test _or_ a written letter of verification | _____ |
| **H-3** | Health records for children including results of complete health evaluation, immunizations, emergency contact information, names of people authorized to pick up the child, and pertinent health history | _____ |
| **H-4a** | Written policy regarding sick children<br>Release authorization forms | _____ |
| **H-5** | Sign-in and out sheets for children | _____ |
| **H-6** | Vehicle license, inspection and maintenance records | _____ |
| **H-8** | Accident reports | _____ |

Center Profile

**H-10**             Documentation of first-aid training including CPR and
                     emergency management of choking                              _____

**H-11b**            Medical emergency plan
                     Parental consent for emergency treatment                     _____

**H-14b**            Signs displaying appropriate handwashing procedures          _____

**H-18d**            Certification of nontoxic building materials                 _____

**H-20b**            Written permission to administer medication                  _____

**H-21a**            Documentation of monthly evacuation practice
                     Written emergency procedures posted                          _____

**H-22c**            Emergency telephone numbers are posted                       _____

**I-1**              Evidence of menus that reflect compliance with USDA
                     recommendations                                              _____

**I-2a**             Written menus provided to parents                            _____

**I-2b**             Feeding times and consumption provided to parents
                     of infants and toddlers                                      _____

**I-3**              Written menus provide foods indicative of children's
                     cultural backgrounds                                         _____

**I-4**              Nutritional information and recommendations for foods
                     brought from home                                            _____

**I-5**              Food inspection certificate                                  _____

**J-1a–e**           Records of staff evaluation                                  _____

**J-1f**             Training plan                                                _____

**J-2a; J-2b**       Annual program evaluation and written goals for
                     improvement                                                  _____

**J-3**              Records of child assessment (may consist of
                     anecdotal records, classroom and playground
                     observations, individually administered tests, locally
                     or nationally developed progress checklists, dated
                     compilations of children's work case studies)

# Worksheet for collecting information on Staff Qualifications

Staff member name _____

Job title _____

Group staff member is assigned to _____

Hours staff member is assigned to group _____

Years of experience working with young children _____

Date of employment in this program _____

## Check highest level of formal education completed

❑ Some high school ❑ High-school graduate ❑ Some college

❑ College graduate (specify major) _____

## Check highest level of early childhood training completed

Note: **An ECE/CD unit is defined as 16 classroom hours or 1 credit hour of study in early childhood education or child development (ECE/CD).** ECE/CD units may be earned through college-level courses, vocational-technical courses, or other forms of professional development (i.e., workshops, conferences, etc.). **To determine units for staff members, total the number of hours of professional development and divide by 16. For example, 100 clock hours of professional development ÷ 16 (1 unit) = 6 units in ECE/CD.**

**Total number of hours of professional development:** _____ **÷ 16 =** _____ **units.**

❑ 1–6 units in ECE/CD ❑ 7–12 units in ECE/CD

❑ 13 or more units in ECE/CD (specify number _____)

❑ A.A. degree in ECE/CD ❑ B.A./B.S. degree in ECE/CD ❑ Other degree _____

❑ Graduate work in ECE/CD (specify hours _____)

❑ Master's degree in ECE/CD ❑ Doctorate degree in ECE/CD

## Check all credentials or certificates completed

❑ CDA Credential ❑ State certificate in early childhood education ❑ State certificate in elementary education

❑ Other credential or certificate (Specify the name of the credential, the institution it was awarded by, and the number of

ECE/CD units required.) _____

---

If staff members participate in a comprehensive training plan, please identify the number of training modules completed and briefly describe the plan.

A degree in elementary education is **not** equivalent to a degree in early childhood education or child development. For staff members that possess a degree in elementary education, total the number of semester hours of coursework that is applicable to ECE/CD.

# Section 5

## Teaching-Staff Questionnaire

Directions for use
Sample Teaching-Staff Questionnaire
Sample Summary Sheet
Open-Ended Teaching Staff Survey

# Section 5
# Teaching-Staff Questionnaire

**What is the purpose of the Teaching-Staff Questionnaire?**

Many of NAEYC's Criteria for High-Quality Early Childhood Programs relate to the quality of life experienced by the staff and the aspects of the program that help the staff do their jobs well. The purpose of the Teaching-Staff Questionnaire is to give staff members an opportunity to evaluate those criteria. This is important because the quality of life experienced by adults indirectly affects the quality of care and education provided for children. Staff members whose health is protected and who are satisfied with their jobs are more likely to express positive feelings toward children and are more likely to remain in their positions for longer periods of time.

In this section of the *Guide* you will find

(1) a copy of the Academy's Teaching-Staff Questionnaire that is used in preparing the Program Description,

(2) a copy of the summary sheet that is used to tabulate the results to be reported on the Program Description, and

(3) a sample open-ended teaching-staff survey that you may wish to use with your staff during the self-study if you have not addressed these issues previously. This survey is for your use and is not required by the Academy.

Multiple copies of the Academy's Teaching-Staff Questionnaire (on blue paper) and a blank copy of the Summary Sheet are sent to the program along with the self-study materials. The Open-Ended Staff Survey may be photocopied from the *Guide*.

## Directions for use

**Who completes the Teaching-Staff Questionnaire?**

All staff members who work directly with children should be given an opportunity to complete the questionnaire. The program should strive for 100% of the Teaching-Staff Questionnaire to be completed. Practicum students and interns should complete the questionnaires if they are in the classroom to maintain ratios.

**How should the Teaching-Staff Questionnaire be used during the self-study?**

Staff members should be asked to respond anonymously. The Teaching-Staff Questionnaire should be used as an aid in the evaluation process during the self-study. The questionnaire can be used in several ways depending on the individual needs of the program. If these issues have been addressed before among the staff, the questionnaire may be used to guide discussion of how the issues currently are being met, before staff actually complete the questionnaire. The questionnaire also could be used to generate topics for staff meetings to provide open discussion of these issues.

> The Academy recommends that the program use the Open-Ended Teaching-Staff Survey prior to the Teaching-Staff Questionnaire to obtain more in-depth information about the staff's feelings on these issues. The survey can be found on **pages 121 to 125 of the *Guide.***

During the self-study, the staff and director should look at the criteria that relate to staff members' needs, identify areas that are strengths and areas in need of improvement, and make improvements where possible. When the program is ready to go on and seek accreditation, the Teaching-Staff Questionnaire (on blue paper) is used to collect the current information that becomes part of the Program Description. Sometimes after staff complete the Teaching-Staff Questionnaire, directors find that additional improvements need to be made before seeking accreditation. If so, you may make improvements and have staff complete the questionnaire a second time (additional copies can be made). **The Teaching-Staff Questionnaire is used to verify the director's rating from the Administrator Report on the criterion and should reflect the situation after improvements are made.**

## When should the Teaching-Staff Questionnaire be completed?

The Teaching-Staff Questionnaire is used as one source of evidence of how well the program meets certain criteria when the program is ready to seek accreditation. **The final Teaching-Staff Questionnaire should be filled out no more than three months before the Program Description is sent to the Academy to be sure that the results represent the current situation.** Once the issues have been examined during the self-study process, completing the questionnaire should take only about 30 minutes of the staff members time. When the questionnaire is distributed a date for it to be returned should be specified or it could be completed during a staff meeting.

> Programs are *not* limited to only completing the Teaching-Staff Questionnaire one time. The questionnaire can be completed several times during the self-study process. The results that are reported to the Academy should reflect the current ratings.

## How are the results reported on the Program Description?

A copy of the Summary Sheet appears on pages 119 and 120 of the *Guide.* To complete the Summary Sheet, the director or staff member assigned to this task:

- counts the number of times each criterion is rated [1], [2], or [3],
- records the totals on the Summary Sheet, and
- copies the totals onto Part 3 of the Program Description in the boxes marked "Staff Questionnaire."

The Teaching-Staff Questionnaire is only one part of the self-study/validation process. The questionnaire is designed to evaluate the way in which the program addresses staff needs and helps staff do their jobs well. Staff members study other aspects of the program using the Classroom Observation.

# Teaching-Staff Questionnaire

This questionnaire is for teaching-staff members in an early childhood program to evaluate the aspects of the program staff know best. The letters and numbers to the left of each item refer to a specific criterion. For further explanation of the criteria refer to the *Accreditation Criteria & Procedures of the National Association for the Education of Young Children*.

## Instructions

Each statement on the left side of the page is the criterion to be rated. Criteria about staff should be rated based on your own experience and knowledge. Evaluate the early childhood program in which you work by rating the degree to which each statement on the questionnaire describes your program. For example, **H-9a** states, "Staff know procedures for reporting child abuse." To rate this item, ask yourself, "Do I know the procedures?" If you know and fully understand the procedures, you would rate the criterion a [3], fully met.

| [1]<br>Not met | [2]<br>Partially met | [3]<br>Fully met |
|---|---|---|
| The criterion is not met.<br><br>There is **little evidence** that this statement accurately describes the program. | The criterion is partially met.<br><br>There is **some evidence** that this statement accurately describes the program. | The criterion is completely met.<br><br>There is a **great deal** of evidence that this statement accurately describes the program throughout the day. |

Rate each criterion by circling only **one** of the numbers: [1], [2], or [3]. Explain your ratings under the "Comments" column if

- the criterion is not met [1].
- the criterion is partially met [2].
- the criterion is met through an alternate means (explain how and why).
- the program exceeds the criterion.
  No explanation is needed if the criterion is fully met [3].

**Reminder:** The final Teaching-Staff Questionnaire should be administered no more than three months prior to submitting the results to the Academy.

Date completed _____

# B. Curriculum

| Criterion | Rating | | | Comments |
|---|---|---|---|---|
| | Not met | Partially met | Fully met | |

**B-1.** The program has a written statement of its philosophy and goals for children that is available to staff and families.

[1] [2] [3]

_____
_____
_____

**B-2a.** The program has written curriculum plans, based on knowledge of child development and assessment of individual needs and interests.

[1] [2] [3]

_____
_____
_____

**B-2b.** The learning environment and activities for children reflect the program's philosophy and goals.

[1] [2] [3]

_____
_____
_____
_____

**B-3a.** Teachers have clearly defined goals for individual children that guide curriculum planning. Teachers accurately assess the skills and progress of each child in the program. Teachers adapt curriculum plans to meet the wide range of individual needs and interests of all children in the group. Teachers identify children who have difficulties in behavior or development and form a plan to help them acquire the necessary skills. Teachers are prepared to meet the individual special needs of each child, including children with disabilities.

[1] [2] [3]

_____
_____
_____
_____
_____
_____
_____

**B-3b.** The program is designed to be inclusive of all children, including those with identified disabilities and special learning and developmental needs. Modifications are made in the environment and staffing patterns for children with special needs. Staff are aware of the identified/diagnosed special needs of individual children and trained to follow through on specific intervention plans. Therapy is developed appropriately and incorporated within classroom activities as much as possible rather than removing the child from the classroom. Staff make appropriate professional referrals when necessary. Family members are involved in development and use of Individualized Education Plans. Staff address the priorities and concerns of families of children with special needs.

[1] [2] [3]

_____
_____
_____
_____
_____
_____
_____
_____

# B. Curriculum *continued*

|  | | Rating | | Comments |
|--|--|--------|--|----------|
| **Criterion** | Not met | Partially met | Fully met | |

**B-11.** Teachers plan with families to make toileting, feeding, and the development of other self-regulation skills a positive experience for children.
[1] [2] [3]

# C. Interactions among Teachers and Families

**C-3a.** Teachers work in collaborative partnerships with families, establishing and maintaining regular, ongoing, two-way communication with children's parents to build trust and mutual understanding and to ensure that children's learning and developmental needs are met.
[1] [2] [3]

**C-4a.** Family members are welcome visitors in the program at all times (for example, to observe, eat lunch with a child, or volunteer in the classroom).
[1] [2] [3]

**C-4b.** Parents and other family members are encouraged to be involved in the program in various ways, taking into consideration working parents and those with little spare time.
[1] [2] [3]

**C-5a.** A verbal and/or written system is established for sharing among both staff and parents the day-to-day happenings that affect children. (For example, information is exchanged between teachers at shift changes and passed on to parents at pick-up time.)
[1] [2] [3]

**C-5b.** Changes in a child's physical or emotional state are reported to parents regularly.
[1] [2] [3]

**C-6a.** Teachers and parents work together to make decisions about how to best support children's development and learning or to handle problems or differences of opinion as they arise.
[1] [2] [3]

# C. Interactions among Teachers and Families *continued*

| Criterion | Rating | | | Comments |
|---|---|---|---|---|
| | Not met | Partially met | Fully met | |

**C-6b.** Conferences are held at least once a year and at other times, as needed, to discuss children's progress, accomplishments, and difficulties at home and at the program.

1    2    3

**C-6c.** Teachers solicit and incorporate parents' knowledge about their children into ongoing assessment and planning.

1    2    3

**C-7.** Families are informed about the program and the curriculum and about policy or regulatory changes and other critical issues that could potentially affect the program and/or the early childhood profession through newsletters, bulletin boards, and other appropriate means.

1    2    3

**C-8a.** Staff and families communicate to ensure that children experience smooth transitions from home to the program or from one program to another during the day.

1    2    3

**C-8b.** Teachers and families communicate to ensure that the programs *(or classrooms)* from which children come and to which they go from one year to the next provide continuity over time.

1    2    3

**C-9a.** Communication between staff and families conveys trust and respect.

1    2    3

**C-9b.** Communication among teachers and families is frequent. (For example, teachers greet parents when they arrive and depart. Frequent friendly notes/telephone calls are used to communicate if parents do not bring their children to the program.)

1    2    3

# C. Interactions among Teachers and Families *continued*

| Criterion | Rating | | | Comments |
|---|---|---|---|---|
| | Not met | Partially met | Fully met | |
| **C-9c.** Staff show sensitivity in their interactions with families. (For example, show sensitivity in interactions with families who are experiencing difficulties; include child in conversation when a child must be discussed in the child's presence; maintain privacy when discussions are held between parents and staff about problems and concerns regarding specific children.) | 1 | 2 | 3 | |
| **C-9d.** Teachers show acceptance of various family structures and cultural perspectives. (For example, teachers speak positively about families to the children and among themselves.) | 1 | 2 | 3 | |
| **C-9e.** Major changes that affect children, such as changes in room or teacher and use of special services, are discussed with parents before decisions are made. | 1 | 2 | 3 | |
| **C-9f.** Teachers seek parents' specific ideas for dealing with the child when at the program. | 1 | 2 | 3 | |
| **C-10a.** Administrators and teachers are familiar with and make appropriate use of community resources including social services; mental and physical health agencies; and educational programs such as museums, libraries, and neighborhood centers. | 1 | 2 | 3 | |
| **C-10b.** Administrators and teachers link families with appropriate community resources, upon indication by family members that they would like to make use of a resource. (Some resources might be available through services offered by the program, but community resources that are not part of the program are also equally acceptable.) | 1 | 2 | 3 | |

Teaching-Staff Questionnaire

## C. Interactions among Teachers and Families *continued*

| Criterion | Rating | | | Comments |
|---|---|---|---|---|
| | Not met | Partially met | Fully met | |

**C-11.** Policies ensure that staff and parents have an effective way of negotiating difficulties and differences that arise in their interactions. The program has a variety of known and accepted techniques to handle differences, such as a parent policy council, an appeals committee, special conferences, or individual meetings.

Rating: 1  2  3

## D. Staff Qualifications and Development

**D-3.** New staff, volunteers, and substitutes are adequately oriented about the goals and philosophy of the program, emergency health and safety procedures, individual needs of children assigned to the staff member's care, guidance and classroom management techniques, child abuse and neglect reporting procedures, planned daily activities of the program, and expectations for ethical conduct.

Rating: 1  2  3

**D-4a.** The program provides regular opportunities for staff to participate in ongoing professional development to improve skills in working with children and families or to prepare them to assume more responsible positions.

Rating: 1  2  3

**D-4b.** Ongoing professional development provides continuing education and other opportunities for staff to keep abreast of the latest developments in the field, including new programs and practices and pending policy, legislation, or regulatory changes. The amount and kind of continuing education provided varies, depending on the needs of the program, the pre-service qualifications of the staff, and the number of staff pursuing higher education while employed.

Rating: 1  2  3

# E. Administration

| | | Rating | | | Comments |
|---|---|---|---|---|---|

**Criterion**

| | | Not met | Partially met | Fully met | |

**E-1a.** At least annually, the director and staff conduct an assessment to identify strengths and weaknesses of the program and to set program goals for the year.

[1] [2] [3]

**E-1b.** The annual program evaluation examines the adequacy of staff compensation and benefits and rate of staff turnover, and a plan is developed to increase salaries and benefits to ensure recruitment and retention of qualified staff and continuity of relationships.

[1] [2] [3]

**E-2a.** The program has written policies and procedures for operating, including hours, fees, illness, holidays, refund information, and termination of enrollment. Child enrollment and termination policies protect children's rights as outlined in the Americans with Disabilities Act.

[1] [2] [3]

**E-2b.** The program has a child abuse and neglect policy that includes reporting requirements for staff as well as procedures to be followed should a staff member be accused of abuse or neglect.

[1] [2] [3]

**E-3a.** The program has written personnel policies, including job descriptions; salary scales with increments based on professional qualification, length of employment, and performance; benefits; resignation and termination; and grievance procedures.

[1] [2] [3]

**E-3c.** Every effort is made to hire staff who reflect diverse cultural, racial, and linguistic characteristics as needed to communicate with the children and families served. When staff are not of the linguistic and cultural background of the children/families, increased efforts are made to ensure communication with families, such as regular conferences with a translator present.

[1] [2] [3]

Teaching-Staff
Questionnaire

# E. Administration *continued*

| Criterion | Rating | | | Comments |
|---|---|---|---|---|
| | Not met | Partially met | Fully met | |
| **E-4.** Benefits packages for full-time staff include paid leave (annual, sick, and personal), medical insurance, and retirement. Other benefits such as subsidized child care or continued education may be negotiated as unique to the situation. Benefits for part-time staff who are employed at least half-time are available on a prorated basis. | 1 | 2 | 3 | |
| **E-9a.** Staff interactions reflect mutual trust, respect, and support for each other. | 1 | 2 | 3 | |
| **E-9b.** Staff members seek out and acknowledge each other's ideas and opinions. Staff give positive recognition to each other's skills and accomplishments. | 1 | 2 | 3 | |
| **E-9c.** Staff provide appropriate supports for each other when dealing with stress. | 1 | 2 | 3 | |
| **E-9d.** Staff respect each other's rights to confidentiality. | 1 | 2 | 3 | |
| **E-9e.** Staff communicate with each other to ensure smooth operations. | 1 | 2 | 3 | |
| **E-10a.** Staff and administrators plan and consult together frequently about the program, children, and families. | 1 | 2 | 3 | |

# E.  Administration *continued*

| Criterion | Rating: Not met | Partially met | Fully met | Comments |
|---|---|---|---|---|

**E-10b.** Staff plan and consult together.

[ 1 ]  [ 2 ]  [ 3 ]

**E-10c.** Regular staff meetings are held for staff to consult on program planning, to plan for implementing and attaining goals, to plan for individual children, and to discuss program and working conditions (may be meetings of small group of or full staff).

[ 1 ]  [ 2 ]  [ 3 ]

**E-10d.** Teachers are provided weekly paid planning time, away from responsibility for children.

[ 1 ]  [ 2 ]  [ 3 ]

**E-11.** Staff are provided space and time away from children during the day. (When staff work directly with children for more than four hours, staff are provided breaks of at least 15 minutes in each four-hour period.)

[ 1 ]  [ 2 ]  [ 3 ]

**E-12.** Staff keep information about children, families, and associates confidential. Staff refrain from commenting about children or families in the presence of other adults or children.

[ 1 ]  [ 2 ]  [ 3 ]

**E-13.** An appropriate person on-site is designated to assume authority and to take action in an emergency, in the event of the director's absence.

[ 1 ]  [ 2 ]  [ 3 ]

Teaching-Staff Questionnaire

# F.    Staffing

**F-1 and F-2. Recommended staff-child ratios within group size***

| Age of children | 6 | 8 | 10 | 12 | 14 | 16 | 18 | 20 | 22 | 24 | 30 |
|---|---|---|---|---|---|---|---|---|---|---|---|
| | | | | | | | | **Group size** | | | |
| Infants (birth to 12 months) | 1:3 | 1:4 | | | | | | | | | |
| Toddlers (12 to 24 months) | 1:3 | 1:4 | 1:5 | 1:4 | | | | | | | |
| 2-year-olds (24 to 30 months) | | 1:4 | 1:5 | 1:6 | | | | | | | |
| 2½-year-olds (30 to 36 months) | | | 1:5 | 1:6 | 1:7 | | | | | | |
| 3-year-olds | | | | | 1:7 | 1:8 | 1:9 | 1:10 | | | |
| 4-year-olds | | | | | | 1:8 | 1:9 | 1:10 | | | |
| 5-year-olds | | | | | | 1:8 | 1:9 | 1:10 | | | |
| Kindergartners | | | | | | | | 1:10 | 1:11 | 1:12 | |
| 6- to 8-year-olds | | | | | | | | 1:10 | 1:11 | 1:12 | 1:15 |
| 9- to 12-year-olds | | | | | | | | | 1:12 | 1:15 | |

*Smaller group sizes and lower staff-child rations have been found to be strong predictors of compliance with indiciators of quality such as positive interactions among staff and children and developmentally appropriate curriculum. Variations in group sizes and ratios are acceptable in cases where the program demonstrates a very high level of compliance with criteria for interactions (A), curriculum (B), staff qualifications (D), health and safety (H), and physical environment (G).

| Criterion | | Rating | | | Comments |
|---|---|---|---|---|---|
| | Not met | Partially met | Fully met | | |

**F-1.**    The number of children in a group is limited in accordance with NAEYC Criteria to facilitate adult-child interaction and constructive activity among children. Groups of children may be age-determined or multiage. (A group is the number of children assigned to a staff member or a team of staff members occupying an individual classroom or well-defined space, with clear physical boundaries that prevent intermingling of children, within a larger room.)

*(Using the chart on this page, determine which groups meet or exceed the required group sizes.)*

Rating boxes: [1] Not met    [2] Partially met    [3] Fully met

# F. Staffing *continued*

| Criterion | Not met | Partially met | Fully met | Comments |
|---|---|---|---|---|
| | **Rating** | | | **Comments** |

**F-2a.** Sufficient staff with primary responsibility for working with children are available to provide frequent personal contact, meaningful learning activities, and supervision and to offer immediate care as needed.

*(Using the chart on the previous page, determine which groups meet or exceed the required staff-child ratios.)*

[1] [2] [3]

_____
_____
_____
_____

**F-2b.** Substitutes are provided to maintain staff-child ratios when regular staff are absent. Substitutes for infants and toddlers are familiar with the children and oriented to children's schedules and individual differences in a systematic way before assignment. Volunteers who work with children complete a pre-assignment orientation and participate in ongoing training.

[1] [2] [3]

_____
_____
_____
_____

**F-3a.** Each staff member has primary responsibility for and develops a deeper attachment to an identified group of children.

[1] [2] [3]

_____
_____
_____

**F-3b.** Every attempt is made to have continuity of adults who work with children within each day and over extended periods of time (several years of the child's enrollment), particularly infants and toddlers.

[1] [2] [3]

_____
_____
_____

**F-3c.** Infants and toddlers spend the majority of the time interacting with the same person each day.

[1] [2] [3]

❑ **Not applicable**

_____
_____
_____
_____
_____
_____

## F. Staffing *continued*

|  | Rating | | | Comments |
|---|---|---|---|---|
| **Criterion** | Not met | Partially met | Fully met | |
| **F-3d.** The program is organized and staffed to minimize the number of group transitions an individual child experiences during the time the child is enrolled in the program. Every attempt is made to maintain continuity of relationships between teachers and children and among groups of children. | 1 | 2 | 3 | |
| **F-4.** A majority of the child's day is spent in activities utilizing recommended staff-child ratios and group-size limitations while minimizing the number of transitions or regroupings children experience and maintaining relationships among groups of children as much as possible. | 1 | 2 | 3 | |

## G. Physical Environment

| Criterion | Not met | Partially met | Fully met | Comments |
|---|---|---|---|---|
| **G-10a.** The work environment for staff, including classrooms and staff rooms, is comfortable, well-organized, and in good repair. | 1 | 2 | 3 | |
| **G-10b.** The environment includes a place for adults to take a break or work away from children, an adult-sized bathroom, a secure place for staff to store their personal belongings, and an administrative area that is separated from the children's areas for planning or preparing materials. | 1 | 2 | 3 | |

## H. Health and Safety

| Criterion | Not met | Partially met | Fully met | Comments |
|---|---|---|---|---|
| **H-4a.** The program has a written policy, given to all families, specifying the conditions under which sick children are excluded, included but isolated, or included in the regular classroom, in accordance with local licensing and public health regulations. | 1 | 2 | 3 | |

# H. Health and Safety *continued*

| | Rating | | | Comments |
|---|---|---|---|---|

**Criterion**

Rating columns: Not met (1), Partially met (2), Fully met (3)

**H-7b.** There is specific accountability for each child by one staff member. Systems are in place for accounting for children's whereabouts at regular intervals, especially during periods of transition.

Rating: 1   2   3

**H-8.** Staff are alert to the health of each child. Individual medical problems and accidents are recorded and reported to staff and families, and a written record is kept of such incidents.

Rating: 1   2   3

**H-9a.** Staff know procedures for reporting suspected incidents of child abuse and/or neglect.

Rating: 1   2   3

**H-9b.** Suspected incidents of child abuse and/or neglect by families, staff, volunteers, or others are reported to the appropriate local agencies.

Rating: 1   2   3

**H-11a.** Adequate first-aid supplies are readily available.

Rating: 1   2   3

**H-11b.** A plan exists for dealing with medical emergencies that includes a source of emergency care, written parental consent forms, and transportation arrangements.

Rating: 1   2   3

**H14b.** Staff and volunteers know and follow proper procedures during handwashing, including washing with soap and warm, running water for at least 10 seconds; using single use or disposable towels; and avoiding recontamination from faucets by turning off faucets with towel.

Rating: 1   2   3

Teaching-Staff Questionnaire

# H. Health and Safety *continued*

| Criterion | Rating | | | Comments |
|---|---|---|---|---|
| | Not met | Partially met | Fully met | |

**H-14d.** Staff and volunteers follow universal precautions to prevent transmission of blood-borne diseases.

    [1]   [2]   [3]

**H-16a.** Individual bedding is washed at least once a week and used by only one child between washings. Individual cribs, cots, and mats are washed if soiled.

    [1]   [2]   [3]

❑ **Not applicable**

**H-21a.** Staff and volunteers are familiar with primary and secondary evacuation routes and practice evacuation procedures monthly with children.

    [1]   [2]   [3]

**H-22a.** Staff and volunteers are familiar with emergency procedures and procedures for severe storm warnings.

    [1]   [2]   [3]

# J. Evaluation

**J-1a.** All staff are evaluated at least annually by the director or other appropriate supervisor.

    [1]   [2]   [3]

**J-1b.** Results of staff evaluation are written and confidential. They are discussed privately with the staff member.

    [1]   [2]   [3]

**J-1c.** Staff evaluations include classroom observation. Evaluation is based on the employee's job description and previously established goals for improvement.

    [1]   [2]   [3]

# J.   Evaluation *continued*

**Rating**  **Comments**

| Criterion | Not met | Partially met | Fully met | |
|---|---|---|---|---|
| **J-1d.** Staff are informed of evaluation criteria in advance. | 1 | 2 | 3 | |
| **J-1e.** Staff have an opportunity to evaluate their own performance. | 1 | 2 | 3 | |
| **J-1f.** A plan for staff training is generated from the staff-evaluation process. | 1 | 2 | 3 | |
| **J-2a.** At least annually, administrators, families, staff, school-age children, and other routinely participating adults are involved in evaluating the program's effectiveness in meeting the needs of children and families. | 1 | 2 | 3 | |
| **J-2b.** The program regularly establishes goals for continuous improvement and innovation. | 1 | 2 | 3 | |
| **J-3.** Individual descriptions of children's development and learning are written and compiled as a basis for planning appropriate learning activities, as a means of facilitating optimal development of each child, as a means of identifying children who may be in need of more systematic diagnosis of a learning or developmental problem, and as records for use in communications with families. | 1 | 2 | 3 | |

*Teaching-Staff Questionnaire*

NAEYC #934

# Teaching-Staff Questionnaire Summary Sheet

Total number of Teaching-Staff Questionnaires received: ___11___ out of ___12___.

| Criterion reference number | Not met 1 | Partially met 2 | Fully met 3 |
|---|---|---|---|
| B-1 | | | 11 |
| B-2a | | 1 | 10 |
| B-2b | | 1 | 10 |
| B-3a | | 2 | 9 |
| B-3b | 1 | 1 | 9 |
| B-11 | | | 11 |
| C-3a | | | 11 |
| C-4a | | | 11 |
| C-4b | | | 11 |
| C-5a | | | 11 |
| C-5b | 1 | 1 | 9 |
| C-6a | | 3 | 8 |
| C-6b | | | 11 |
| C-6c | | 1 | 10 |
| C-7 | | | 11 |
| C-8a | | | 11 |
| C-8b | 1 | | 10 |
| C-9a | | | 11 |
| C-9b | | | 11 |
| C-9c | | | 11 |
| C-9d | | 2 | 9 |
| C-9e | | 1 | 10 |

| Criterion reference number | Not met 1 | Partially met 2 | Fully met 3 |
|---|---|---|---|
| C-9f | 1 | | 10 |
| C-10a | | | 11 |
| C-10b | | | 11 |
| C-11 | 1 | 3 | 7 |
| D-3 | | | 11 |
| D-4a | | 2 | 9 |
| D-4b | | 2 | 9 |
| E-1a | | | 11 |
| E-1b | | | 11 |
| E-2a | | | 11 |
| E-2b | | 1 | 10 |
| E-3a | | | 11 |
| E-3c | | 2 | 9 |
| E-4 | | | 11 |
| E-9a | 1 | | 10 |
| E-9b | | 1 | 10 |
| E-9c | | | 11 |
| E-9d | | 1 | 10 |
| E-9e | | 1 | 10 |
| E-10a | | | 11 |
| E-10b | | | 11 |
| E-10c | | | 11 |

Record number of responses

| Criterion reference number | Record number of responses | | |
|---|---|---|---|
| | Not met 1 | Partially met 2 | Fully met 3 |
| E-10d | | | 11 |
| E-11 | | | 11 |
| E-12 | | 1 | 10 |
| E-13 | | | 11 |
| F-1 | | 1 | 10 |
| F-2a | | | 11 |
| F-2b | | 1 | 10 |
| F-3a | | | 11 |
| F-3b | 1 | 2 | 8 |
| F-3c | | | 11 |
| F-3d | | | 11 |
| F-4 | | 1 | 10 |
| G-10a | | | 11 |
| G-10b | | | 11 |
| H-4a | | | 11 |
| H-7b | | 1 | 10 |
| H-8 | | 1 | 10 |
| H-9a | | | 11 |

| Criterion reference number | Record number of responses | | |
|---|---|---|---|
| | Not met 1 | Partially met 2 | Fully met 3 |
| H-9b | | | 11 |
| H-11a | | | 11 |
| H-11b | | | 11 |
| H-14b | | | 11 |
| H-14d | | 1 | 10 |
| H-16a | | | 11 |
| H-21a | | | 11 |
| H-22a | | 2 | 9 |
| J-1a | | 3 | 8 |
| J-1b | | 3 | 8 |
| J-1c | | 3 | 8 |
| J-1d | | 3 | 8 |
| J-1e | | 3 | 8 |
| J-1f | | 3 | 8 |
| J-2a | | 3 | 8 |
| J-2b | | | 11 |
| J-3 | | | 11 |

NAEYC #935

# Open-Ended Teaching-Staff Survey

This survey is to help staff members think about the aspects of the program that directly affect staff. The most important determinant of the quality of an early childhood program is the quality of the staff who directly care for and educate children. However, the ability of staff members to do their best is affected by how their own needs are met and the support they receive.

Directions: Check the box or boxes that best describe your experience with the program. This survey is intended to be used prior to the Teaching-Staff Questionnaire.

1. **How long have you been employed in this program?**
   - ❑ Less than one year
   - ❑ More than one year

2. **Have you received a written copy of your job description?** (Criterion **E-3**)
   - ❑ Yes
   - ❑ No

3. **Which of these areas are included in the program's written personnel policies?** (Criterion **E-3**)
   - ❑ Description of job responsibilities
   - ❑ Salary information
   - ❑ Professional development
   - ❑ Benefits
   - ❑ Resignation and termination policies
   - ❑ Grievance procedures (how to appeal a decision about your job status)

   **What other information about your job would you like to see in writing?**

4. **Which of these benefits are provided for full-time employees? If part-time, are any of these benefits provided on a pro-rated basis?** (Criterion **E-4**)

   |  | Provided | Not provided | Not needed |
   |---|---|---|---|
   | Paid leave (annual, sick, and/or personal) | ❑ | ❑ | ❑ |
   | Medical insurance | ❑ | ❑ | ❑ |
   | Retirement plan | ❑ | ❑ | ❑ |
   | Subsidized child care | ❑ | ❑ | ❑ |
   | Educational benefits | ❑ | ❑ | ❑ |
   | Flexible work plan | ❑ | ❑ | ❑ |

   **What other benefits are you provided or other options would you like to have provided?**

**5. How effective was the orientation you received for your job?** (Criterion **D-3**)

❑ Very effective ❑ Adequate ❑ Inadequate

**6. How were these topics addressed in the orientation process?** (Criterion **D-3** and **B-3**)

|  | Effectively | Adequately | Inadequately |
|---|---|---|---|
| Goals and philosophy of the program | ❑ | ❑ | ❑ |
| Health and safety procedures and policies | ❑ | ❑ | ❑ |
| Discipline techniques | ❑ | ❑ | ❑ |
| Daily plan of activities | ❑ |  |  |
| Developmentally appropriate programming | ❑ | ❑ | ❑ |
| Special needs of children assigned to you | ❑ | ❑ | ❑ |
| Expectations for ethical conduct (see NAEYC's Code of Ethical Conduct) | ❑ | ❑ | ❑ |

**What other topics would you like to see addressed?**

**7. How would you rate the quality of the communication between staff and administrators?** (Criterion **E-9**)

❑ Effectively ❑ Adequately ❑ Inadequately

**How could communication among staff and administrators be improved?**

**8. How would you rate the quality of communication among staff members?** (Criterion **E-9**)

❑ Effectively ❑ Adequately ❑ Inadequately

**How could communication among staff members be improved?**

9. **How would you rate the communication among staff and administrators on these topics?**

| | Effective | Adequate | Inadequate |
|---|:---:|:---:|:---:|
| Discussion of working conditions (**G-10**) | ❑ | ❑ | ❑ |
| Plans for individual children (**B-3**) | ❑ | ❑ | ❑ |
| Plan for children with special needs (**B-3**) | ❑ | ❑ | ❑ |
| Discussion of program planning (**E-10**) | ❑ | ❑ | ❑ |
| Evaluation of program (**E-1**) | ❑ | ❑ | ❑ |
| Evaluation of staff (**J-1**) | ❑ | ❑ | ❑ |
| Professional development opportunities (**D-4**) | ❑ | ❑ | ❑ |

**What other topics would you like to see addressed among staff and administrators?**

10. **How would you rate these systems designed to meet your personal needs?**

| | Effective | Adequate | Inadequate |
|---|:---:|:---:|:---:|
| Time for breaks (**E-11**) | ❑ | ❑ | ❑ |
| Staff lounge or area for taking a break (**G-10**) | ❑ | ❑ | ❑ |
| Space for storing your personal belongings (**G-10**) | ❑ | ❑ | ❑ |

**What other systems are needed?**

**11. How would you rate these systems designed to help you perform your job optimally?**

| | Effective | Adequate | Inadequate |
|---|---|---|---|
| Opportunities to consult with other staff (E-10) | ❑ | ❑ | ❑ |
| Paid planning time (E-10) | ❑ | ❑ | ❑ |
| Sufficient resources on-site (E-10) | ❑ | ❑ | ❑ |
| Opportunities for in-service training (D-4) | ❑ | ❑ | ❑ |
| Classroom observation (J-1) | ❑ | ❑ | ❑ |
| Individual training plan (J-1) | ❑ | ❑ | ❑ |

**What other systems are needed?**

**12. How would you rate these opportunities to improve your professional knowledge and skills?** (Criterion D-4)

| | Effective | Adequate | Inadequate |
|---|---|---|---|
| Off-site workshops/seminars | ❑ | ❑ | ❑ |
| Visits to other programs | ❑ | ❑ | ❑ |
| Access to resource materials | ❑ | ❑ | ❑ |
| In-service sessions provided on-site | ❑ | ❑ | ❑ |
| College level/technical school courses | ❑ | ❑ | ❑ |
| Professional memberships/conferences | ❑ | ❑ | ❑ |
| Off-site workshops/seminars | ❑ | ❑ | ❑ |

**What other opportunities are needed?**

13. **Comment on the effectiveness of the in-service training in which you have participated. Which forms of in-service training were most helpful to you? In what other areas would you find training helpful?**

14. **How frequently are you observed in the classroom?** (Criterion J-1)
    - ❑ Quarterly or more
    - ❑ Twice a year
    - ❑ Once a year
    - ❑ Less than once a year
    - ❑ Never

15. **How frequently is your job performance evaluated?** (Criterion J-1)
    - ❑ Quarterly or more
    - ❑ Twice a year
    - ❑ Once a year
    - ❑ Less than once a year
    - ❑ Never

16. **How would you rate these aspects of your performance evaluation?** (Criterion J-1)

| | Effective | Adequate | Inadequate |
|---|---|---|---|
| Director observes classroom | ❑ | ❑ | ❑ |
| Director discusses evaluation | ❑ | ❑ | ❑ |
| Evaluations are written and confidential | ❑ | ❑ | ❑ |
| Opportunities exist to evaluate self | ❑ | ❑ | ❑ |

**What other ways of evaluating your job performance would you like?**

# Section 6

## Family Questionnaire

Sample Family Questionnaire
Sample Summary Sheet
Open-Ended Family Survey

# Family Questionnaire

**What is the purpose of the Family Questionnaire?**

Many of NAEYC's Criteria for High-Quality Early Childhood Programs relate to parents who have children in the program. Whenever a program serves young children, it also serves their families. The purpose of the Family Questionnaire is to obtain information from parents about how well the program meets the criteria that directly relate to parents, such as the criteria on Relationships among Teachers and Families.

In this section of the *Guide* you will find

(1) A copy of the Academy's Family Questionnaire and introductory letter. This questionnaire (on yellow paper) is used in preparing the Program Description.

(2) A copy of the Summary Sheet that is used to tabulate the results to be reported on the Program Description.

(3) A sample open-ended family survey that we suggest you use with parents as part of your self-study. This survey is for your use only, as a preliminary to the Family Questionnaire, and is not required by the Academy.

Multiple copies of the Academy's Family Questionnaire (on yellow paper) and a blank copy of the Summary Sheet are sent to the program with the self-study materials.

## Directions for use

**How should parents be involved in the self-study?**

Parents should be informed that the early childhood program has decided to engage in the NAEYC accreditation process. It is important that parents understand the importance of self-study and the value that the process will bring to the program.

Some of the Criteria relate directly to families. Parents are the best source of information about how well those criteria are met. It is important to remember that parents are the consumers of the service offered by an early childhood program. Parents should be seen as a valuable source of information to help identify the strengths and weaknesses of the program and to make suggestions for improvements.

There are many ways to involve parents in the self-study. One way is to ask all parents to complete the Open-Ended Family Survey to get as much information as possible about how well your program is meeting the needs of its clients. You may photocopy the Open-Ended Family Survey that is found on pages 139 to 142 of this section. This survey will serve as an important tool in opening the dialogue between administrators, teachers, and families. Another way of involving parents might be to ask for volunteers for a parent committee that could interview or survey parents or members of the community about their needs and how well they are met by the program. Parent meetings also provide good opportunities for exploring issues about quality in an open forum with parents and updating them on the progress of self-study.

During the self-study, the staff, director, and parents should look at the criteria that relate to parents' needs, identify areas that are strengths and areas in need of improvement, and make improvements where possible. When the program is ready to continue and seek accreditation the Academy's Family Questionnaire is distributed to parents to collect the current information that becomes part of the Program Description.

## Who completes the Family Questionnaire?

Each family that the program serves should have an opportunity to complete the questionnaire. Responses from the parents should be viewed as feedback to help improve the quality of your early childhood program. A sample of the questionnaire appears in this section of the *Guide*.

## When is the questionnaire completed?

The Family Questionnaire is used as one source of evidence about how well the program meets the criteria related to parents. The Open-Ended Family Survey can be distributed early in the self-study process to allow time for the program to provide clarification or information to parents that they are unsure of. **To ensure the results represent the current situation, the final questionnaire should be distributed no more than three months before the Program Description is sent to the Academy.**

The questionnaire has a brief letter of introduction. The director (or appropriate person) should fill in the name of the program and the date by which the questionnaire should be returned (usually within three days) and sign it. After three days, parents should be reminded or encouraged to complete the questionnaire if they have not done so. It should take only 10 to 15 minutes of the parents' time.

## What if all the questionnaires are not returned?

A return rate of at least 50% is required by the Academy. You should try to obtain as many of the questionnaires as possible. Report the number distributed and number of questionnaires returned on the Family Questionnaire Summary Sheet. Also, report what efforts, if any, you made to increase the number returned. If your return rate is less than 50% the Academy will advise you of what action needs to be taken prior to the validation visit.

> To improve the return rate; the Academy suggest asking parents to complete the questionnaire on-site when they drop off or pick up their children.

## How are the results reported on the Program Description?

The results of the Family Questionnaire are recorded on the Summary Sheet, a copy of which appears on pages 137 and 138 of the *Guide*. The Summary Sheet shows which items on the Family Questionnaire relate to which criteria. The Summary Sheet is used to count the responses to the questionnaire. The director (or person assigned to this task) counts the numbers of "don't know," "no," "yes," and "not applicable" responses and records the total on the Summary Sheet. That person should also record the number of questionnaires that were returned out of the total number distributed. The totals from the Summary Sheet are copied onto the Program Description in the boxes marked with Family Questionnaire numbers.

**For example:**

*Family Questionnaire #5*

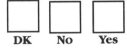

DK   No   Yes

## How are the results used?

The results from the Family Questionnaire that are reported on the Program Description are used during the validation visit to verify administrative criteria that are rated by the director. In order to validate administrative criteria rated by the director and staff members, there needs to be consistency or agreement between the administrator and staff and/or families.

# Family Questionnaire

*Prepared by the National Association
for the Education of Young Children*

Dear family members:

_____
(Name of program)

is working toward being accredited by the National Association for the Education of Young Children (NAEYC). NAEYC operates a national, voluntary accreditation system for any public or private school or center serving children from birth through kindergarten and/or school-age child care. The accreditation process identifies high-quality early childhood programs and schools.

NAEYC feels that family members can provide valuable information about the quality of their children's program. As part of the accreditation process, family members are asked to fill out the questionnaire that follows. The questions on it are related to the standards for accreditation.

You may want to say more about the program, so feel free to write any comments on the form. You do not need to sign your name. We would be grateful if you would return the completed questionnaire by

_____.
(Date)

Thank you very much for your help.

Sincerely yours,

Program Director

*Please turn the page.*

Family Questionnaire

# Family Questionnaire

How long has your child (or children) been enrolled in this program? Check one box.

❑ Less than six months          ❑ One to two years
❑ Six months to one year        ❑ More than two years

How old is your child (or children) who are enrolled in this program? _____

## Directions

For each statement, circle "Yes" or "No" or "DK" for "don't know." If the statement does not apply to your child's program, circle "NA" for "not applicable."

1. The program gives information to families about

DK   No   Yes          (a) the program's philosophy and goals for children.

DK   No   Yes   NA     (b) payments and refunds.

DK   No   Yes          (c) hours the program is open and holidays and closings.

DK   No   Yes          (d) rules about attendance of sick children.

DK   No   Yes          (e) meals and snacks given to children.

DK   No   Yes   NA     (f) times when infants and toddlers are fed and what they eat.


DK   No   Yes   2. Families are able to give ideas about the program's policies and procedures and about planning to meet the needs of their children.


DK   No   Yes   3. The program has a plan for helping new children to feel comfortable by either including a visit before enrollment, having a parent meeting, or gradually bringing in new children. This helps ease the transition as the child separates from her or his parent(s) to a new school.


DK   No   Yes   4. Teachers work with parents to establish and maintain regular, ongoing, two-way communication.


DK   No   Yes   5. Teachers listen to parents and have respect for the family's goals and preferences for the child.


DK   No   Yes   6. Teachers and families work together positively about how the family and staff handle different aspects of childrearing such as discipline, feeding, toileting, and other important issues.

DK   No   Yes   7. Family members are welcome visitors in the program at all times. They feel welcome when they enter the classroom.

DK   No   Yes   8. There are ways for parents (even those who work and/or are very busy) to take part in the program, such as visiting and helping in the classroom, taking field trips, joining in at parties, or sharing a meal/snack.

DK   No   Yes   9. The program informs parents about day-to-day happenings and special events, such as field trips, that affect children.

DK   No   Yes   10. Families are given information about what happened to their children during the day, especially information about injuries and any changes in children's health or eating habits.

DK   No   Yes   11. Teachers and parents work together to decide how to best help the child to develop and learn, or to talk about any problems that may arise.

DK   No   Yes   12. Parent-teacher conferences are held to discuss children's progress, accomplishments, and/or difficulties at least once a year (conferences are held more often if parents want them).

DK   No   Yes   13. Parents are informed about the program and any policy or regulatory changes that affect it through newsletters, newspaper articles, bulletin boards, or other ways.

DK   No   Yes   14. Teachers communicate with parents to ensure that children experience smooth transitions during the day (from home to program or from one program to another).

DK   No   Yes   15. Teachers communicate with parents to ensure that the programs from which children come and go from one year to the next provide continuity over time.

DK   No   Yes   16. Personally, I feel that communication between parents and staff shows trust and respect.

DK   No   Yes   17. Communication is frequent between parents and staff, such as when children are dropped off and picked up, or through notes and telephone calls.

DK   No   Yes   18. Personally, I feel that staff are sensitive to the feelings of family members.

DK     No     Yes        19.  I feel that teachers are accepting of my family. They speak positively about families to the children and among themselves.

DK     No     Yes        20.  Changes that affect children, such as changes in room or teacher or use of special services, are discussed with parents before decisions are made.

DK     No     Yes        21.  Teachers seek parents' specific ideas for dealing with the child when at the program.

DK     No     Yes        22.  The program has an effective way of negotiating difficulties and differences that arise. Some techniques to handle differences might include a parent-policy council, an appeals committee, special conferences, or individual meetings.

DK     No     Yes        23.  Children are generally taught by the same teacher(s), so the children do not have to constantly adjust to new adults.

DK     No     Yes        24.  At least once a year, parents are asked to evaluate how well the program is meeting their child's needs.

**For parents of children with special needs:**

DK     No     Yes     NA     25.  Staff involve parents in development and use of Individualized Education Plans (IEPs) designed to meet the child's needs. Staff also address the needs of parents of children with special needs.

**Please feel free to write any comments on what you like about the program or what you would like to see changed.**

# Family Questionnaire Summary Sheet

Total number of Family Questionnaires received: __86__ out of __94__. What efforts, if any, did the program make to increase the number of questionnaires returned? We told parents in advance and then provided space and coffee and donuts to enjoy while completing the questionnaire after they dropped off their children.

| Question number on Family Questionnaire | Criterion reference number | Number of "don't know" responses | Number of "no" responses | Number of "yes" responses | Number of "not applicable" responses |
|---|---|---|---|---|---|
| 1a | B-1; C-1a | | | 86 | |
| 1b | C-1b | | | 86 | |
| 1c | C-1b | | | 86 | |
| 1d | C-1b; H-4a | 2 | | 84 | |
| 1e | I-2a | 1 | 1 | 84 | |
| 1f | I-2b | | 2 | 84 | |
| 2 | C-1c | | | 86 | |
| 3 | C-2 | | 5 | 81 | |
| 4 | C-3a | | | 86 | |
| 5 | C-3b | | | 86 | |
| 6 | B-11 | | 1 | 85 | |
| 7 | C-4a | | | 86 | |
| 8 | C-4b | 1 | | 85 | |
| 9 | C-5a; H-7c | 1 | | 85 | |
| 10 | C-5b; H-8 | | 3 | 83 | |
| 11 | C-6a; C-6c | 4 | | 82 | |
| 12 | C-6b | 1 | | 85 | |
| 13 | C-7 | | 1 | 85 | |
| 14 | C-8a | | | 86 | |
| 15 | C-8b | 10 | 1 | 75 | |
| 16 | C-9a | | | 86 | |

Family Questionnaire

| Question number on Family Questionnaire | Criterion reference number | Number of "don't know" responses | Number of "no" responses | Number of "yes" responses | Number of "not applicable" responses |
|---|---|---|---|---|---|
| 17 | C-9b | 1 | 1 | 81 | 3 |
| 18 | C-9c | 11 | 3 | 72 | |
| 19 | C-9d | 6 | | 80 | |
| 20 | C-9e | | | 86 | |
| 21 | C-9f | | | 86 | |
| 22 | C-11 | | | 86 | |
| 23 | F-3b | | | 86 | |
| 24 | J-2a | | 1 | 85 | |
| 25 | B-3b | | | 8 | 78 |

NAEYC #938

# Open-Ended Family Survey

<hr>

(Name of program)

is collecting information about how well we are meeting the needs of children and families. Please answer the following questions and feel free to add any comments. You do not need to put your name on this form.

Please return it by _____
(date)

Directions: Check the box (or boxes) that best describes your experience with this program.

**1. What information have you received about the program?**

| | Received information | Haven't received, but would be helpful | Not needed |
|---|:---:|:---:|:---:|
| Statement of program philosophy and goals | ❑ | ❑ | ❑ |
| Payment information (fees, refunds) | ❑ | ❑ | ❑ |
| Hours of operation | ❑ | ❑ | ❑ |
| Holidays, closings | ❑ | ❑ | ❑ |
| Termination of enrollment | ❑ | ❑ | ❑ |
| What to do when child is sick | ❑ | ❑ | ❑ |
| Transportation and pick-up arrangements | ❑ | ❑ | ❑ |
| What parents are expected to provide (such as children's food, clothing) | ❑ | ❑ | ❑ |
| Daily activities provided for children | ❑ | ❑ | ❑ |
| Special events/field trips | ❑ | ❑ | ❑ |
| How discipline is handled | ❑ | ❑ | ❑ |
| How difficulties or differences are handled (negotiation techniques) | ❑ | ❑ | ❑ |
| Opportunities for family involvement | ❑ | ❑ | ❑ |

**What other information would be helpful?**

2. **The introduction to the program made me and my child feel welcome.**
   ❑ Do not agree at all        ❑ Somewhat agree        ❑ Fully agree

   **What could the program do to make the introduction better for your child and family?**

3. **Communication between administrators, teaching staff, and my family is effective.**
   ❑ Do not agree at all        ❑ Somewhat agree        ❑ Fully agree

4. **The frequency and amount of communication between staff members seems sufficient.**
   ❑ Do not agree at all        ❑ Somewhat agree        ❑ Fully agree

5. **Do you feel that you are kept informed about these aspects of your child's experience?**

| | Feel informed | Would like more information | Not needed |
|---|---|---|---|
| Changes in child's health or behavior | ❑ | ❑ | ❑ |
| Injuries to child | ❑ | ❑ | ❑ |
| Child's meals/snacks | ❑ | ❑ | ❑ |
| Events of child's day | ❑ | ❑ | ❑ |
| Child's developmental progress | ❑ | ❑ | ❑ |
| Teacher changes | ❑ | ❑ | ❑ |
| Transitions | ❑ | ❑ | ❑ |

**I feel comfortable sharing my ideas and concerns with staff members regarding my child?**
❑ Do not agree at all        ❑ Somewhat agree        ❑ Fully agree

**What other information about your child would you like?**

**6. How would you rate these ways of communicating with staff members?**

| | Effective | Needs improvement | Not needed |
|---|:---:|:---:|:---:|
| Welcoming of parental input | ❑ | ❑ | ❑ |
| Personal conversation at beginning or end of day | ❑ | ❑ | ❑ |
| Written notes | ❑ | ❑ | ❑ |
| Newsletter | ❑ | ❑ | ❑ |
| Bulletin board | ❑ | ❑ | ❑ |
| Conferences | ❑ | ❑ | ❑ |
| Telephone calls | ❑ | ❑ | ❑ |

**What other ways of communicating with staff members would be helpful?**

**Do you feel that there is mutual trust, respect, and communication between families and staff members?**

❑ Do not agree at all    ❑ Somewhat agree    ❑ Fully agree

**7. In which of the following activities have you participated or would you like to participate?**

| | Have participated | Would like to | No opportunity | Not interested |
|---|:---:|:---:|:---:|:---:|
| Observed classroom activities | ❑ | ❑ | ❑ | ❑ |
| Helped with classroom activities | ❑ | ❑ | ❑ | ❑ |
| Helped on field trips | ❑ | ❑ | ❑ | ❑ |
| Attended party or other social activity | ❑ | ❑ | ❑ | ❑ |
| Sharing a meal/snack | ❑ | ❑ | ❑ | ❑ |
| Attended parent meeting | ❑ | ❑ | ❑ | ❑ |
| Assisted in fundraising or other work | ❑ | ❑ | ❑ | ❑ |
| Helped with program planning | ❑ | ❑ | ❑ | ❑ |
| Served on parent council/board | ❑ | ❑ | ❑ | ❑ |

**In which other activities would you like to participate?**

Open-Ended Family Survey

8.  **How do you think staff members feel about your child?**

9.  **How do you think staff members feel about you? Do they respect your opinions? Are they open to your suggestions?**

10. **Do you and your family members feel welcome in the program?**

# Section 7

## How to Prepare Your Program Description
### Information about the Program Description
### Directions for completing the Program Description

## Sample Program Description
### Part 1—Center Profile
### Part 2—Results of Classroom Observations
### Part 3—Results of Administrator Report

# Section 7

## How to Prepare Your Program Description

In this section of the *Guide,* you will find
(1) information about the Program Description,
(2) directions for completing the Program Description, and
(3) a sample copy of the Program Description.

With the self-study materials, you are sent
(1) A copy of the Program Description to fill out and return to the Academy when you decide to seek accreditation. Do not write in this form until you are ready to request a validation visit.
(2) A copy of the Classroom Observation Summary Sheet to return to the Academy with the completed Program Description.
(3) A return envelope for mailing the completed Program Description and Classroom Observation Summary Sheet to the Academy.

## Information about the Program Description

**What is the purpose of the Program Description?**

The Program Description is used for three steps in the accreditation process:
(1) The director uses this form to describe how the program meets the Criteria by reporting the results of the self-study.
(2) The validator(s) uses this form during the on-site visit, to record the results of the validation, and to verify the accuracy of the Program Description.
(3) Commissioners use the validated Program Description to make the accreditation decision.

**What information is on the Program Description?**

The Program Description has three parts:
*Part 1—Center Profile.* The Center Profile is where the director describes the program. The Center Profile includes information about enrollment, age groups served, length of day, purpose and philosophy of the program, how the program is organized in terms of groups and staffing, and the qualifications of staff members.
*Part 2—Results of Classroom Observations.* Part 2 is where the director reports the program's compliance with the criteria that are assessed in each classroom using the Early Childhood Classroom Observation. In Part 2 the director reports the program's average score for each observed criterion. The form provides space for the director to make comments about how the program meets these criteria.

Program Description

*145*

*Part 3—Results of Administrator Report.* Part 3 is where the director reports the program's compliance with the criteria that are rated for the entire program. These criteria include policies and procedures related to the overall administration of the program. Some of these criteria are also rated by staff members and parents. Part 3 of the Program Description provides space for reporting the director's rating for each administrative criterion and for reporting the responses to the Teaching-Staff and Family Questionnaires.

## Why is the Program Description used in the accreditation process?

The Program Description is designed to make the reporting process as easy as possible for directors. The form is also designed to ensure that every Program Description is the same length and organized the same way. This helps validators and commissioners, and it also helps directors who do not have time to write lengthy descriptions of how their programs meet each criterion. The Program Description is also designed to be used by a variety of programs.

Although the Program Description form is structured, directors should not feel limited or constrained by it. In addition to rating each item, directors should feel free to write additional comments or explanations in the space provided. Although no comment is necessary if the criterion is rated a [3], directors should comment if the item is rated less than a [3], and can provide additional information if they feel they exceed the criterion.

## When is the Program Description completed?

The Program Description should be completed after the self-study is finished and the staff and director have made any improvements they wish to make. Once the Program Description is completed it should be sent to the Academy, indicating that the program is ready for the validation visit. The information reported on the Program Description is what the validators will verify during the on-site visit. It is important that the information be up-to-date and reflect the current situation (as of three months), not what it was when the self-study began or what is planned for the future.

## Who completes the Program Description?

Although the information reported on the Program Description is collected by many people, including staff and parents, one person should take responsibility for compiling all the information and completing the Program Description. That person should be the director (or the most appropriate administrator) who will also need to be available to work with the validators during the on-site visit.

# Directions for completing the Program Description

In completing the Program Description, do not write in spaces that are identified for "Validation Purposes." **Write legibly and in black ink.**

**How to fill out Part 1—Center Profile**

(pages 3 to 15 of the Program Description)

**1. Write the Program ID Number on the form.** Each program is assigned a Program Identification Number by the Academy that should be used in all contact with the Academy and should be written on the Center Profile. The program will be identified only by the ID number when Commissioners consider whether to accredit the program. If you have misplaced your Program Identification Number, contact the Academy before submitting your Program Description.

**2. Answer all questions on the Center Profile.** You may need additional space to answer some of the questions, such as the program philosophy. If so, please be brief. An example of a completed Center Profile is provided on pages 81 to 93 in Section 4 of the *Guide.*

> **Please note: Licensing is a prerequisite for accreditation.** If your program is exempt from licensing, you should be prepared to provide evidence of that exemption, and also to write a report of your voluntary compliance with state licensing standards including which standards you do not meet and why. All programs need to present valid certification that it is in compliance with all legal requirements for protection of the health and safety of children in group settings, such as building codes, sanitation, water quality, and fire protection.

*3. Fill out the Staffing Pattern and Staff Qualifications chart.* Examples for completing the Staffing Pattern and Staff Qualifications charts are provided in Section 4 (pages 84 to 93) of the *Guide.* The Staffing Pattern presents all of the following information in one place: organization of the groups, ages of children in each group, average attendance by hour, number of staff per hour, work hours of each staff member, and ratio of staff to children for each group throughout the day. Staff members should always be identified by group throughout the day. **Staff members should be identified by first name and last initial on this chart and on the Staff Qualifications chart**. If your grouping system is very complicated, the Staffing Pattern may be difficult. If you feel you cannot present it on this chart, attach a copy of your own staff pattern, **but be sure to include all the same information.** If you need clarification contact your regional coordinator at the Academy.

If your program employs an open space organizational structure, please attach a clear description of the arrangement of the environment (a floor plan) and how the children are grouped within it. Clarify how the intent of the criteria for staffing (F-1, F-2, and F-3) are met in this environment.

> Remember—information about staff-child ratios, group sizes, and how groups of children are organized is very important. The Commission must be able to grasp a clear picture of how the program is staffed.

## How to fill out Part 2—Results of Classroom Observations

(pages 17 to 49 of the Program Description)

**1. Record the program's average rating for each criterion.** After all the observations are finished and the teaching staff and the director agree on a whole number rating to report for each classroom or group of children, the Classroom Observation Summary Sheet is completed.

**To complete the Classroom Observation Summary Sheet:**

- Record the final ratings for each classroom
- Add the sum of scores and calculate the average score across classrooms for each criterion that is rated
- On Part 2 of the Program Description, record the average rating in the box marked "Average rating."

**2. Comment about criteria that are not met or are exceeded.** Below the average rating box is a space marked "Director's comments on rating."

**The director should use this space to**

- Explain any criterion that is not met or is partially met, that is any criterion with an average rating of 2.7 or less.
- Comment if you feel that you meet the criterion in a different way. For instance, if your program does not have its own playground, but provides outdoor play through use of a neighboring park, explain this difference.
- Comment if the program does more than is required, pointing out any particular strengths of the program.
- If the criterion does not apply to the program, the director should check "not applicable."

> Reminder: The right-hand side of the page is for validators only. The director should not write in these spaces. The validator will record ratings for the classrooms observed during the validation visit, you should not record the results from your observations in the Program Description.

# How to fill out Part 3—Results of the Administrator Report

(pages 50 to 102 of the Program Description)

**1. Circle the appropriate number [1], [2], or [3] indicating your rating for each criterion,** in the space marked "Director's rating." As director you have already thought about how your program meets these criteria using the Administrator Report during the self-study. Now rate the program based on the current situation, after improvements were made.

**2. Comment about criteria that are partially met or not met (ratings of [2] or [1] or that are exceeded.** Below the director's rating box is a space marked "Director's comments on rating."

**The director should use this space to**

- Explain any rating that is partially met or not met.
- Explain how the criterion is met in a different way. For example, criterion **F-3a** states that "Each staff member has primary responsibility for and develops a deeper attachment to an identified group of children. There is specific accountability for each child by one staff member." The director states that the criterion is partially met and comments that "Two teachers work with the 20 preschool children, and both are responsible for all children."
- Indicate areas where your program does more than what is required by a criterion.

**3. Report the results of the Teaching-Staff and Family Questionnaires.** The questionnaires are used as another source of evidence to demonstrate compliance with some of the administrative criteria. The results are reported next to the appropriate criterion in the far right column marked, "Validation procedure."

**Using the Teaching-Staff and Family Questionnaire Summary Sheets:**

- Report the return rate for the Teaching-Staff and Family Questionnaires on page 51 of the Program Description.
- Write in the total number of times each criterion is rated [1], [2], or [3] by staff for the criteria in the boxes marked "Staff Questionnaire."
- Write in the total number of parents who responded either "don't know," "no," or "yes" to each item on the Family Questionnaire in the boxes marked "Family Questionnaire."

Program Description

*The item numbers on the Family Questionnaire do not match the criterion numbers, but the Program Description indicates which Family Questionnaire number to fill in on Part 3. For example,

## C.   Relationships among Teachers and Families

**Director's rating**

**Validation procedure**

**Criterion**

| Not met | Partially met | Fully met |
|---|---|---|
| 1 | 2 | (3) |

**C-6a.** Teachers and parents work together to make decisions about how to best support children's development and learning or to handle problems or differences of opinion as they arise.

*Staff Questionnaire C-6a*

| 0 | 1 | 5 |
|---|---|---|
| 1 | 2 | 3 |

**Validation decision**

❏ V   ❏ NV

*Director's comments on rating*

*Family Questionnaire #11*

| 0 | 5 | 45 |
|---|---|---|
| DK | No | Yes |

_____

_____

*For validator* _____

In this case, the director circled [3], indicating that she feels the criterion is fully met. Criterion **C-6a** appears on the Teaching-Staff Questionnaire and was rated a [3] by five staff members and [2] by one staff member. Question #11 on the Family Questionnaire is related to this criterion. Five parents answered "no" and 45 answered "yes" to that question.

---

Do not throw away the final set of Family and Teaching-Staff Questionnaires and summary sheets. The validator will need to sample these during the validation visit.

# Submitting your Program Description to the Academy for your validation visit

**Check over the Program Description**

Check to make sure that you have rated all criteria. Check to be certain that you have filled in all of the boxes marked "Staff Questionnaire" and "Family Questionnaire." Make sure that the report reflects the program's current situation. If you find that the Program Description contains many ratings of [2] and [1], you may not be ready for accreditation or you might have rated your program too hard. In either case, review the criteria and ratings before submitting your Program Description to the Academy. You should not submit until you feel that you will be successful, the program is in substantial compliance with the criteria.

Carefully read and sign the Accreditation Release Form located on page 4 of the Program Description. Accreditation is null and void if false information is knowingly submitted to the Academy at any time.

**Make a copy of the Program Description**

You will put a lot of work into preparing your Program Description. Sometimes things become lost in the mail. You should make a copy for your records. Following the validation visit and Commission decision, the validated Program Description will be returned to you.

**What is mailed to the Academy?**

Using the return envelope, mail the following by certified or registered mail:
- Completed Program Description with the signed release form;
- Classroom Observation Summary Sheet; and
- payment for your validation visit (check, money order, purchase order, VISA, or MasterCard).

**How long will it take for the Academy to arrange the validation visit?**

The Academy staff requires 40 working days (8 to 10 weeks) to arrange your validation visit. The spring is a very busy time. It is very difficult for the Academy to deliver the validation visit within the 8- to 10-week window during this peak time. Make sure that your Program Description is submitted in a timely manner to ensure that the visit can be arranged before the end of the program or school-year. To avoid lengthy delays, may we request submitting for validation prior to February. If your Program Description is submitted to the Academy but does not allow enough time to arrange the validation visit prior to the closing of your program, your Program Description will be held for a validation visit until the program re-opens. In this case you are not required to re-do the self-study. You will however, be required to update the Program Description to reflect the current program at the time of validation.

Programs applying for **reaccreditation** should submit their Program Description for validation ninety (90) days prior to their expiration date in order for the Academy to ensure enough time for a validation visit and the Commission to render a decision prior to the expiration.

*National Association for the Education of Young Children*

# Early Childhood Program Description

**What is the purpose of the Program Description?**

The form is used for three steps in the accreditation process:

(1)  The program director uses this form to report the results of the program's self-study describing how the program meets the Criteria.

(2)  The validator(s) uses this form during the on-site visit to record the results of the validation verifying the accuracy of the Program Description.

(3)  The commissioners use the validated Program Description to make the accreditation decision.

**How is the Program Description organized?**

The Program Description has three parts:

*Part 1—Center Profile* describes the program such as the number of children enrolled, hours of operation, staffing, and the staff qualifications of staff members.

*Part 2—Results of Classroom Observations* is used by the program director to report the average rating of each criterion that is observed in individual classrooms and the director's comments about that average rating; is used by the validator(s) to compare the results of her observations of a sample of classrooms with the program's ratings and to record the results of the discussion with the director of each nonvalidated criterion.

*Part 3—Results of Administrator Report* is used by the program director to report the program's compliance with those criteria that are assessed through the Administrator Report, the Teaching Staff Questionnaire and/or the Family Questionnaire; is used by the validator(s) to compare the sources of evidence to validate the accuracy of the report and to record the results of the discussion with the director of each nonvalidated criterion.

**Note to director and validator(s): Please write legibly and in black ink.**

**Program ID Number**

# Early Childhood Program Description
## *Part 1—Center Profile*

**Program identification—This page is removed before the Commission considers the Program Description.**

Name of program _____

Name and title of person completing this form _____

_____

Name and title of person legally responsible for administration of program (if different from above)

_____

_____

**Location(s) of program** (overseas programs should provide mailing address)

(1)  Street _____

City _____ State _____ ZIP code _____

Telephone ( _____ ) _____

Program FAX ( _____ ) _____

Program e-mail _____

**For multisite applications:**
**No more than three sites may apply under one Program Description.**

(2)  Street _____

City _____ State _____ ZIP code _____

Telephone ( _____ ) _____

(2)  Street _____

City _____ State _____ ZIP code _____

Telephone ( _____ ) _____

Number of sites applying for accreditation under this Program Description _____. Sites must be within 15 minutes from one another; additional sites cannot serve more than 60 children per site.

Program Description

National Association for the Education of Young Children

# Validation/Accreditation Release Form

Please read carefully and sign.

As _____

(Title)

of _____

(Name of program)

which is applying for accreditation by the National Academy of Early Childhood Programs, I verify that this program has completed a self-study and Program Description, which is attached, and requested a validation visit to verify the Program Description. I certify that I understand the accreditation procedures, that I knowingly and voluntarily present this program for review. I understand that the Academy may deny accreditation to this program if the Academy determines that this program does not comply with the Academy's Criteria and that if accreditation is granted it may be revoked upon a determination that this program is no longer in compliance with the Criteria or that this program has failed to comply with Academy procedures. I understand that if accreditation is granted, it is null and void if false information is knowingly submitted to the Academy at any time.

_____

(Name of program)

hereby releases the Academy, the National Association for the Education of Young Children, and their employees and agents from liability in connection with actions and decisions taken with respect to this application for review and accreditation, except for cases of gross negligence or willful misconduct.

I further understand that this program has the right of advance notice of the validator(s) who will conduct the on-site visit and date(s) for the visit. I understand that I may request a different validator if a conflict of interest exists with the person assigned. I enclose the validation fee in the amount of $ _____.

Please make checks payable to NAEYC.

_____

Signature of program director or authorized administrator

_____

Name (please print)

_____

Date

Program ID Number

# Early Childhood Program Description
## *Part 1—Center Profile*

1.  How long has the program been in operation? _____
    (years/months)

    If applicable, at site 2? _____
    (years/months)

    If applicable, at site 3? _____
    (years/months)

2.  Does the program currently meet local licensing regulations?

    If yes, by what agencies is the program licensed/accredited? _____

    _____

    If no, explain. _____

    _____

3.  What are your program's hours of operation? _____

    Days per week _____ Months per year _____

    Does your program change during summer?

    If yes, what is the last day of the regular school year? _____

    In what way does the program change for the summer? _____

    _____

4.  What funding sources support the program? Please provide the estimated percentage of funding received from each source.

    _____ Parent tuition                      _____ Public funds (federal/state)

    _____ Community funds (United Way, etc.)   _____ Church contributions

    _____ Employer contributions               _____ Other (please specify below)

5. If the program has a governing board or policy or advisory group, describe the composition of the group and its functions.

6. What is the purpose of the program? (Describe the type of program, for example, a full-day child care center, half-day preschool, public school kindergarten, parent cooperative, Head Start, or Montessori School.)

7. What is the philosophy of the program? (Provide a brief description of the program's goals and objectives for children. Use the space below or attach additional sheets if necessary.)

8. What is the total number of children enrolled in the program? _____

   Daily enrollment (if different from total above) _____ Monday _____ Tuesday _____ Wednesday

   _____ Thursday _____ Friday _____ Saturday _____ Sunday

9. Provide the number of children enrolled by developmental level.

   _____ Infants (birth through 12 months)

   _____ Toddlers (13 months to 35 months)

   _____ Preschoolers (3- through 5-year-olds)

   _____ Kindergarteners (attending public or private kindergarten program)

   _____ School-agers (6-year-olds and older)

10. Staffing Pattern—use the following chart to describe how the program is staffed. For each hour of the day indicate the number of children enrolled in the group, the number of staff members assigned to the group (use first name and last initial only), and the hours worked by the staff members. A *group* is the number of children assigned to a staff member or team of staff members occupying an individual classroom or well-defined space within a larger room. Each group should be listed separately on the Staffing Pattern. **If your program is not organized into self-contained classrooms but employs an open-space organizational structure, please attach clear information about the arrangements of the environment (a floor plan) and how the children are grouped within it.** Clarify how the staffing criteria (group size and staff-child ratio) are met in this environment throughout the day.

## Staffing Pattern

| Group of children | Staffing Pattern | | | | | | | | | | | | | |
|---|---|---|---|---|---|---|---|---|---|---|---|---|---|---|
| **Group name** | **AM** | **Number of children enrolled each hour** | | | | | | | | | | | | **PM** |
| | 6:00 | 7:00 | 8:00 | 9:00 | 10:00 | 11:00 | 12:00 | 1:00 | 2:00 | 3:00 | 4:00 | 5:00 | 6:00 | 7:00 |
| | | | | | | | | | | | | | | |
| | **Number of staff in attendance each hour** | | | | | | | | | | | | | |
| **Age range    Number** | | | | | | | | | | | | | | |
| Infants _____ | Hours of each staff member | | | | | | | | | | | | | |
| Toddlers _____ | | | | | | | | | | | | | | |
| Preschoolers _____ | | | | | | | | | | | | | | |
| Kindergartners _____ | | | | | | | | | | | | | | |
| School-agers _____ | | | | | | | | | | | | | | |
| **Group name** | **AM** | **Number of children enrolled each hour** | | | | | | | | | | | | **PM** |
| | 6:00 | 7:00 | 8:00 | 9:00 | 10:00 | 11:00 | 12:00 | 1:00 | 2:00 | 3:00 | 4:00 | 5:00 | 6:00 | 7:00 |
| | | | | | | | | | | | | | | |
| | **Number of staff in attendance each hour** | | | | | | | | | | | | | |
| **Age range    Number** | | | | | | | | | | | | | | |
| Infants _____ | Hours of each staff member | | | | | | | | | | | | | |
| Toddlers _____ | | | | | | | | | | | | | | |
| Preschoolers _____ | | | | | | | | | | | | | | |
| Kindergartners _____ | | | | | | | | | | | | | | |
| School-agers _____ | | | | | | | | | | | | | | |
| **Group name** | **AM** | **Number of children enrolled each hour** | | | | | | | | | | | | **PM** |
| | 6:00 | 7:00 | 8:00 | 9:00 | 10:00 | 11:00 | 12:00 | 1:00 | 2:00 | 3:00 | 4:00 | 5:00 | 6:00 | 7:00 |
| | | | | | | | | | | | | | | |
| | **Number of staff in attendance each hour** | | | | | | | | | | | | | |
| **Age range    Number** | | | | | | | | | | | | | | |
| Infants _____ | Hours of each staff member | | | | | | | | | | | | | |
| Toddlers _____ | | | | | | | | | | | | | | |
| Preschoolers _____ | | | | | | | | | | | | | | |
| Kindergartners _____ | | | | | | | | | | | | | | |
| School-agers _____ | | | | | | | | | | | | | | |

Program Description

## Staffing Pattern *continued*

| Group of children | Staffing Pattern | | | | | | | | | | | | | | |
|---|---|---|---|---|---|---|---|---|---|---|---|---|---|---|---|

**Group name**

| AM | Number of children enrolled each hour | | | | | | | | | | | | | PM |
|---|---|---|---|---|---|---|---|---|---|---|---|---|---|---|
| 6:00 | 7:00 | 8:00 | 9:00 | 10:00 | 11:00 | 12:00 | 1:00 | 2:00 | 3:00 | 4:00 | 5:00 | 6:00 | 7:00 |
|  |  |  |  |  |  |  |  |  |  |  |  |  |  |

Number of staff in attendance each hour

|  |  |  |  |  |  |  |  |  |  |  |  |  |  |
|---|---|---|---|---|---|---|---|---|---|---|---|---|---|

**Age range**    **Number**

Infants _____

Toddlers _____

Preschoolers _____

Kindergartners _____

School-agers _____

Hours of each staff member

---

**Group name**

| AM | Number of children enrolled each hour | | | | | | | | | | | | | PM |
|---|---|---|---|---|---|---|---|---|---|---|---|---|---|---|
| 6:00 | 7:00 | 8:00 | 9:00 | 10:00 | 11:00 | 12:00 | 1:00 | 2:00 | 3:00 | 4:00 | 5:00 | 6:00 | 7:00 |
|  |  |  |  |  |  |  |  |  |  |  |  |  |  |

Number of staff in attendance each hour

|  |  |  |  |  |  |  |  |  |  |  |  |  |  |
|---|---|---|---|---|---|---|---|---|---|---|---|---|---|

**Age range**    **Number**

Infants _____

Toddlers _____

Preschoolers _____

Kindergartners _____

School-agers _____

Hours of each staff member

---

**Group name**

| AM | Number of children enrolled each hour | | | | | | | | | | | | | PM |
|---|---|---|---|---|---|---|---|---|---|---|---|---|---|---|
| 6:00 | 7:00 | 8:00 | 9:00 | 10:00 | 11:00 | 12:00 | 1:00 | 2:00 | 3:00 | 4:00 | 5:00 | 6:00 | 7:00 |
|  |  |  |  |  |  |  |  |  |  |  |  |  |  |

Number of staff in attendance each hour

|  |  |  |  |  |  |  |  |  |  |  |  |  |  |
|---|---|---|---|---|---|---|---|---|---|---|---|---|---|

**Age range**    **Number**

Infants _____

Toddlers _____

Preschoolers _____

Kindergartners _____

School-agers _____

Hours of each staff member

---

**Group name**

| AM | Number of children enrolled each hour | | | | | | | | | | | | | PM |
|---|---|---|---|---|---|---|---|---|---|---|---|---|---|---|
| 6:00 | 7:00 | 8:00 | 9:00 | 10:00 | 11:00 | 12:00 | 1:00 | 2:00 | 3:00 | 4:00 | 5:00 | 6:00 | 7:00 |
|  |  |  |  |  |  |  |  |  |  |  |  |  |  |

Number of staff in attendance each hour

|  |  |  |  |  |  |  |  |  |  |  |  |  |  |
|---|---|---|---|---|---|---|---|---|---|---|---|---|---|

**Age range**    **Number**

Infants _____

Toddlers _____

Preschoolers _____

Kindergartners _____

School-agers _____

Hours of each staff member

## Staffing Pattern *continued*

| Group of children | Staffing Pattern | | | | | | | | | | | | | | |
|---|---|---|---|---|---|---|---|---|---|---|---|---|---|---|---|

**Group name**

| AM | | Number of children enrolled each hour | | | | | | | | | | | | PM |
|---|---|---|---|---|---|---|---|---|---|---|---|---|---|---|
| 6:00 | 7:00 | 8:00 | 9:00 | 10:00 | 11:00 | 12:00 | 1:00 | 2:00 | 3:00 | 4:00 | 5:00 | 6:00 | 7:00 |
| | | | | | | | | | | | | | |

**Number of staff in attendance each hour**

| | | | | | | | | | | | | | |
|---|---|---|---|---|---|---|---|---|---|---|---|---|---|

Hours of each staff member

| Age range | Number |
|---|---|
| Infants | _____ |
| Toddlers | _____ |
| Preschoolers | _____ |
| Kindergartners | _____ |
| School-agers | _____ |

**Group name**

| AM | | Number of children enrolled each hour | | | | | | | | | | | | PM |
|---|---|---|---|---|---|---|---|---|---|---|---|---|---|---|
| 6:00 | 7:00 | 8:00 | 9:00 | 10:00 | 11:00 | 12:00 | 1:00 | 2:00 | 3:00 | 4:00 | 5:00 | 6:00 | 7:00 |
| | | | | | | | | | | | | | |

**Number of staff in attendance each hour**

| | | | | | | | | | | | | | |
|---|---|---|---|---|---|---|---|---|---|---|---|---|---|

Hours of each staff member

| Age range | Number |
|---|---|
| Infants | _____ |
| Toddlers | _____ |
| Preschoolers | _____ |
| Kindergartners | _____ |
| School-agers | _____ |

**Group name**

| AM | | Number of children enrolled each hour | | | | | | | | | | | | PM |
|---|---|---|---|---|---|---|---|---|---|---|---|---|---|---|
| 6:00 | 7:00 | 8:00 | 9:00 | 10:00 | 11:00 | 12:00 | 1:00 | 2:00 | 3:00 | 4:00 | 5:00 | 6:00 | 7:00 |
| | | | | | | | | | | | | | |

**Number of staff in attendance each hour**

| | | | | | | | | | | | | | |
|---|---|---|---|---|---|---|---|---|---|---|---|---|---|

Hours of each staff member

| Age range | Number |
|---|---|
| Infants | _____ |
| Toddlers | _____ |
| Preschoolers | _____ |
| Kindergartners | _____ |
| School-agers | _____ |

**Group name**

| AM | | Number of children enrolled each hour | | | | | | | | | | | | PM |
|---|---|---|---|---|---|---|---|---|---|---|---|---|---|---|
| 6:00 | 7:00 | 8:00 | 9:00 | 10:00 | 11:00 | 12:00 | 1:00 | 2:00 | 3:00 | 4:00 | 5:00 | 6:00 | 7:00 |
| | | | | | | | | | | | | | |

**Number of staff in attendance each hour**

| | | | | | | | | | | | | | |
|---|---|---|---|---|---|---|---|---|---|---|---|---|---|

Hours of each staff member

| Age range | Number |
|---|---|
| Infants | _____ |
| Toddlers | _____ |
| Preschoolers | _____ |
| Kindergartners | _____ |
| School-agers | _____ |

Program Description

## Staffing Pattern *continued*

| Group of children | Staffing Pattern | | | | | | | | | | | | | |
|---|---|---|---|---|---|---|---|---|---|---|---|---|---|---|

**Group name**

| AM | Number of children enrolled each hour | | | | | | | | | | | | PM |
|---|---|---|---|---|---|---|---|---|---|---|---|---|---|
| 6:00 | 7:00 | 8:00 | 9:00 | 10:00 | 11:00 | 12:00 | 1:00 | 2:00 | 3:00 | 4:00 | 5:00 | 6:00 | 7:00 |
| | | | | | | | | | | | | | |

**Number of staff in attendance each hour**

| | | | | | | | | | | | | | |
|---|---|---|---|---|---|---|---|---|---|---|---|---|---|

| Age range | Number | | Hours of each staff member |
|---|---|---|---|
| Infants | _____ | | |
| Toddlers | _____ | | |
| Preschoolers | _____ | | |
| Kindergartners | _____ | | |
| School-agers | _____ | | |

**Group name**

| AM | Number of children enrolled each hour | | | | | | | | | | | | PM |
|---|---|---|---|---|---|---|---|---|---|---|---|---|---|
| 6:00 | 7:00 | 8:00 | 9:00 | 10:00 | 11:00 | 12:00 | 1:00 | 2:00 | 3:00 | 4:00 | 5:00 | 6:00 | 7:00 |
| | | | | | | | | | | | | | |

**Number of staff in attendance each hour**

| | | | | | | | | | | | | | |
|---|---|---|---|---|---|---|---|---|---|---|---|---|---|

| Age range | Number | | Hours of each staff member |
|---|---|---|---|
| Infants | _____ | | |
| Toddlers | _____ | | |
| Preschoolers | _____ | | |
| Kindergartners | _____ | | |
| School-agers | _____ | | |

**Group name**

| AM | Number of children enrolled each hour | | | | | | | | | | | | PM |
|---|---|---|---|---|---|---|---|---|---|---|---|---|---|
| 6:00 | 7:00 | 8:00 | 9:00 | 10:00 | 11:00 | 12:00 | 1:00 | 2:00 | 3:00 | 4:00 | 5:00 | 6:00 | 7:00 |
| | | | | | | | | | | | | | |

**Number of staff in attendance each hour**

| | | | | | | | | | | | | | |
|---|---|---|---|---|---|---|---|---|---|---|---|---|---|

| Age range | Number | | Hours of each staff member |
|---|---|---|---|
| Infants | _____ | | |
| Toddlers | _____ | | |
| Preschoolers | _____ | | |
| Kindergartners | _____ | | |
| School-agers | _____ | | |

**Group name**

| AM | Number of children enrolled each hour | | | | | | | | | | | | PM |
|---|---|---|---|---|---|---|---|---|---|---|---|---|---|
| 6:00 | 7:00 | 8:00 | 9:00 | 10:00 | 11:00 | 12:00 | 1:00 | 2:00 | 3:00 | 4:00 | 5:00 | 6:00 | 7:00 |
| | | | | | | | | | | | | | |

**Number of staff in attendance each hour**

| | | | | | | | | | | | | | |
|---|---|---|---|---|---|---|---|---|---|---|---|---|---|

| Age range | Number | | Hours of each staff member |
|---|---|---|---|
| Infants | _____ | | |
| Toddlers | _____ | | |
| Preschoolers | _____ | | |
| Kindergartners | _____ | | |
| School-agers | _____ | | |

## Staffing Pattern *continued*

| Group of children | Staffing Pattern | | | | | | | | | | | | | |
|---|---|---|---|---|---|---|---|---|---|---|---|---|---|---|
| **Group name** | **AM** | **Number of children enrolled each hour** | | | | | | | | | | | | **PM** |
| | 6:00 | 7:00 | 8:00 | 9:00 | 10:00 | 11:00 | 12:00 | 1:00 | 2:00 | 3:00 | 4:00 | 5:00 | 6:00 | 7:00 |
| | | | | | | | | | | | | | | |
| | **Number of staff in attendance each hour** | | | | | | | | | | | | | |
| **Age range    Number** | | | | | | | | | | | | | | |
| Infants _____ | Hours of each staff member | | | | | | | | | | | | | |
| Toddlers _____ | | | | | | | | | | | | | | |
| Preschoolers _____ | | | | | | | | | | | | | | |
| Kindergartners _____ | | | | | | | | | | | | | | |
| School-agers _____ | | | | | | | | | | | | | | |
| **Group name** | **AM** | **Number of children enrolled each hour** | | | | | | | | | | | | **PM** |
| | 6:00 | 7:00 | 8:00 | 9:00 | 10:00 | 11:00 | 12:00 | 1:00 | 2:00 | 3:00 | 4:00 | 5:00 | 6:00 | 7:00 |
| | | | | | | | | | | | | | | |
| | **Number of staff in attendance each hour** | | | | | | | | | | | | | |
| **Age range    Number** | | | | | | | | | | | | | | |
| Infants _____ | Hours of each staff member | | | | | | | | | | | | | |
| Toddlers _____ | | | | | | | | | | | | | | |
| Preschoolers _____ | | | | | | | | | | | | | | |
| Kindergartners _____ | | | | | | | | | | | | | | |
| School-agers _____ | | | | | | | | | | | | | | |
| **Group name** | **AM** | **Number of children enrolled each hour** | | | | | | | | | | | | **PM** |
| | 6:00 | 7:00 | 8:00 | 9:00 | 10:00 | 11:00 | 12:00 | 1:00 | 2:00 | 3:00 | 4:00 | 5:00 | 6:00 | 7:00 |
| | | | | | | | | | | | | | | |
| | **Number of staff in attendance each hour** | | | | | | | | | | | | | |
| **Age range    Number** | | | | | | | | | | | | | | |
| Infants _____ | Hours of each staff member | | | | | | | | | | | | | |
| Toddlers _____ | | | | | | | | | | | | | | |
| Preschoolers _____ | | | | | | | | | | | | | | |
| Kindergartners _____ | | | | | | | | | | | | | | |
| School-agers _____ | | | | | | | | | | | | | | |
| **Group name** | **AM** | **Number of children enrolled each hour** | | | | | | | | | | | | **PM** |
| | 6:00 | 7:00 | 8:00 | 9:00 | 10:00 | 11:00 | 12:00 | 1:00 | 2:00 | 3:00 | 4:00 | 5:00 | 6:00 | 7:00 |
| | | | | | | | | | | | | | | |
| | **Number of staff in attendance each hour** | | | | | | | | | | | | | |
| **Age range    Number** | | | | | | | | | | | | | | |
| Infants _____ | Hours of each staff member | | | | | | | | | | | | | |
| Toddlers _____ | | | | | | | | | | | | | | |
| Preschoolers _____ | | | | | | | | | | | | | | |
| Kindergartners _____ | | | | | | | | | | | | | | |
| School-agers _____ | | | | | | | | | | | | | | |

Program Description

11. Staff Qualifications—complete the chart below for each administrator and staff member who works directly with children. Check the highest level achieved in formal education and early childhood/child development training. Check all credentials completed. An ECE/CD unit = 16 classroom hours or 1 credit hour of study in early childhood education or child development. ECE/CD units may be earned through college level courses, vocational-technical courses, or other forms of ongoing professional development. Be sure to identify all staff members in this chart and on the Staffing Pattern using the same first name and last initials.

## Administrative Staff Qualifications

| | Staff members | | | | | |
|---|---|---|---|---|---|---|
| Staff member (use first name and last initial only) | | | | | | |
| Job title | | | | | | |
| Years of relevant experience | | | | | | |
| Date of employment in this program | | | | | | |
| Formal education completed<br>    Some high school | | | | | | |
|     High school graduate | | | | | | |
|     Some college | | | | | | |
| College graduate (specify major) | | | | | | |
| Early childhood training completed<br>    1–6 units in ECE/CD | | | | | | |
|     7–12 units in ECE/CD | | | | | | |
|     13 or more units in ECE/CD (specify number) | | | | | | |
|     A.A. degree in ECE/CD | | | | | | |
|     B.A./B.S. degree in ECE/CD | | | | | | |
|     Graduate work in ECE/CD (specify units) | | | | | | |
|     Master's degree in ECE/CD | | | | | | |
|     Doctorate degree in ECE/CD | | | | | | |
| Administrative training completed (Specify the credential or comprehensive training program and the number of administrative units required.)<br><br>    Administrative credential<br><br>    Administrative training | | | | | | |

## Teaching Staff Qualifications

| | Teaching staff members | | | | | |
|---|---|---|---|---|---|---|
| Staff member (use first name and last initial only) | | | | | | |
| Job title | | | | | | |
| Years of relevant experience | | | | | | |
| Date of employment in this program | | | | | | |
| Formal education completed<br>    Some high school | | | | | | |
|     High school graduate | | | | | | |
|     Some college | | | | | | |
| College graduate (specify major) | | | | | | |
| Early childhood training completed<br>    1–6 units in ECE/CD | | | | | | |
|     7–12 units in ECE/CD | | | | | | |
|     13 or more units in ECE/CD<br>    (specify number) | | | | | | |
|     A.A. degree in ECE/CD | | | | | | |
|     B.A./B.S. degree in ECE/CD | | | | | | |
|     Graduate work in ECE/CD<br>    (specify units) | | | | | | |
|     Master's degree in ECE/CD | | | | | | |
|     Doctorate degree in ECE/CD | | | | | | |
| Credentials/certificates<br>    CDA (year received) | | | | | | |
|     State certificate in early child-<br>    hood education | | | | | | |
|     State certificate in elementary<br>    education | | | | | | |
| Other (specify the credential or comprehensive training program and the number of ECE/CD units required) | | | | | | |

Program Description

## Teaching Staff Qualifications

| | Teaching staff members | | | | | |
|---|---|---|---|---|---|---|
| Staff member (use first name and last initial only) | | | | | | |
| Job title | | | | | | |
| Years of relevant experience | | | | | | |
| Date of employment in this program | | | | | | |
| Formal education completed<br>    Some high school | | | | | | |
|    High school graduate | | | | | | |
|    Some college | | | | | | |
| College graduate (specify major) | | | | | | |
| Early childhood training completed<br>    1–6 units in ECE/CD | | | | | | |
|    7–12 units in ECE/CD | | | | | | |
|    13 or more units in ECE/CD<br>    (specify number) | | | | | | |
|    A.A. degree in ECE/CD | | | | | | |
|    B.A./B.S. degree in ECE/CD | | | | | | |
|    Graduate work in ECE/CD<br>    (specify units) | | | | | | |
|    Master's degree in ECE/CD | | | | | | |
|    Doctorate degree in ECE/CD | | | | | | |
| Credentials/certificates<br>    CDA (year received) | | | | | | |
|    State certificate in early childhood education | | | | | | |
|    State certificate in elementary education | | | | | | |
| Other (specify the credential or comprehensive training program and the number of ECE/CD units required) | | | | | | |

## Teaching Staff Qualifications

| | Teaching staff members | | | | | |
|---|---|---|---|---|---|---|
| Staff member (use first name and last initial only) | | | | | | |
| Job title | | | | | | |
| Years of relevant experience | | | | | | |
| Date of employment in this program | | | | | | |
| Formal education completed  Some high school | | | | | | |
| High school graduate | | | | | | |
| Some college | | | | | | |
| College graduate (specify major) | | | | | | |
| Early childhood training completed  1–6 units in ECE/CD | | | | | | |
| 7–12 units in ECE/CD | | | | | | |
| 13 or more units in ECE/CD (specify number) | | | | | | |
| A.A. degree in ECE/CD | | | | | | |
| B.A./B.S. degree in ECE/CD | | | | | | |
| Graduate work in ECE/CD (specify units) | | | | | | |
| Master's degree in ECE/CD | | | | | | |
| Doctorate degree in ECE/CD | | | | | | |
| Credentials/certificates  CDA (year received) | | | | | | |
| State certificate in early childhood education | | | | | | |
| State certificate in elementary education | | | | | | |
| Other (specify the credential or comprehensive training program and the number of ECE/CD units required) | | | | | | |

## Teaching Staff Qualifications

| | Teaching staff members | | | | | |
|---|---|---|---|---|---|---|
| Staff member (use first name and last initial only) | | | | | | |
| Job title | | | | | | |
| Years of relevant experience | | | | | | |
| Date of employment in this program | | | | | | |
| Formal education completed<br>   Some high school | | | | | | |
|    High school graduate | | | | | | |
|    Some college | | | | | | |
| College graduate (specify major) | | | | | | |
| Early childhood training completed<br>   1–6 units in ECE/CD | | | | | | |
|    7–12 units in ECE/CD | | | | | | |
|    13 or more units in ECE/CD (specify number) | | | | | | |
|    A.A. degree in ECE/CD | | | | | | |
|    B.A./B.S. degree in ECE/CD | | | | | | |
|    Graduate work in ECE/CD (specify units) | | | | | | |
|    Master's degree in ECE/CD | | | | | | |
|    Doctorate degree in ECE/CD | | | | | | |
| Credentials/certificates<br>   CDA (year received) | | | | | | |
|    State certificate in early childhood education | | | | | | |
|    State certificate in elementary education | | | | | | |
| Other (specify the credential or comprehensive training program and the number of ECE/CD units required) | | | | | | |

There are _____ lead teachers; _____ of the leads were employed here 12 months ago.
     (total number of)         (number of)

There are _____ Assistant Teachers; _____ of the Assistant Teachers were employed here 12 months ago.
     (total number of)         (number of)

Comment on the turnover data. (Add additional pages if necessary.)

# Early Childhood Program Description
## *Part 2—Results of Classroom Observations*

**How is Part 2 used in the program?**

Part 2 is used to report how well the program meets the criteria that are observed in each individual classroom or group of children. These criteria are related to Interactions among Teachers and Children, Curriculum, Physical Environment, Health and Safety, and Nutrition and Food Service.

Each classroom is observed and rated by the teaching staff and director. They come to an agreement about the rating for each criterion. Then the ratings of all classrooms are averaged to determine the program's rating form. The director may comment about the program's compliance with any criterion. If the program does not meet or only partially meets a criterion (with an average of 2.7 or less), the director should provide a written explanation or comment. If the program exceeds a criterion, the director should also comment. No comment is needed if the average rating is a [3]. The Classroom Observation Summary Sheet is sent to the Academy along with the Program Description to be used by the validator(s).

**How is Part 2 validated?**

The validator observes and rates a sample of the classrooms in the program. In small programs, all classrooms may be observed. Using the space provided on this form, the validator compares her or his ratings of individual classrooms with the ratings reported by the program. Using the decision rules below, the validator decides if the criterion is validated (V). For all nonvalidated criteria (NV), the validator records the director's comments on this form.

Decision rules for validating observable criteria:

(1)   If one or two classrooms are rated, the program's reported ratings and the validator's ratings must agree for that criterion to be validated (V).

(2)   If three or more classrooms are rated, there can be no more than one case of a one-point difference and there can be no cases of a two-point difference for that criterion to be validated (V).

Decision rules for large programs:

(3)   If seven or more classrooms are rated, there can be no more than two cases of a one-point difference, and there can be no cases of a two-point difference for a criterion to be validated (V).

Program Description

# A. Interactions among Teachers and Children

**Ratings of Center and Validator**

**Criterion**

**Groups**

| | Average rating | C | V | C | V | C | V | C | V | C | V | C | V | C | V | C | V | C | V |
|---|---|---|---|---|---|---|---|---|---|---|---|---|---|---|---|---|---|---|---|

**A-1.** Teachers interact frequently with children showing affection, interest, and respect.

❏ Teachers interact nonverbally by smiling, touching, holding.

❏ Teachers speak with children at eye level, often, throughout the day.

❏ Teachers talk with and listen to individual children during activities and routines (arriving/departing, eating).

❏ Teachers actively seek meaningful conversations with children.

❏ Teachers give one-to-one attention to infants during feeding and diapering, allowing time for infants' responses.

*Director's comments on rating*

**Validation decision**   ❏ **V**    ❏ **NV**

*For validator* _____

_____

_____

_____

_____

_____

_____

_____

_____

| | Average rating | C | V | C | V | C | V | C | V | C | V | C | V | C | V | C | V | C | V |
|---|---|---|---|---|---|---|---|---|---|---|---|---|---|---|---|---|---|---|---|

**A-2.** Teachers are available and responsive to children.

❏ Quickly comfort infants in distress.

❏ Reassure crying toddlers.

❏ Listen to children with attention and respect.

❏ Respond to children's questions and requests.

❏ Teachers are aware of the activities of the entire group even when dealing with a smaller group; staff position themselves strategically and look up often from involvement.

❏ Teachers spend time observing each child without interrupting an actively involved child.

*Director's comments on rating*

**Validation decision**   ❏ **V**    ❏ **NV**

*For validator* _____

_____

_____

_____

_____

_____

_____

_____

_____

# A. Interactions among Teachers and Children *continued*

**Ratings of Center and Validator**

**Criterion**

| Groups | | | | | | | | | | | | | | | | | | | |
|---|---|---|---|---|---|---|---|---|---|---|---|---|---|---|---|---|---|---|---|
| C | V | C | V | C | V | C | V | C | V | C | V | C | V | C | V | C | V | C | V |

**A-3a.** Teachers speak with children in a friendly, positive, courteous manner.

**Average rating**

❏ Speak with individual children often.
❏ Ask open-ended questions.
❏ Call children by name.
❏ Include child in conversations; describe actions, experiences, and events; listen and respond to children's comments and suggestions.

*Director's comments on rating*

**Validation decision**   ❏ V    ❏ NV

*For validator* _____

_____

_____

_____

_____

_____

_____

_____

---

**A-3b.** Teachers talk with individual children, and encourage children of all ages to use language.

**Average rating**

| C | V | C | V | C | V | C | V | C | V | C | V | C | V | C | V | C | V |
|---|---|---|---|---|---|---|---|---|---|---|---|---|---|---|---|---|---|

*For example,*
Repeat infants' sounds, talk about things toddlers see, help 2-year-olds name things, ask preschoolers open-ended questions, provide opportunities for school-agers to talk about their day. Talk positively to children about family members, family events, traditions, and routines.

*Director's comments on rating*

**Validation decision**   ❏ V    ❏ NV

*For validator* _____

_____

_____

_____

_____

_____

_____

_____

---

**A-4a.** Teachers treat children of all races, religions, family backgrounds, and cultures with equal respect and consideration.

**Average rating**

| C | V | C | V | C | V | C | V | C | V | C | V | C | V | C | V | C | V |
|---|---|---|---|---|---|---|---|---|---|---|---|---|---|---|---|---|---|

*For example,*
Teachers initiate activities and discussions to build positive self-identity and teach the value of differences.

Teachers make it a firm rule that a person's identity (age, race, ethnicity, family life, physical appearance, and ability) is never used to tease or reject anyone.

Teachers talk positively about each child's physical characteristics and cultural heritage.

Teachers react to teasing or rejecting among children by intervening to discuss similarities and differences.

*Director's comments on rating*

**Validation decision**   ❏ V    ❏ NV

*For validator* _____

_____

_____

_____

_____

_____

_____

_____

Program Description

# A. Interactions among Teachers and Children *continued*

**Criterion**

**Ratings of Center and Validator**

**Groups**

**A-4b.** Teachers provide children of both sexes with equal opportunities to take part in all activities.

| Average rating | C | V | C | V | C | V | C | V | C | V | C | V | C | V | C | V | C | V |
|---|---|---|---|---|---|---|---|---|---|---|---|---|---|---|---|---|---|---|
| | | | | | | | | | | | | | | | | | | |

*For example,*
Provide models, props, and visual images that counter traditional sex-role limitations (i.e., female firefighters, male nurses).

Value positive levels of noise and activity involving both girls and boys.

When acknowledging individual children, avoid gender stereotypes in language references (i.e., use words such as *strong, gentle, pretty, helpful* for both girls and boys).

*Director's comments on rating*

**Validation decision**  ❏ **V**    ❏ **NV**

*For validator*

**A-5.** Teachers encourage children's development of independent functioning, as appropriate. Teachers foster the development of age-appropriate self-help skills such as picking up toys, wiping spills, personal grooming (toileting, handwashing), obtaining and caring for materials, and other skills. (Cultural perspectives of family or community may influence expectations for independence.)

| Average rating | C | V | C | V | C | V | C | V | C | V | C | V | C | V | C | V | C | V |
|---|---|---|---|---|---|---|---|---|---|---|---|---|---|---|---|---|---|---|
| | | | | | | | | | | | | | | | | | | |

*Director's comments on rating*

**Validation decision**  ❏ **V**    ❏ **NV**

*For validator*

*For example,*
Infants: safe places for independent play

Older infants: finger feeding self

Toddlers: washing hands, selecting own toys

Three and fours: dressing, picking up toys

Kindergartners: doing responsible jobs within the school building, setting table, cleaning, acquiring self-help skills

School-agers: performing responsible jobs, participating in community activities

# A. Interactions among Teachers and Children *continued*

**Ratings of Center and Validator**

**Criterion**

**A-6a.** Teachers facilitate the development of responsibility, self-regulation, and self-control in children.

- ❑ Teachers set clear, consistent, fair limits for classroom behavior and in the case of older children, help them to set their own limits.
- ❑ Teachers use children's mistakes as learning opportunities, describing the situation and encouraging children's evaluation of the problem rather than imposing the solution.
- ❑ Teachers anticipate and eliminate potential problems, redirecting children to more acceptable behavior or activity.
- ❑ Teachers listen and acknowledge children's feelings and frustrations and respond with respect.
- ❑ Teachers guide children to resolve conflicts and model skills that help children to solve their own problems.
- ❑ Teachers encourage appropriate behavior, patiently reminding children of rules and their rationale as needed.
- ❑ Teachers apply logical or natural consequences in problem situations.

| Average rating | | Groups | | | | | | | | | | | | | | | |
|---|---|---|---|---|---|---|---|---|---|---|---|---|---|---|---|---|---|
| | | C | V | C | V | C | V | C | V | C | V | C | V | C | V | C | V |

*Director's comments on rating*

**Validation decision**   ❑ V     ❑ NV

*For validator*

---

**A-6b.** Teachers do not use corporal punishment or other negative discipline methods that hurt, humiliate, or frighten children.

- ❑ Food or beverage is never withheld as a form of discipline.
- ❑ The environment is arranged so that a minimal number of "No's" are necessary, especially for young children.

| Average rating | | C | V | C | V | C | V | C | V | C | V | C | V | C | V | C | V |
|---|---|---|---|---|---|---|---|---|---|---|---|---|---|---|---|---|---|

*Director's comments on rating*

**Validation decision**   ❑ V     ❑ NV

*For validator*

Program Description

# A. Interactions among Teachers and Children *continued*

**Criterion**

**Ratings of Center and Validator**

**Groups**

**A-7.** Overall sound of group is pleasant most of the time.

| Average rating | C | V | C | V | C | V | C | V | C | V | C | V | C | V | C | V | C | V |
|---|---|---|---|---|---|---|---|---|---|---|---|---|---|---|---|---|---|---|

*For example,*
Happy laughter, excitement, busy activity, pleasant conversation rather than harsh, stressful noise or enforced quiet

Adult voices do not predominate.

*Director's comments on rating*

**Validation decision**   ❑ V     ❑ NV

_____

_____

_____

_____

*For validator* _____

_____

_____

_____

**A-8.** Teachers support children's emotional development, assisting them to be comfortable, relaxed, happy, and involved in play and other activities.

| Average rating | C | V | C | V | C | V | C | V | C | V | C | V | C | V | C | V | C | V |
|---|---|---|---|---|---|---|---|---|---|---|---|---|---|---|---|---|---|---|

*Director's comments on rating*

**Validation decision**   ❑ V     ❑ NV

❑ Comfort and reassure children who are hurt, fearful, or otherwise upset.

❑ Help children deal with anger, frustration, or sadness by comforting, identifying, and reflecting feelings.

❑ Help children use various strategies to express emotions and solve social problems, as appropriate for age of child.

❑ Intervene quickly when children's responses to each other become physically aggressive, discuss the inappropriateness of such action, and help children to develop more positive strategies to solve conflicts.

❑ Encourage children to verbalize feelings and ideas, including both positive and negative emotions. For example, supply words for very young children to describe feelings; discuss alternative solutions with children 2 years and older.

*For validator* _____

# A. Interactions among Teachers and Children *continued*

**Ratings of Center and Validator**

**Criterion**

**A-9.** Teachers recognize and encourage prosocial behaviors among children, such as cooperation, helping taking turns, talking to solve problems, and concern for others. Expectations of children's social behavior are developmentally appropriate. Teachers support children's beginning friendships and provide opportunities for children to learn from each other as well as adults.

*For example,*
Infants interact (look, touch gently, vocalize) freely with one another as teachers observe, alert to respond and model safe interaction when necessary.

Two pieces of the same popular equipment are available so toddlers are not forced to share too often.

Preschoolers are encouraged to cooperate in small groups.

Kindergartners work with small, flexible groups on extended projects and participate in group problem-solving.

School-agers have opportunities to participate in group games or to work or play alone.

| Average rating | Groups | | | | | | | | |
|---|---|---|---|---|---|---|---|---|---|
| | C V | C V | C V | C V | C V | C V | C V | C V | C V |

*Director's comments on rating*

**Validation decision** ☐ V ☐ NV

*For validator*

**A-10.** Teachers use a variety of teaching strategies to enhance children's learning and development throughout the day.
- ☐ Stimulate children's thinking and extend their learning using verbal methods such as posing problems, asking questions, and making comments and suggestions.
- ☐ Introduce children to new experiences, ideas, or challenges.
- ☐ Coach and/or directly guide children in the acquisition of specific skills as needed, being careful to challenge, but not frustrate any child.

| Average rating | | | | | | | | | |
|---|---|---|---|---|---|---|---|---|---|
| | C V | C V | C V | C V | C V | C V | C V | C V | C V |

*Director's comments on rating*

**Validation decision** ☐ V ☐ NV

*For validator*

Program Description

# B.    Curriculum

## Criterion

**B-4.**    The daily schedule provides a balance of activities in consideration of the child's total daily experience—what happens before, during, and after the program with attention to the following dimensions of scheduling:

**Ratings of Center and Validator**

| Groups | | | | | | | | | | | | | | | | | |
|---|---|---|---|---|---|---|---|---|---|---|---|---|---|---|---|---|---|
| C | V | C | V | C | V | C | V | C | V | C | V | C | V | C | V | C | V |
| | | | | | | | | | | | | | | | | | |

**B-4a.**    All age groups play outdoors daily, permitting conditions protect children's health and safety.

Average rating

*Director's comments on rating*        **Validation decision**        ❑ **V**        ❑ **NV**

*For validator* _____

_____                _____

_____                _____

_____                _____

_____                _____

**B-4b.**    The schedule provides for alternating periods of quiet and active play.

Average rating

| C | V | C | V | C | V | C | V | C | V | C | V | C | V | C | V | C | V |
|---|---|---|---|---|---|---|---|---|---|---|---|---|---|---|---|---|---|
| | | | | | | | | | | | | | | | | | |

*Director's comments on rating*        **Validation decision**        ❑ **V**        ❑ **NV**

*For validator* _____

_____                _____

_____                _____

_____                _____

_____                _____

_____                _____

_____                _____

_____                _____

_____                _____

# B.   Curriculum *continued*

**Ratings of Center and Validator**

**Criterion**

**B-4c.**   A balance of large-muscle/ small-muscle activities is provided in the daily schedule.

| Average rating | Groups | | | | | | | | | |
|---|---|---|---|---|---|---|---|---|---|---|
| | C V | C V | C V | C V | C V | C V | C V | C V | C V | C V |

*Director's comments on rating*       **Validation decision**   ❑ **V**      ❑ **NV**

_____       *For validator* _____

_____       _____

_____       _____

_____       _____

**B-4d.**   More than one option for grouping (such as individual, small group, or large group) is available to children most of the day. Infants and toddlers are not expected to function as a large group.

| Average rating | | | | | | | | | | |
|---|---|---|---|---|---|---|---|---|---|---|
| | C V | C V | C V | C V | C V | C V | C V | C V | C V | C V |

*Director's comments on rating*       **Validation decision**   ❑ **V**      ❑ **NV**

_____       *For validator* _____

_____       _____

_____       _____

_____       _____

**B-4e.**   A balance of child-initiated and teacher-initiated activity is provided. The amount of time spent in large-group, teacher-initiated activity is limited.

| Average rating | | | | | | | | | | |
|---|---|---|---|---|---|---|---|---|---|---|
| | C V | C V | C V | C V | C V | C V | C V | C V | C V | C V |

*Director's comments on rating*       **Validation decision**   ❑ **V**      ❑ **NV**

_____       *For validator* _____

_____       _____

_____       _____

_____       _____

_____       _____

_____       _____

Program Description

## B.  Curriculum *continued*

**Criterion**

**Ratings of Center and Validator**

**B-5a.** Materials and equipment appropriate to the age group, (including books, dolls, toys, dress-up props, photos, pictures, music) that project diverse racial, gender, and age attributes are provided.

❑ Materials reflect the lives of the children and families served.
❑ Materials and equipment reflect the diversity found in society in general.

| Average rating | Groups | | | | | | | | | | | | | | | | | |
|---|---|---|---|---|---|---|---|---|---|---|---|---|---|---|---|---|---|---|
| | C | V | C | V | C | V | C | V | C | V | C | V | C | V | C | V | C | V |
| | | | | | | | | | | | | | | | | | | |

*Director's comments on rating*

**Validation decision**     ❑ V          ❑ NV

*For validator* _____

_____    _____

_____    _____

_____    _____

**B-5b.** Developmentally appropriate materials and equipment are available for *infants.*

❑ Simple, lightweight, open-ended, easily washable toys such as containers, balls, pop-beads, nesting cups
❑ Rattles, squeak toys, action/reaction toys
❑ Cuddle toys
❑ Toys to mouth such as teethers, rings
❑ Pictures of real objects
❑ Crawling area with sturdy, stable furniture to pull self up

| Average rating | C | V | C | V | C | V | C | V | C | V | C | V | C | V | C | V | C | V |
|---|---|---|---|---|---|---|---|---|---|---|---|---|---|---|---|---|---|---|
| | | | | | | | | | | | | | | | | | | |

❑ **Not applicable**

**Validation decision**     ❑ V          ❑ NV

*Director's comments on rating*     *For validator* _____

_____    _____

_____    _____

_____    _____

**B-5c.** Developmentally appropriate materials and equipment are available for *toddlers.*

❑ Push and pull toys
❑ Manipulatives such as stacking toys, large wooden spools/beads/cubes, pounding bench, simple puzzles
❑ Sturdy picture books, music
❑ Toys for pretending, such as play telephone, dolls
❑ Large paper, crayons
❑ Sturdy furniture to hold on to while walking
❑ Sand and water toys

| Average rating | C | V | C | V | C | V | C | V | C | V | C | V | C | V | C | V | C | V |
|---|---|---|---|---|---|---|---|---|---|---|---|---|---|---|---|---|---|---|
| | | | | | | | | | | | | | | | | | | |

❑ **Not applicable**

**Validation decision**     ❑ V          ❑ NV

*Director's comments on rating*     *For validator* _____

_____    _____

_____    _____

_____    _____

_____    _____

# B. Curriculum *continued*

**Criterion**

**Ratings of Center and Validator**

| | Groups | | | | | | | | | | | | | | | | | |
|---|---|---|---|---|---|---|---|---|---|---|---|---|---|---|---|---|---|---|

**B-5d.** Developmentally appropriate materials and equipment are available for *preschoolers*.

- ❑ Active play equipment for climbing and balancing
- ❑ Unit blocks and accessories
- ❑ Puzzles, manipulative toys
- ❑ Picture books, audio recordings/tapes, musical instruments
- ❑ Art materials such as finger and tempera paints, crayons, safe scissors, and paste
- ❑ Dramatic play materials such as dolls, dress-up clothes and props, child-sized furniture, puppets
- ❑ Sand and water toys

Average rating

| C | V | C | V | C | V | C | V | C | V | C | V | C | V | C | V | C | V |
|---|---|---|---|---|---|---|---|---|---|---|---|---|---|---|---|---|---|

❑ **Not applicable**

**Validation decision** ❑ V ❑ NV

*Director's comments on rating*

*For validator* _____

_____     _____

_____     _____

_____     _____

_____     _____

_____     _____

**B-5e.** Developmentally appropriate materials and equipment are available for *kindergartners*.

- ❑ Active play equipment for climbing and balancing
- ❑ Unit blocks and accessories such as figures, signs, cars, trees
- ❑ Construction materials
- ❑ Complex puzzles and manipulative toys for counting, sorting
- ❑ Picture books and early readers
- ❑ Audio recordings/tapes, musical instruments, computers with appropriate software
- ❑ Materials for writing and complex art projects
- ❑ A variety of dramatic play materials and props
- ❑ Board and card games

Average rating

| C | V | C | V | C | V | C | V | C | V | C | V | C | V | C | V | C | V |
|---|---|---|---|---|---|---|---|---|---|---|---|---|---|---|---|---|---|

❑ **Not applicable**

**Validation decision** ❑ V ❑ NV

*Director's comments on rating*

*For validator* _____

_____     _____

_____     _____

_____     _____

_____     _____

_____     _____

_____     _____

_____     _____

_____     _____

_____     _____

_____     _____

Program Description

# B.    Curriculum *continued*

**Ratings of Center and Validator**

**Criterion**

| | Groups | | | | | | | | | | | | | | | | |
|---|---|---|---|---|---|---|---|---|---|---|---|---|---|---|---|---|---|
| Average rating | C | V | C | V | C | V | C | V | C | V | C | V | C | V | C | V | C | V |
| | | | | | | | | | | | | | | | | | | |

**B-5f.**    Developmentally appropriate materials are available for *school-agers.*

❑ Active play equipment and materials such as bats and balls for organized games
❑ Construction materials for woodworking, unit blocks, accessories for blocks
❑ Materials for hobby and art projects, science projects
❑ Materials for dramatics, cooking
❑ Books, audio recordings/tapes, musical instruments, computers with appropriate software
❑ Board and card games
❑ Complex manipulative toys (connecting or interlocking toys) jigsaw puzzles

❑ **Not applicable**

*Director's comments on rating*

_____

_____

_____

_____

_____

**Validation decision**    ❑ **V**    ❑ **NV**

*For validator* _____

_____

_____

_____

_____

_____

| | C | V | C | V | C | V | C | V | C | V | C | V | C | V | C | V | C | V |
|---|---|---|---|---|---|---|---|---|---|---|---|---|---|---|---|---|---|---|
| Average rating | | | | | | | | | | | | | | | | | | |
| | | | | | | | | | | | | | | | | | | |

**B-6a.**    Active media that children can control, such as videotaping, cameras, audiotaping and developmentally appropriate computer software may be used in the classroom as active learning materials, along with other materials that children can choose. If such technology is used, the program provides equal access for all children. Teachers help children use these media as independently as possible.

*This criterion applies to children 3 years of age and older; it is not applicable to infants and toddlers. (Note: If no such media are used, score "Not applicable.")*

❑ **Not applicable**

*Director's comments on rating*

_____

_____

_____

_____

_____

_____

_____

_____

_____

**Validation decision**    ❑ **V**    ❑ **NV**

*For validator* _____

_____

_____

_____

_____

_____

_____

_____

_____

_____

# B. Curriculum *continued*

**Criterion**

**Ratings of Center and Validator**

| | Groups | | | | | | | | | | | | | | | | | | |
|---|---|---|---|---|---|---|---|---|---|---|---|---|---|---|---|---|---|---|---|
| Average rating | C | V | C | V | C | V | C | V | C | V | C | V | C | V | C | V | C | V |
| | | | | | | | | | | | | | | | | | | | |

**B-6b.** The use of passive media, such as television, films, videotapes, and audiotapes is limited to developmentally appropriate programming.

- ❑ Programs are previewed by adults prior to use.
- ❑ Another option for activity is always available.
- ❑ No child is required to view the program.
- ❑ Teachers discuss what is viewed with the children to develop critical viewing skills.
- ❑ Passive media are used only as infrequent events, rather than as regular, daily routines.

❑ **Not applicable**

**Validation decision**  ❑ V  ❑ NV

*Director's comments on rating*

*For validator* _____

_____

_____

_____

_____

_____

Program Description

# B.   Curriculum *continued*

**B-7.**   Teachers provide a variety of developmentally appropriate activities and materials that are selected to emphasize concrete experiential learning and to achieve the following goals:

**B-7a.**   Foster positive identity and sense of emotional well-being.

### Ratings of Center and Validator

| Average rating | Groups | | | | | | | | | | | | | | | | | | |
|---|---|---|---|---|---|---|---|---|---|---|---|---|---|---|---|---|---|---|---|
| | C | V | C | V | C | V | C | V | C | V | C | V | C | V | C | V | C | V |
| | | | | | | | | | | | | | | | | | | |

*Director's comments on rating*    **Validation decision**    ❑ V     ❑ NV

_____    *For validator* _____

_____    _____

_____    _____

_____    _____

_____    _____

_____    _____

*For example,*

**Infants/ toddlers**

Hold and touch, make frequent eye contact, and communicate with babies especially during caregiving.

Talk and sing to babies.

Allow infants to achieve mastery of their bodies through self-initiated motor behavior such as rolling, sitting.

Allow toddlers to feed themselves and encourage their development of self-help skills when ready.

Encourage and support each toddler's developmental achievements such as pulling up self, walking, and climbing.

Listen and respond to toddler's emerging language.

**Preschoolers**

Allow time for children to talk about what they see, do, and like.

Use children's names frequently in songs, games.

Display children's work and photos of children and their families.

Encourage children to draw pictures and tell stories about self, family, and cultural practices.

Provide many opportunities for children to initiate activity, develop and demonstrate control of their bodies and self-help skills.

**Kindergartners**

Provide learning experiences that respond to children's individual differences in ability and interests.

Display children's unique products and work.

Engage children in experiences that demonstrate the explicit valuing of each child, such as sending a card to a sick classmate.

Provide learning experiences in which children can succeed most of the tme and yet be challenged to work on the edge of their developing capabilities.

**School-agers**

Provide opportunities to express growing independence/self-reliance such as the ability to make choices, initiate own activities.

Allow opportunities to work or play alone.

Provide ways to ensure privacy.

Plan cooperative rather than competitive activities.

Recognize preference for self-selected peer groups.

Encourage children to draw pictures and tell stories about self, family, and cultural practices.

Display children's work and photos of children and their families.

Provide opportunities to explore cultural heritage.

# B. Curriculum *continued*

**Criterion**

---

**B-7b.** Develop social skills.

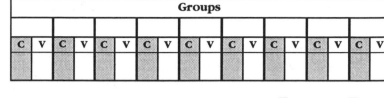

| Average rating | Groups | | | | | | | | | | | | | | | | | |
|---|---|---|---|---|---|---|---|---|---|---|---|---|---|---|---|---|---|---|
| | C | V | C | V | C | V | C | V | C | V | C | V | C | V | C | V | C | V |
| | | | | | | | | | | | | | | | | | | |

*Director's comments on rating*     **Validation decision**     ❏ V     ❏ NV

_____     *For validator* _____

_____     _____

_____     _____

_____     _____

_____     _____

_____     _____

_____     _____

_____     _____

*For example,*
**Infants/toddlers**

Hold, pat, and touch babies.

Talk to, sing to, and play with each baby on a one-to-one basis.

Respond to and expand on cues coming from child.

Interpret infants' actions to other children to help them get along in the group. ("Mary had it first.")

Assist toddlers in social interaction.

**Preschoolers**

Create space and time for small groups of children to build blocks together or enjoy dramatic play.

Coach children who have difficulty entering a play situation or making constructive use of child-chosen activity.

Provide opportunities for sharing, caring, and helping, such as making cards for a sick child or caring for pets.

Explore ways to respond to biased comments and behaviors.

**Kindergartners**

Use a variety of ways of flexibly grouping children.

Provide opportunities for children to collaborate and cooperate during play and projects.

Coach children in social problem-solving and conflict-resolution skills.

Engage children in setting and enforcing classroom rules.

Provide opportunities for sharing, caring, and helping, such as making cards for a sick child or caring for pets.

Provide opportunities to support children's beginning friendships.

**School-agers**

Arrange planned and spontaneous activities in team sports, group games, interest clubs, board and card games.

Allow time to sit and talk with friend or adult.

Focus on activities rather than outcomes (scores, winners).

# B.    Curriculum *continued*

**Criterion**

**B-7c.**   Encourage children to think, reason, question, and experiment.

**Ratings of Center and Validator**

| Average rating | Groups | | | | | | | | | | | | | | | | | | | |
|---|---|---|---|---|---|---|---|---|---|---|---|---|---|---|---|---|---|---|---|---|
| | C | V | C | V | C | V | C | V | C | V | C | V | C | V | C | V | C | V | C | V |
| | | | | | | | | | | | | | | | | | | | | |

*Director's comments on rating*

_____

_____

_____

_____

_____

_____

_____

**Validation decision**      ❑ **V**      ❑ **NV**

*For validator* _____

_____

_____

_____

_____

_____

---

*For example,*
**Infants/toddlers**

Provide an appropriately challenging, safe environment for infants and toddlers to explore and manipulate.

Provide light colorful objects for babies to look at which they can reach for and grasp.

Play naming and hiding games such as peek-a-boo, pat-a-cake.

Provide simple toys that respond to infants' initiations so they may pay attention to cause and effect.

Provide large containers full of objects for toddlers to carry, dump, and refill.

Help toddlers develop awareness by reflecting their experiences. ("You're pointing to the street. Is it because you hear the garbage truck?")

Provide opportunities for making choices without interfering with selections.

Avoid interruptions of children's activities.

**Preschoolers**

Plan activities for labeling, classifying, sorting objects by shape, color, size.

Discuss daily and weekly routines in terms of time concepts, season of the year.

Extend children's thinking and learning during activities by adding new materials, asking open-ended questions, offering ideas or suggestions, joining in their play, and providing assistance in solving problems.

Observe natural events such as seeds growing, life cycle of pets.

Create opportunities to use numbers, counting objects.

Take walks around building or neighborhood.

Plan trips to provide new learning experiences for preschoolers.

Encourage water and sand play.

**Kindergartners**

Provide opportunities to learn basic science and math concepts through sand and water exploration, constructing with blocks and working with levers, pulleys, scales, and other simple machines.

Involve children in observing and investigating natural events and objects, sorting and classifying, searching for patterns, noting differences and similarities, and drawing and discussing what they see.

Engage children in sustained project work, seeking solutions to concrete problems; observe and record changes in the environment, work with tools.

Read for information and reference.

Engage children in representing their understanding in various ways, such as drawing, writing, speaking.

Plan trips to provide new learning experiences.

**School-agers**

Provide activities such as cooking, money-making projects, gardening, science experiments, trips in the community, interacting with visitors, multicultural experiences, computer projects.

Provide opportunities to complete homework if desired including peer or adult tutoring for children who request assistance.

# B. Curriculum *continued*

**Criterion**

**B-7d.** Encourage language and literacy development

**Ratings of Center and Validator**

| Average rating | Groups | | | | | | | | | | | | | | | | | |
|---|---|---|---|---|---|---|---|---|---|---|---|---|---|---|---|---|---|---|
| | C | V | C | V | C | V | C | V | C | V | C | V | C | V | C | V | C | V |
| | | | | | | | | | | | | | | | | | | |

*Director's comments on rating*   **Validation decision**   ❑ V   ❑ NV

_____   *For validator* _____

_____   _____

_____   _____

_____   _____

_____   _____

_____   _____

_____   _____

*For example,*
**Infants/toddlers**
Engage in many one-to-one, face-to-face interactions with infants.

Look at simple books and pictures.

Talk in a pleasant, calm voice, using simple language and frequent eye contact while being responsive to the infant's cues.

Verbally label objects and events within the infant's experience.

Respond to sounds infant makes, occasionally imitating infant's vocalization.

Describe children's and adult's actions and the events that occur in the child's environment.

Respond to toddlers' attempts at language in supportive ways, such as expanding their utterances and answering their questions, engaging in meaningful conversation about everyday experiences.

**Preschoolers**
Read books and poems, tell stories about experiences, talk about pictures, write down experience stories children dictate.

Provide time for conversation, ask child questions that require more than a one-word answer.

Answer children's questions.

Add more information to what a child says.

Label things in room, use written words with pictures and spoken language, provide a print-rich environment.

Use flannel board, puppets, songs, finger plays, rhyming games.

Encourage children's emerging interest in writing (scribbling, drawing, copying, and using invented spelling).

**Kindergartners**
Actively work to increase children's vocabulary every day.

Read books and poems, tell stories about experiences, talk about pictures, write down experience stories children dictate.

Help children develop book-handling skills and familiarity with the conventions of print (such as story/chapter titles, punctuation, and capital letters).

Help children develop the full range of strategies for reading, for instance, using letter-sound relationships, pictures, and their understanding of the text to figure out unknown words.

Provide many opportunities every day for children to write for reasons that make sense to them (such as making lists, labeling their work, and writing notes to their parents).

Give children frequent practice and help in composing, editing, and revising stories and other written products.

Observe and make plans to ensure each child's continual progress in oral language, reading, and writing.

**School-agers**
Provide opportunities to read books.

Write and produce plays, publish newspapers, write stories.

Share experiences with friends or adults.

Use audio-visual equipment such as tape recorders.

Make own filmstrips, recordings.

# B. Curriculum *continued*

**Criterion**

**Ratings of Center and Validator**

| | Groups | | | | | | | | | | | | | | | | | |
|---|---|---|---|---|---|---|---|---|---|---|---|---|---|---|---|---|---|---|
| **Average rating** | C | V | C | V | C | V | C | V | C | V | C | V | C | V | C | V | C | V |
| | | | | | | | | | | | | | | | | | | |

**B-7e.** Enhance physical development and skills.

*Director's comments on rating*

**Validation decision**  ❏ **V**   ❏ **NV**

*For validator* _____

_____    _____

_____    _____

_____    _____

_____    _____

_____

*For example,*
**Infants/toddlers**
Allow infants' self-initiated motor development such as rolling, sitting, walking at their own pace.
Provide open carpeted space as well as hard surfaces such as wood floors for crawling.
Provide low, sturdy furniture for child to pull up self or hold on to while walking.
Provide accessible outdoor activities for infants.
Provide simple objects infants may reach for and grasp.
Allow nonmobile infants to move and breathe comfortably, lying freely on their backs while looking about, kicking, reaching, practicing eye-hand coordination.
Provide toddlers objects for carrying, such as baskets, large empty plastic bottles, balls.
Provide toddlers simple puzzles, nesting toys, stacking toys, and pop-beads.

**Preschoolers**
Provide time and space for active play such as jumping, running, balancing, climbing, riding tricycles.
Provide creative movement activity using obstacle course or activity songs and records.
Provide fine-motor activities such as complex manipulative toys, pegboards, puzzles, lacing cards, and woodworking.
Provide art materials for drawing, modeling, writing.

**Kindergartners**
Provide equipment, time, and space for active play such as jumping rope, running, balancing, climbing, and playing group games.
Provide creative movement activity, music, songs, and recordings.

Provide fine-motor activities such as jigsaw puzzles, sewing, woodworking, objects that can be taken apart and put back together, dolls and accessories.
Provide variety of art and writing materials and daily opportunities for drawing, painting, cutting, and writing.

**School-agers**
Provide opportunities to get physical exercise and use variety of outdoor equipment.
Encourage participation in group games, individual and team sports.
Provide fine-motor activities and hobbies such as sewing, macramé, pottery, leatherwork, carpentry, computers.

# B. Curriculum *continued*

## Criterion

**Ratings of Center and Validator**

**B-7f.** Encourage and demonstrate sound health, safety, and nutritional practices.

| Average rating | | Groups | | | | | | | | | | | | | | | | | |
|---|---|---|---|---|---|---|---|---|---|---|---|---|---|---|---|---|---|---|---|
| | C | V | C | V | C | V | C | V | C | V | C | V | C | V | C | V | C | V | C | V |

*Director's comments on rating*      **Validation decision**   ❏ V      ❏ NV

_____      *For validator* _____

_____      _____

_____      _____

_____      _____

*For example,*
**All ages**
Cook and serve a variety of nutritious foods.
Discuss good nutrition.
Do activities to develop safety awareness in the center, home, and community.
Encourage health practices such as washing hands, brushing teeth, getting regular exercise and enough rest.
Talk about visiting doctor, dentist.
For infants/toddlers: Describe routine health activities as they are implemented.
For preschoolers, kindergartners, and school-agers: Study topics such as human body, nutrition, life skills.

**B-7g.** Encourage creative expression, representation, and appreciation for the arts.

| Average rating | | C | V | C | V | C | V | C | V | C | V | C | V | C | V | C | V | C | V | C | V |
|---|---|---|---|---|---|---|---|---|---|---|---|---|---|---|---|---|---|---|---|---|

*Director's comments on rating*      **Validation decision**   ❏ V      ❏ NV

_____      *For validator* _____

_____      _____

_____      _____

_____      _____

*For example,*
**Infants/toddlers**
Occasionally use music for movement, singing, or listening.
Sing to baby, appreciate infants' vocalizations and sounds.
Display interesting things to look at.
Provide time and space for movement and play.
Encourage scribbling with crayons.

**Preschoolers**
Do creative art activities such as brush painting, drawing, collage, and playdough.
Provide time and space for dancing, movement activities, creative dramatics.
Do musical activities such as singing, listening to records, playing instruments.
Most art activities are offered as an exploratory process rather than to produce a product.

Adult-made models, patterns, and pre-drawn forms are used infrequently.
Provide materials representative of a variety of cultures.

**Kindergartners**
Provide opportunities for children to represent ideas and feelings and learn fundamental concepts and skills in the fine arts.
Do creative art projects, painting, drawing, collage, and modeling.
Provide time and space for dancing, movement activities, creative dramatics.
Do musical activities such as singing, listening to recordings, playing instruments.
Adult-made models, patterns, and pre-drawn forms are used infrequently.

Provide visits by artists, materials representative of a variety of cultures.
Develop appreciation for the arts by taking trips to galleries, concerts, cultural events.

**School-agers**
Provide planned and spontaneous activities in arts and crafts such as mural and easel painting, ceramics, carpentry, weaving.
Encourage dancing, creative dramatics, listening to recordings, singing, playing instruments.
Provide materials representative of a variety of cultures.
Provide visits by artists, materials representative of a variety of cultures.
Develop appreciation for the arts by taking trips to galleries, concerts, cultural events.

Program Description

# B.   Curriculum *continued*

**Criterion**

**B-7h.**   Respect cultural diversity.

*For example,*

**All ages, as appropriate to age group**

Build sense of the group as a community, bringing each child's home culture and language into the shared culture of the school so each child feels accepted and gains a sense of belonging.

Provide books, materials, images, and experiences that reflect diverse cultures that children may not likely see, as well as those that represent their family life and cultural group.

Initiate discussions and activities to teach respect and appreciation for similarities and differences among people.

Talk positively about each child's physical characteristics, family, and cultural heritage.

Cook or serve foods from children's various contemporary cultures.

Avoid stereotyping any group through materials, objects, language.

Invite families' participation in all aspects of the program.

Take trips to museums, cultural resources of community.

Infuse all curriculum topics with diverse cultural perspectives, avoiding a "tourist" approach.

| Average rating | Groups | | | | | | | | | | | | | | | | | | | |
|---|---|---|---|---|---|---|---|---|---|---|---|---|---|---|---|---|---|---|---|---|
| | C | V | C | V | C | V | C | V | C | V | C | V | C | V | C | V | C | V | C | V |
| | | | | | | | | | | | | | | | | | | | | |

*Director's comments on rating*        **Validation decision**   ❑ **V**      ❑ **NV**

_____        *For validator* _____

_____        _____

_____        _____

_____        _____

_____        _____

_____        _____

_____        _____

_____        _____

_____        _____

_____        _____

**B-8.**   Teachers provide materials and time for children to select their own activities during the day.

❑ Infants and toddlers have objects and materials for free choice.

❑ Several alternative activities are available for children's choice.

❑ Teachers respect the child's right not to participate in some activities.

❑ Teachers pick up on activities that children start or interests that children show.

❑ Kindergartners and schoolagers help prepare materials, plan and choose their own activities at times during the day.

| Average rating | C | V | C | V | C | V | C | V | C | V | C | V | C | V | C | V | C | V |
|---|---|---|---|---|---|---|---|---|---|---|---|---|---|---|---|---|---|---|---|
| | | | | | | | | | | | | | | | | | | |

*Director's comments on rating*        **Validation decision**   ❑ **V**      ❑ **NV**

_____        *For validator* _____

_____        _____

_____        _____

_____        _____

_____        _____

_____        _____

_____        _____

_____        _____

_____        _____

# B. Curriculum *continued*

**Criterion**

**Groups**

**B-9.** Teachers conduct smooth and unregimented transitions between activities.

| Average rating | C | V | C | V | C | V | C | V | C | V | C | V | C | V | C | V | C | V |
|---|---|---|---|---|---|---|---|---|---|---|---|---|---|---|---|---|---|---|
| | | | | | | | | | | | | | | | | | | |

- ❑ Children are given advanced notice to prepare them for transitions ahead of time.
- ❑ Children are not always required to move as a group from one activity to another.
- ❑ The new activity is prepared before the transition from the completed activity to avoid prolonged waiting.
- ❑ School-age children help plan and participate in the change of activity, have time to adjust to change from school to program.

*Director's comments on rating*

**Validation decision**　❑ **V**　　❑ **NV**

*For validator*

---

**B-10.** Teachers are flexible enough to change planned or routine activities.

| Average rating | C | V | C | V | C | V | C | V | C | V | C | V | C | V | C | V | C | V |
|---|---|---|---|---|---|---|---|---|---|---|---|---|---|---|---|---|---|---|
| | | | | | | | | | | | | | | | | | | |

*For example,*
Staff follow needs or interests of the children.

Staff adjust to changes in weather or other unexpected situations in a relaxed way without upsetting children.

*Director's comments on rating*

**Validation decision**　❑ **V**　　❑ **NV**

*For validator*

Program Description

## B. Curriculum *continued*

**Ratings of Center and Validator**

**Criterion**

**B-11.** Routine tasks are incorporated into the program as a means of furthering children's learning, self-help, and social skills.

❑ For infants and toddlers, routines are used as a time for pleasant interaction and learning.

❑ Routines such as diapering or toileting, eating, dressing, and sleeping or resting are handled in a relaxed, reassuring, and individualized manner based on developmental needs.

❑ Teachers plan with families to make toileting, feeding, and the development of other self-regulation skills a positive experience for children.

*For example,*
Respect infants' individual sleeping schedules; provide alternatives to preschoolers who are early risers; offer kindergartners choices or permit preferences whenever possible; provide school-agers with a place to rest if they choose; respect school-agers' increasing interest in personal grooming.

| Average rating | | Groups | | | | | | | | | | | | | | | | | | |
|---|---|---|---|---|---|---|---|---|---|---|---|---|---|---|---|---|---|---|---|---|
| | | C | V | C | V | C | V | C | V | C | V | C | V | C | V | C | V | C | V |
| | | | | | | | | | | | | | | | | | | | | |

*Director's comments on rating*    **Validation decision**   ❑ V    ❑ NV

*For validator* _____

## G. Physical Environment

**G-1a.** There is enough usable space indoors so children are not crowded.

| Average rating | | C | V | C | V | C | V | C | V | C | V | C | V | C | V | C | V | C | V |
|---|---|---|---|---|---|---|---|---|---|---|---|---|---|---|---|---|---|---|---|
| | | | | | | | | | | | | | | | | | | | |

*Director's comments on rating*    **Validation decision**   ❑ V    ❑ NV

*For validator* _____

# G. Physical Environment *continued*

**Ratings of Center and Validator**

**Criterion**

| | Groups | | | | | | | | |
|---|---|---|---|---|---|---|---|---|---|

**G-1b.** There is enough usable space for outdoor play for each age group.

| Average rating | C | V | C | V | C | V | C | V | C | V | C | V | C | V | C | V | C | V |
|---|---|---|---|---|---|---|---|---|---|---|---|---|---|---|---|---|---|---|

*For example,*
Age groups use different areas or are scheduled at different times.

*Director's comments on rating*

**Validation decision**   ❑ **V**   ❑ **NV**

*For validator* _____

_____

_____

_____

_____

_____

_____

_____

_____

_____

---

**G-2.** Space is arranged to accommodate children individually, in small groups, or in a large group.

| Average rating | C | V | C | V | C | V | C | V | C | V | C | V | C | V | C | V | C | V |
|---|---|---|---|---|---|---|---|---|---|---|---|---|---|---|---|---|---|---|

❑ There are clear pathways for children to move from one area to another without disturbing activities.

❑ Areas are organized for easy supervision by staff.

*Director's comments on rating*

**Validation decision**   ❑ **V**   ❑ **NV**

*For validator* _____

_____

_____

_____

_____

_____

_____

_____

_____

_____

Program Description

# G.  Physical Environment *continued*

**Criterion**

**Ratings of Center and Validator**

**Groups**

| C | V | C | V | C | V | C | V | C | V | C | V | C | V | C | V | C | V |
|---|---|---|---|---|---|---|---|---|---|---|---|---|---|---|---|---|---|

**G-3.** Space is arranged to facilitate a variety of activities for each age group.

**Average rating**

❑ Nonwalkers (infants/younger toddlers) are provided open space for crawling/toddling and protected space for play, separating groups of nonmobile and mobile infants for safety.

❑ Older toddlers, preschoolers, and kindergartners have space arranged for a variety of individual and small-group activities including block building, dramatic play, art, music, science, math, manipulatives, quiet book reading.

❑ Older toddlers, preschoolers, and kindergartners are occasionally offered sand and water play and woodworking.

❑ School-agers are provided separate space for their program including both active and quiet activities to permit sustained work on projects.

*Director's comments on rating*

**Validation decision**    ❑ **V**        ❑ **NV**

*For validator*

**G-4.** A variety of age-appropriate materials and equipment are available for children indoors and outdoors.

**Average rating**

| C | V | C | V | C | V | C | V | C | V | C | V | C | V | C | V | C | V |
|---|---|---|---|---|---|---|---|---|---|---|---|---|---|---|---|---|---|

❑ A sufficient quantity of materials and equipment is provided to avoid problems with sharing or waiting.

❑ Materials are durable and in good repair.

❑ Materials are organized consistently on low, open shelves to encourage independent use by children.

❑ Extra materials are accessible to staff to add variety to usual activities.

❑ Materials are rotated and adapted to maintain children's interest.

*Director's comments on rating*

**Validation decision**    ❑ **V**        ❑ **NV**

*For validator*

# G. Physical Environment *continued*

**Criterion**

**Ratings of Center and Validator**

| | | Groups | | | | | | | | | | | | | | | | | | |
|---|---|---|---|---|---|---|---|---|---|---|---|---|---|---|---|---|---|---|---|---|

**G-5.** Individual space is provided for each child's belongings.

❑ There is a place to hang or store clothing and places for storing other belongings such as art-work to be taken home.

| Average rating | | C | V | C | V | C | V | C | V | C | V | C | V | C | V | C | V | C | V |
|---|---|---|---|---|---|---|---|---|---|---|---|---|---|---|---|---|---|---|---|---|

*Director's comments on rating*

**Validation decision**     ❑ V          ❑ NV

_____     *For validator* _____

_____     _____

_____     _____

_____     _____

_____     _____

**G-6.** Private areas where children can play or work alone or with a friend are available indoors and outdoors.

*For example,*
Book corners, tunnels, or playhouses that are easy for adults to supervise

| Average rating | | C | V | C | V | C | V | C | V | C | V | C | V | C | V | C | V | C | V |
|---|---|---|---|---|---|---|---|---|---|---|---|---|---|---|---|---|---|---|---|---|

*Director's comments on rating*

**Validation decision**     ❑ V          ❑ NV

_____     *For validator* _____

_____     _____

_____     _____

_____     _____

_____     _____

**G-7.** The environment includes soft elements.

*For example,*
Rugs, cushions, soft furniture, soft toys, comfortable chairs for adults to hold children in their laps

| Average rating | | C | V | C | V | C | V | C | V | C | V | C | V | C | V | C | V | C | V |
|---|---|---|---|---|---|---|---|---|---|---|---|---|---|---|---|---|---|---|---|---|

*Director's comments on rating*

**Validation decision**     ❑ V          ❑ NV

_____     *For validator* _____

_____     _____

_____     _____

_____     _____

_____     _____

Program Description

# G. Physical Environment *continued*

**Criterion**

**Ratings of Center and Validator**

**Groups**

**G-8.** Sound-absorbing materials such as ceiling tile and rugs are used to cut down noise.

| Average rating |
|---|

| C | V | C | V | C | V | C | V | C | V | C | V | C | V | C | V | C | V |
|---|---|---|---|---|---|---|---|---|---|---|---|---|---|---|---|---|---|

*Director's comments on rating*

**Validation decision**  ❑ **V**  ❑ **NV**

*For validator* _____

_____

_____

_____

_____

_____

---

**G-9a.** A variety of activities can go on outdoors throughout the year.

❑ Balance of shade and sun
❑ Variety of surfaces such as hard area for wheel toys, grass, sand and soil, hills, flat sections
❑ Variety of age-appropriate equipment such as for crawling, pulling up to stand, riding, climbing, balancing, individual playing

| Average rating |
|---|

| C | V | C | V | C | V | C | V | C | V | C | V | C | V | C | V | C | V |
|---|---|---|---|---|---|---|---|---|---|---|---|---|---|---|---|---|---|

*Director's comments on rating*

**Validation decision**  ❑ **V**  ❑ **NV**

*For validator* _____

_____

_____

_____

_____

_____

---

**G-9b.** The outdoor play area is protected from access to streets and other dangers by fences or by natural barriers.

*For example,*
Programs need to exercise professional judgment in situations where community conditions of violence or extreme weather threaten children's health or safety. If conditions for outdoor play are not safe, the program should provide regular, alternative activities to meet children's needs for fresh air and exercise.

| Average rating |
|---|

| C | V | C | V | C | V | C | V | C | V | C | V | C | V | C | V | C | V |
|---|---|---|---|---|---|---|---|---|---|---|---|---|---|---|---|---|---|

*Director's comments on rating*

**Validation decision**  ❑ **V**  ❑ **NV**

*For validator* _____

_____

_____

_____

_____

_____

# H.  Health and Safety

**Criterion**

**Ratings of Center and Validator**

**H-7a.**  Children are under adult supervision at all times.

❑ Infants and toddlers are never
left unattended.
❑ Preschoolers are supervised by
sight and sound.
❑ Kindergartners and school-
agers may not be in sight, but
staff know where children are
and what they are doing.

| Average rating | Groups | | | | | | | | | |
|---|---|---|---|---|---|---|---|---|---|---|
| | C | V | C | V | C | V | C | V | C | V | C | V | C | V | C | V | C | V |

*Director's comments on rating*    **Validation decision**    ❑ V        ❑ NV

_____    *For validator* _____

_____    _____

_____    _____

_____    _____

**H-12.**  Children are dressed appropriately for active play indoors
and outdoors.

❑ Extra clothing is kept on hand.
❑ Protective clothing such as
smocks and mittens is kept on
hand.

| Average rating | C | V | C | V | C | V | C | V | C | V | C | V | C | V | C | V | C | V |
|---|---|---|---|---|---|---|---|---|---|---|---|---|---|---|---|---|---|---|

*Director's comments on rating*    **Validation decision**    ❑ V        ❑ NV

_____    *For validator* _____

_____    _____

_____    _____

_____    _____

**H-13a.**  As children use the facility,
staff and children keep areas
reasonably clean.

❑ Tables are washed and floors
are swept after meals.
❑ Toys are picked up after use.

| Average rating | C | V | C | V | C | V | C | V | C | V | C | V | C | V | C | V | C | V |
|---|---|---|---|---|---|---|---|---|---|---|---|---|---|---|---|---|---|---|

*Director's comments on rating*    **Validation decision**    ❑ V        ❑ NV

_____    *For validator* _____

_____    _____

_____    _____

_____    _____

_____    _____

Program Description

# H. Health and Safety *continued*

**Criterion**

**Ratings of Center and Validator**

**Groups**

**H-13b.** Toileting and diapering areas are sanitary.

| Average rating | C | V | C | V | C | V | C | V | C | V | C | V | C | V | C | V | C | V |
|---|---|---|---|---|---|---|---|---|---|---|---|---|---|---|---|---|---|---|
| | | | | | | | | | | | | | | | | | | |

❑ Soiled diapers are disposed of or held for laundry in closed containers out of reach of children.

❑ Changing table is disinfected after each use.

*Director's comments on rating*

**Validation decision**    ❑ **V**    ❑ **NV**

*For validator* _____

_____

_____

_____

_____

**H-14a.** Staff wash their hands with liquid soap and water at appropriate times:

| Average rating | C | V | C | V | C | V | C | V | C | V | C | V | C | V | C | V | C | V |
|---|---|---|---|---|---|---|---|---|---|---|---|---|---|---|---|---|---|---|
| | | | | | | | | | | | | | | | | | | |

❑ Upon arrival

❑ Before preparing or serving food

❑ Before feeding children

❑ After diapering or assisting children with toileting or nose wiping

❑ After handling pets or animals

❑ After contact with any potentially infectious materials, including bodily fluids

*Director's comments on rating*

**Validation decision**    ❑ **V**    ❑ **NV**

*For validator* _____

_____

_____

_____

_____

**H-14b.** Staff follow proper procedures during handwashing.

| Average rating | C | V | C | V | C | V | C | V | C | V | C | V | C | V | C | V | C | V |
|---|---|---|---|---|---|---|---|---|---|---|---|---|---|---|---|---|---|---|
| | | | | | | | | | | | | | | | | | | |

❑ Wash with liquid soap and warm, running water for at least 10 seconds.

❑ Use single use or disposable towels.

❑ Avoid recontamination from faucets by turning off faucets with towel.

*Director's comments on rating*

**Validation decision**    ❑ **V**    ❑ **NV**

*For validator* _____

_____

_____

_____

_____

# H.  Health and Safety *continued*

**Criterion**

**Ratings of Center and Validator**

**Groups**

**H-14c.** A sink with running water of comfortable temperature is very close to diapering and toileting areas. Signs are posted reminding staff of proper handwashing procedures.

| Average rating | C | V | C | V | C | V | C | V | C | V | C | V | C | V | C | V | C | V |
|---|---|---|---|---|---|---|---|---|---|---|---|---|---|---|---|---|---|---|
| | | | | | | | | | | | | | | | | | | |

*Director's comments on rating*          **Validation decision**     ❏ **V**          ❏ **NV**

_____          *For validator* _____

_____          _____

_____          _____

_____          _____

**H-15a.** The building, play yard, and all equipment are maintained in safe, clean condition and in good repair.

❏ No sharp edges, splinters, protruding or rusty nails, or missing parts
❏ Glass, trash is removed from children's play areas.
❏ Outdoor sandboxes are covered when not in use.
❏ The water play table is cleaned and sanitized with a bleach solution daily, when in use.

| Average rating | C | V | C | V | C | V | C | V | C | V | C | V | C | V | C | V | C | V |
|---|---|---|---|---|---|---|---|---|---|---|---|---|---|---|---|---|---|---|
| | | | | | | | | | | | | | | | | | | |

*Director's comments on rating*          **Validation decision**     ❏ **V**          ❏ **NV**

_____          *For validator* _____

_____          _____

_____          _____

_____          _____

_____          _____

**H-15b.** Infants' and toddlers' toys are large enough to prevent swallowing or choking.

| Average rating | C | V | C | V | C | V | C | V | C | V | C | V | C | V | C | V | C | V |
|---|---|---|---|---|---|---|---|---|---|---|---|---|---|---|---|---|---|---|
| | | | | | | | | | | | | | | | | | | |

❏ **Not applicable**                    **Validation decision**     ❏ **V**          ❏ **NV**

*Director's comments on rating*          *For validator* _____

_____          _____

_____          _____

_____          _____

_____          _____

Program Description

# H.   Health and Safety *continued*

**Ratings of Center and Validator**

**Criterion**

**H-16b.** Sides of infants' cribs are in a locked position when cribs are occupied. Young infants should be placed on their backs when sleeping.

| Average rating | | Groups | | | | | | | | | | | | | | | |
|---|---|---|---|---|---|---|---|---|---|---|---|---|---|---|---|---|---|
| | C | V | C | V | C | V | C | V | C | V | C | V | C | V | C | V | C | V |

❑ **Not applicable**            **Validation decision**     ❑ **V**     ❑ **NV**

*Director's comments on rating*          *For validator* _____

_____          _____

_____          _____

_____          _____

_____          _____

**H-17a.** Toilets, drinking water, and handwashing facilities are easily accessible to children.

*For example,*
Facilities are either child-sized or made accessible by nonslip stools; infants and toddlers have hands washed; infants and toddlers are offered drinking water or other beverages.

| Average rating | | C | V | C | V | C | V | C | V | C | V | C | V | C | V | C | V | C | V |
|---|---|---|---|---|---|---|---|---|---|---|---|---|---|---|---|---|---|---|

*Director's comments on rating*          **Validation decision**     ❑ **V**     ❑ **NV**

_____          *For validator* _____

_____          _____

_____          _____

_____          _____

**H-17b.** Liquid soap and disposable towels are provided.

| Average rating | | C | V | C | V | C | V | C | V | C | V | C | V | C | V | C | V | C | V |
|---|---|---|---|---|---|---|---|---|---|---|---|---|---|---|---|---|---|---|

*Director's comments on rating*          **Validation decision**     ❑ **V**     ❑ **NV**

_____          *For validator* _____

_____          _____

_____          _____

_____          _____

_____          _____

# H. Health and Safety *continued*

**Criterion**

**Ratings of Center and Validator**

**H-17c.** Children wash hands after toileting and before meals.

- ❑ Staff assist infants and toddlers with face- and handwashing as needed.
- ❑ Children are educated by staff members concerning hand-washing procedures: use of running water, soap, rubbing, and single use or disposable towels.

| Average rating | C | V | C | V | C | V | C | V | C | V | C | V | C | V | C | V | C | V |
|---|---|---|---|---|---|---|---|---|---|---|---|---|---|---|---|---|---|---|
| | | | | | | | | | | | | | | | | | | |

*Director's comments on rating*    **Validation decision**    ❑ V    ❑ NV

_____    *For validator* _____

_____    _____

_____    _____

_____    _____

---

**H-18a.** Areas used by children are well-lighted and ventilated and kept at a comfortable temperature.

| Average rating | C | V | C | V | C | V | C | V | C | V | C | V | C | V | C | V | C | V |
|---|---|---|---|---|---|---|---|---|---|---|---|---|---|---|---|---|---|---|
| | | | | | | | | | | | | | | | | | | |

*Director's comments on rating*    **Validation decision**    ❑ V    ❑ NV

_____    *For validator* _____

_____    _____

_____    _____

_____    _____

_____    _____

---

**H-18b.** Electrical outlets are covered with protective caps. (NA for rooms used by school-agers only.)

| Average rating | C | V | C | V | C | V | C | V | C | V | C | V | C | V | C | V | C | V |
|---|---|---|---|---|---|---|---|---|---|---|---|---|---|---|---|---|---|---|
| | | | | | | | | | | | | | | | | | | |

❑ **Not applicable**    **Validation decision**    ❑ V    ❑ NV

*Director's comments on rating*    *For validator* _____

_____    _____

_____    _____

_____    _____

_____    _____

Program Description

# H.  Health and Safety *continued*

**Criterion**

| | | Groups | | | | | | | | |
|---|---|---|---|---|---|---|---|---|---|---|

**H-18c.** Floor coverings do not cause tripping hazards.

| Average rating |
|---|
|  |

| C | V | C | V | C | V | C | V | C | V | C | V | C | V | C | V | C | V |
|---|---|---|---|---|---|---|---|---|---|---|---|---|---|---|---|---|---|
|  |  |  |  |  |  |  |  |  |  |  |  |  |  |  |  |  |  |

*For example,*
Floor coverings are attached to the floor or backed with nonslip coverings, held down with furniture.

❑ **Not applicable**            **Validation decision**        ❑ V            ❑ NV

*Director's comments on rating*        *For validator* _____

_____        _____

_____        _____

_____        _____

_____        _____

**H-19a.** All pieces of playground equipment are surrounded by a resilient surface (fine, loose sand; wood chips; wood mulch; fine gravel) that extends at least 4 feet beyond the fall zone.

| Average rating |
|---|
|  |

| C | V | C | V | C | V | C | V | C | V | C | V | C | V | C | V | C | V |
|---|---|---|---|---|---|---|---|---|---|---|---|---|---|---|---|---|---|
|  |  |  |  |  |  |  |  |  |  |  |  |  |  |  |  |  |  |

*Director's comments on rating*        **Validation decision**        ❑ V            ❑ NV

        *For validator* _____

_____        _____

_____        _____

_____        _____

_____        _____

**H-19b.** Climbing equipment, swings, and large pieces of furniture are securely anchored. (Program submits verification if anchoring cannot be easily observed.)

| Average rating |
|---|
|  |

| C | V | C | V | C | V | C | V | C | V | C | V | C | V | C | V | C | V |
|---|---|---|---|---|---|---|---|---|---|---|---|---|---|---|---|---|---|
|  |  |  |  |  |  |  |  |  |  |  |  |  |  |  |  |  |  |

*Director's comments on rating*        **Validation decision**        ❑ V            ❑ NV

*For example,*
Permanent equipment outdoors, tall storage shelves indoors. Heavy pieces of furniture such as video monitors are secured so they cannot be tipped over by children.

        *For validator* _____

_____        _____

_____        _____

_____        _____

_____        _____

# H. Health and Safety *continued*

**Criterion**

**Ratings of Center and Validator**

**Groups**

**H-20a.** All chemicals and potentially dangerous products such as medicines or cleaning supplies are stored in original, labeled containers in locked cabinets inaccessible to children (does not apply to diluted bleach solution which must be inaccessible, but not locked).

| Average rating | C | V | C | V | C | V | C | V | C | V | C | V | C | V | C | V | C | V |
|---|---|---|---|---|---|---|---|---|---|---|---|---|---|---|---|---|---|---|
| | | | | | | | | | | | | | | | | | | |

*Director's comments on rating*     **Validation decision** ❑ V      ❑ NV

*For validator* _____

_____     _____

_____     _____

_____     _____

**H-21b.** Written emergency-evacuation procedures are posted in conspicuous places.

| Average rating | C | V | C | V | C | V | C | V | C | V | C | V | C | V | C | V | C | V |
|---|---|---|---|---|---|---|---|---|---|---|---|---|---|---|---|---|---|---|
| | | | | | | | | | | | | | | | | | | |

*Director's comments on rating*     **Validation decision** ❑ V      ❑ NV

*For validator* _____

_____     _____

_____     _____

_____     _____

# I. Nutrition and Food Service

**I-3.** Mealtime is a pleasant social and learning experience for children.

❑ Mealtimes promote good nutrition habits.

❑ Infants are held in an inclined position while bottle fed so social interaction can occur.

❑ At least one adult sits with children during meals to provide a good role model and encourage conversation.

❑ Toddlers, preschoolers, and kindergartners are encouraged to serve and feed themselves and assist with clean-up.

❑ Chairs, tables, and eating utensils are suitable for the size and developmental levels of the children.

| Average rating | C | V | C | V | C | V | C | V | C | V | C | V | C | V | C | V | C | V |
|---|---|---|---|---|---|---|---|---|---|---|---|---|---|---|---|---|---|---|
| | | | | | | | | | | | | | | | | | | |

*Director's comments on rating*     **Validation decision** ❑ V      ❑ NV

*For validator* _____

_____     _____

_____     _____

_____     _____

_____     _____

Program Description

# Early Childhood Program Description
## *Part 3—Results of Administrator Report*

**How is Part 3 used in the program?**

Part 3 is used to report how well the program meets all the criteria that are assessed using the Administrator Report, the Teaching-Staff Questionnaire, and the Family Questionnaire. These criteria are related to Administration, Staff Qualifications and Development, Staffing, Relationships among Teachers and Families, Nutrition and Food Service, Health and Safety, and Evaluation.

Space is provided on this form for directors to report their ratings of the program's compliance for these criteria from the Administrator Report. Space is also provided for the program to report the results of the ratings supplied by staff on the Teaching-Staff Questionnaire and family members on the Family Questionnaire. Directors should comment on or explain any criteria that are not met (rating [1]) or partially met (rating [2]). If the program exceeds a criterion, the director should also comment. If the criterion is rated fully met [3], no comment is needed.

**How is Part 3 validated?**

The "validation procedure" column on the form provides a code for validators. This code indicates what sources of evidence the validator will compare to the director's rating to validate each criterion. If the sources of evidence are consistent, the criterion is validated (V). If the sources are not consistent, the criterion is nonvalidated (NV). **The validator and director discuss all nonvalidated criteria and the validator records the director's comments or explanations on this form during the exit interview.**

**Directions for director**

## Director reports return rate for questionnaires

Using the original questionnaires and the summary sheets, answer the questions below:

1. Total number of Teaching-Staff Questionnaires received _____, out of _____ distributed.

2. Total number of Family Questionnaires received _____, out of _____ distributed. The validation procedures requires at least a 50% return rate. If the return rate is less than 50%, please explain the importance of the questionnaire and re-distribute for a higher return.

## Validation of questionnaire summary sheets

**Directions for validator**

Use the most current questionnaires filled out by the staff and families and the corresponding summary sheets. Count the number of questionnaires returned to compare with numbers reported on the summary sheets. Randomly select 25% of the Teaching-Staff Questionnaires and 10% of the Family Questionnaires. Identify four or five items on both the Teaching-Staff Questionnaires and Family Questionnaires to compare to responses recorded on the summary sheets. If you discover a number of inconsistencies, ask the director to redo the summary sheet(s), correct the Program Description, and initial the correction(s). Report the accuracy of the summary sheets below. If the summary sheets are accurate, move to the next step, validation of the Administrator Report.

**Teaching-Staff Questionnaire Summary Sheet**
- ❑ **V** (summary sheet is accurate)
- ❑ **NV** (director corrects summary sheet)

**Family Questionnaire Summary Sheet**
- ❑ **V** (summary sheet is accurate)
- ❑ **NV** (director corrects summary sheet)

**Validation decision rules when Teaching-Staff Questionnaires and Family Questionnaires are a source of evidence**

1. If the director rates the criterion fully met [3], at least 75% of the questionnaire response must be in agreement in order to be valid.

2. If the director rates the criterion partially met [2] or not met [1], the majority of the questionnaires responses must be in agreement in order to be valid.

75% of the returned Teaching-Staff Questionnaires = _____.

75% of the returned Family Questionnaires = _____.

Program Description

# B.  Curriculum

**Criterion**

**Director's rating**

| Not met | Partially met | Fully met |
|:---:|:---:|:---:|

**Validation procedure**

**B-1.** The program has a written statement of its philosophy and goals for children that is available to staff and families.

| 1 | 2 | 3 |
|:---:|:---:|:---:|

*Director's comments on rating*

*Staff Questionnaire B-1*

| | | |
|:---:|:---:|:---:|
| 1 | 2 | 3 |

**Validation decision**

❑ V    ❑ NV

*Family Questionnaire #1a*

| | | |
|:---:|:---:|:---:|
| DK | No | Yes |

Check documents

*For validator* _____

_____

_____     _____

_____     _____

_____     _____

_____     _____

_____     _____

**B-2a.** The program has written curriculum plans, based on knowledge of child development and assessment of individual needs and interests.

| 1 | 2 | 3 |
|:---:|:---:|:---:|

*Director's comments on rating*

*Staff Questionnaire B-2a*

| | | |
|:---:|:---:|:---:|
| 1 | 2 | 3 |

**Validation decision**

❑ V    ❑ NV

Check documents

*For validator* _____

_____     _____

_____     _____

_____     _____

_____     _____

**B-2b.** The learning environment and activities for children reflect the program's philosophy and goals.

| 1 | 2 | 3 |
|:---:|:---:|:---:|

*Director's comments on rating*

*Staff Questionnaire B-2b*

| | | |
|:---:|:---:|:---:|
| 1 | 2 | 3 |

**Validation decision**

❑ V    ❑ NV

Check documents

*For validator* _____

_____     _____

_____     _____

_____     _____

_____     _____

## B. Curriculum *continued*

**Criterion**

**B-3a.** Teachers have clearly defined goals for individual children that guide curriculum planning.

- ❏ Accurately assess the skills and progress of each child in the program (through the use of observations, assessment tools, activity records).
- ❏ Adapt curriculum plans to meet the wide range of individual needs and interests of all children in the group.
- ❏ Identify children who have difficulties in behavior or development and form a plan to help them acquire the necessary skills.
- ❏ Prepare to meet the individual special needs of each child, including children with disabilities.

**Director's rating**

| Not met | Partially met | Fully met |
|:---:|:---:|:---:|
| 1 | 2 | 3 |

*Director's comments on rating*

_____

_____

_____

_____

_____

_____

**Validation procedure**

*Staff Questionnaire B-3a*

| | | |
|:---:|:---:|:---:|
| 1 | 2 | 3 |

**Validation decision**

❏ V ❏ NV

Interview director; refer to Classroom Observation; check documents.

*For validator* _____

_____

_____

_____

_____

**B-3b.** The program is designed to be inclusive of all children, including those with identified disabilities and special learning and developmental needs.

- ❏ Modifications are made in the environment and staffing patterns for children with special needs.
- ❏ Staff are aware of the identified/diagnosed special needs of individual children and trained to follow through on specific intervention plans.
- ❏ Therapy is developed appropriately and incorporated within classroom activities as much as possible rather than removing the child from the classroom.
- ❏ Staff make appropriate professional referrals when necessary.
- ❏ Family members are involved in development and use of Individualized Education Plans.
- ❏ Staff address the priorities and concerns of families of children with special needs.

| | | |
|:---:|:---:|:---:|
| 1 | 2 | 3 |

*Director's comments on rating*

_____

_____

_____

_____

_____

_____

_____

*Staff Questionnaire B-3b*

| | | |
|:---:|:---:|:---:|
| 1 | 2 | 3 |

*Family Questionnaire #25*

| | | | |
|:---:|:---:|:---:|:---:|
| DK | No | Yes | NA |

**Validation decision**

❏ V ❏ NV

Interview director; check documents.

*For validator* _____

_____

_____

_____

_____

_____

## B. Curriculum *continued*

**Criterion**

**Director's rating**

| Not met | Partially met | Fully met |
|---------|---------------|-----------|
| 1 | 2 | 3 |

**Validation procedure**

**B-11.** Teachers plan with families to make toileting, feeding, and the development of other self-regulation skills a positive experience for children.

*Staff Questionnaire B-11*

| | | |
|---|---|---|
| 1 | 2 | 3 |

**Validation decision**

❏ V    ❏ NV

*Family Questionnaire #6*

| | | |
|---|---|---|
| DK | No | Yes |

*Director's comments on rating*

_____

_____

*For validator* _____

_____

_____

_____

_____

_____

_____

## C. Relationships among Teachers and Families

**C-1a.** A written description of the program's philosophy is available to families.

| 1 | 2 | 3 |
|---|---|---|

*Family Questionnaire #1a*

| | | |
|---|---|---|
| DK | No | Yes |

**Validation decision**

❏ V    ❏ NV

*Director's comments on rating*

Check documents.

_____

*For validator* _____

_____

_____

_____

_____

_____

_____

_____

_____

# C. Relationships among Teachers and Families *continued*

**Director's rating**

**Validation procedure**

**Criterion**

| Not met | Partially met | Fully met |
|:---:|:---:|:---:|
| 1 | 2 | 3 |

**C-1b.** Written operating policies and procedures are available to families.

*Family Questionnaire #1b*     **Validation decision**

❑ V    ❑ NV

| DK | No | Yes | NA |
|:---:|:---:|:---:|:---:|
| | | | |

*Director's comments on rating*

*Family Questionnaire #1c*

| DK | No | Yes |
|:---:|:---:|:---:|
| | | |

_____

*Family Questionnaire #1d*

| DK | No | Yes |
|:---:|:---:|:---:|
| | | |

_____

_____     *For validator* _____

_____     _____

_____     _____

_____     _____

**C-1c.** Families have opportunities to have input regarding policies and procedures and plans for meeting children's individual needs.

| | | |
|:---:|:---:|:---:|
| 1 | 2 | 3 |

*Family Questionnaire #2*     **Validation decision**

❑ V    ❑ NV

| DK | No | Yes |
|:---:|:---:|:---:|
| | | |

*Director's comments on rating*     *For validator* _____

_____     _____

_____     _____

_____     _____

_____     _____

_____     _____

_____     _____

_____     _____

_____     _____

_____     _____

_____     _____

Program Description

# C. Relationships among Teachers and Families *continued*

| Criterion | Director's rating | Validation procedure |
|---|---|---|

**Director's rating**

Not met / Partially met / Fully met

**Validation procedure**

**C-1d.** Programs with non-English speaking families provide materials in the family's native language or arrange for translation.

**Director's rating:** ☐ 1 ☐ 2 ☐ 3

☐ **Not applicable**

*Director's comments on rating*

**Validation decision**
☐ V ☐ NV

Interview director; check documents.

*For validator* _____

---

**C-2.** A process has been developed for orienting children and families to the program that may include a pre-enrollment visit, family orientation meeting, or gradual introduction of children to the program that also supports children and families through the separation process.

**Director's rating:** ☐ 1 ☐ 2 ☐ 3

*Director's comments on rating*

*Family Questionnaire #3*
☐ DK ☐ No ☐ Yes

**Validation decision**
☐ V ☐ NV

*For validator* _____

---

**C-3a.** Teachers work in collaborative partnerships with families, establishing and maintaining regular, ongoing, two-way communication with children's parents to build trust and mutual understanding and to ensure that children's learning and developmental needs are met.

**Director's rating:** ☐ 1 ☐ 2 ☐ 3

*Director's comments on rating*

*Staff Questionnaire C-3a*
☐ 1 ☐ 2 ☐ 3

*Family Questionnaire #4*
☐ DK ☐ No ☐ Yes

**Validation decision**
☐ V ☐ NV

*For validator* _____

# C. Relationships among Teachers and Families *continued*

| Criterion | Director's rating | Validation procedure |
|---|---|---|

**Director's rating**

Not met | Partially met | Fully met

**Validation procedure**

**C-3b.** Teachers listen to parents, seek to understand their goals and preferences for their children, and respect cultural and family differences. When staff are not of the linguistic and cultural background of the children/families, increased efforts are made to ensure communication with families, such as regular conferences with a translator present.

Director's rating: ☐ 1 ☐ 2 ☐ 3

*Director's comments on rating*

_____
_____
_____
_____

*Family Questionnaire #5*

☐ DK ☐ No ☐ Yes

Interview director.

*For validator* _____

_____
_____
_____

**Validation decision**
☐ V   ☐ NV

---

**C-4a.** Family members are welcome visitors in the program at all times (for example, to observe, eat lunch with a child, or volunteer in the classroom).

Director's rating: ☐ 1 ☐ 2 ☐ 3

*Director's comments on rating*

_____
_____
_____
_____

*Staff Questionnaire C-4a*

☐ 1 ☐ 2 ☐ 3

*Family Questionnaire #7*

☐ DK ☐ No ☐ Yes

*For validator* _____

_____
_____
_____

**Validation decision**
☐ V   ☐ NV

---

**C-4b.** Parents and other family members are encouraged to be involved in the program in various ways, taking into consideration working parents and those with little spare time.

Director's rating: ☐ 1 ☐ 2 ☐ 3

*Director's comments on rating*

_____
_____
_____
_____

*Staff Questionnaire C-4b*

☐ 1 ☐ 2 ☐ 3

*Family Questionnaire #8*

☐ DK ☐ No ☐ Yes

*For validator* _____

_____
_____
_____

**Validation decision**
☐ V   ☐ NV

Program Description

## C. Relationships among Teachers and Families *continued*

**Criterion**

**Director's rating**

Not met · Partially met · Fully met

**Validation procedure**

**C-5a.** A verbal and/or written system is established for sharing among both staff and parents the day-to-day happenings that affect children. (For example, information is exchanged between teachers at shift changes and passed on to parents at pick-up time.)

| 1 | 2 | 3 |

*Director's comments on rating*

_____

_____

_____

_____

_____

_____

*Staff Questionnaire C-5a*

| | | |
| 1 | 2 | 3 |

*Family Questionnaire #9*

| | | |
| DK | No | Yes |

If applicable, check documents.

*For validator* _____

_____

_____

_____

**Validation decision**

❑ V    ❑ NV

**C-5b.** Changes in a child's physical or emotional state are reported to parents regularly.

| 1 | 2 | 3 |

*Director's comments on rating*

_____

_____

_____

_____

_____

_____

_____

_____

_____

_____

_____

*Staff Questionnaire C-5b*

| | | |
| 1 | 2 | 3 |

*Family Questionnaire #10*

| | | |
| DK | No | Yes |

*For validator* _____

_____

_____

_____

_____

_____

_____

_____

_____

_____

**Validation decision**

❑ V    ❑ NV

# C. Relationships among Teachers and Families *continued*

**Criterion**

**Director's rating**

**Validation procedure**

| Not met | Partially met | Fully met |
|---------|---------------|-----------|

**C-6a.** Teachers and parents work together to make decisions about how to best support children's development and learning or to handle problems or differences of opinion as they arise.

| 1 | 2 | 3 |
|---|---|---|

*Staff Questionnaire C-6a*

| | | |
|---|---|---|
| 1 | 2 | 3 |

**Validation decision**

❑ V    ❑ NV

*Director's comments on rating*

*Family Questionnaire #11*

| | | |
|---|---|---|
| DK | No | Yes |

_____

_____

*For validator* _____

_____     _____

_____     _____

_____     _____

_____     _____

_____     _____

_____     _____

**C-6b.** Conferences are held at least once a year and at other times, as needed, to discuss children's progress, accomplishments, and difficulties at home and at the program.

| 1 | 2 | 3 |
|---|---|---|

*Staff Questionnaire C-6b*

| | | |
|---|---|---|
| 1 | 2 | 3 |

**Validation decision**

❑ V    ❑ NV

*Director's comments on rating*

*Family Questionnaire #12*

| | | |
|---|---|---|
| DK | No | Yes |

_____

_____

*For validator* _____

_____     _____

_____     _____

_____     _____

_____     _____

_____     _____

_____     _____

_____     _____

Program Description

## C.    Relationships among Teachers and Families *continued*

**Director's rating**

**Validation procedure**

**Criterion**

**C-6c.** Teachers solicit and incorporate parents' knowledge about their children into ongoing assessment and planning.

| Not met | Partially met | Fully met |
|:---:|:---:|:---:|
| 1 | 2 | 3 |

*Director's comments on rating*

_____

_____

_____

_____

_____

_____

_____

_____

*Staff Questionnaire C-6c*

| | | |
|:---:|:---:|:---:|
| 1 | 2 | 3 |

*Family Questionnaire #11*

| | | |
|:---:|:---:|:---:|
| DK | No | Yes |

*For validator* _____

_____

_____

_____

_____

_____

**Validation decision**

❏ V    ❏ NV

---

**C-7.** Families are informed about the program and the curriculum and about policy or regulatory changes and other critical issues that could potentially affect the program and/or the early childhood profession through newsletters, bulletin boards, and other appropriate means.

| | | |
|:---:|:---:|:---:|
| 1 | 2 | 3 |

*Director's comments on rating*

_____

_____

_____

_____

_____

_____

_____

_____

_____

_____

*Staff Questionnaire C-7*

| | | |
|:---:|:---:|:---:|
| 1 | 2 | 3 |

*Family Questionnaire #13*

| | | |
|:---:|:---:|:---:|
| DK | No | Yes |

*For validator* _____

_____

_____

_____

_____

_____

_____

_____

**Validation decision**

❏ V    ❏ NV

# C. Relationships among Teachers and Families *continued*

| | Director's rating | | | Validation procedure | | |
|---|---|---|---|---|---|---|

**Criterion**

**C-8a.** Teachers and families communicate to ensure that children experience smooth transitions from home to the program or from one program to another during the day.

Director's rating

| Not met | Partially met | Fully met |
|---|---|---|
| 1 | 2 | 3 |

*Director's comments on rating*

_____

_____

_____

_____

_____

_____

_____

*Staff Questionnaire C-8a*

| | | |
|---|---|---|
| 1 | 2 | 3 |

*Family Questionnaire #14*

| | | |
|---|---|---|
| DK | No | Yes |

**Validation decision**

❑ V ❑ NV

*For validator* _____

_____

_____

_____

_____

_____

_____

**C-8b.** Teachers and families communicate to ensure that the programs *(or classrooms)* from which children come and to which they go from one year to the next provide continuity over time.

| 1 | 2 | 3 |
|---|---|---|

*Director's comments on rating*

_____

_____

_____

_____

_____

_____

_____

_____

_____

_____

*Staff Questionnaire C-8b*

| | | |
|---|---|---|
| 1 | 2 | 3 |

*Family Questionnaire #15*

| | | |
|---|---|---|
| DK | No | Yes |

**Validation decision**

❑ V ❑ NV

*For validator* _____

_____

_____

_____

_____

_____

_____

_____

_____

_____

Program Description

## C.  Relationships among Teachers and Families *continued*

**Criterion**

|  | Director's rating | | | Validation procedure | |
|---|---|---|---|---|---|

**C-9a.** Communication between staff and families conveys trust and respect.

Director's rating: Not met **1**  Partially met **2**  Fully met **3**

*Staff Questionnaire C-9a*

[ ] [ ] [ ]
1   2   3

**Validation decision**  ❑ V  ❑ NV

*Director's comments on rating*

*Family Questionnaire #16*

[ ] [ ] [ ]
DK   No   Yes

_____

_____

*For validator* _____

_____   _____

_____   _____

_____   _____

_____   _____

_____   _____

_____   _____

_____   _____

_____   _____

**C-9b.** Communication among teachers and families is frequent. (For example, teachers greet parents when they arrive and depart. Frequent friendly notes/telephone calls are used to communicate if parents do not bring their children to the program.)

**1**   **2**   **3**

*Staff Questionnaire C-9b*

[ ] [ ] [ ]
1   2   3

**Validation decision**  ❑ V  ❑ NV

*Director's comments on rating*

*Family Questionnaire #17*

[ ] [ ] [ ]
DK   No   Yes

_____

_____

*For validator* _____

_____   _____

_____   _____

_____   _____

_____   _____

_____   _____

_____   _____

_____   _____

# C. Relationships among Teachers and Families *continued*

| | Director's rating | Validation procedure |
| --- | --- | --- |

**Criterion**

**C-9c.** Staff show sensitivity in their interactions with families. (For example, show sensitivity in interactions with families who are experiencing difficulties; include child in conversation when a child must be discussed in the child's presence; maintain privacy when discussions are held between parents and staff about problems and concerns regarding specific children.)

Director's rating

Not met **1** Partially met **2** Fully met **3**

*Director's comments on rating*

_____

_____

_____

_____

_____

_____

_____

*Staff Questionnaire C-9c*

☐ ☐ ☐
1   2   3

**Validation decision**
❑ V   ❑ NV

*Family Questionnaire #18*

☐ ☐ ☐
DK   No   Yes

*For validator* _____

_____

_____

_____

_____

_____

**C-9d.** Teachers show acceptance of various family structures and cultural perspectives. (For example, teachers speak positively about families to the children and among themselves.)

**1**   **2**   **3**

*Director's comments on rating*

_____

_____

_____

_____

_____

_____

_____

_____

_____

_____

*Staff Questionnaire C-9d*

☐ ☐ ☐
1   2   3

**Validation decision**
❑ V   ❑ NV

*Family Questionnaire #19*

☐ ☐ ☐
DK   No   Yes

*For validator* _____

_____

_____

_____

_____

_____

_____

_____

_____

Program Description

# C. Relationships among Teachers and Families *continued*

| | Director's rating | | | Validation procedure | | |

**Criterion**

**C-9e.** Major changes that affect children, such as changes in room or teacher and use of special services, are discussed with parents before decisions are made.

**Director's rating**

| Not met | Partially met | Fully met |
|---------|---------------|-----------|
| 1 | 2 | 3 |

*Director's comments on rating*

_____

_____

_____

_____

_____

_____

_____

_____

**Validation procedure**

*Staff Questionnaire C-9e*

| | | |
|---|---|---|
| 1 | 2 | 3 |

*Family Questionnaire #20*

| | | |
|---|---|---|
| DK | No | Yes |

**Validation decision**

❏ V    ❏ NV

*For validator* _____

_____

_____

_____

_____

_____

_____

_____

**C-9f.** Teachers seek parents' specific ideas for dealing with the child when at the program.

**Director's rating**

| 1 | 2 | 3 |
|---|---|---|

*Director's comments on rating*

_____

_____

_____

_____

_____

_____

_____

_____

*Staff Questionnaire C-9f*

| | | |
|---|---|---|
| 1 | 2 | 3 |

*Family Questionnaire #21*

| | | |
|---|---|---|
| DK | No | Yes |

**Validation decision**

❏ V    ❏ NV

*For validator* _____

_____

_____

_____

_____

_____

_____

# C. Relationships among Teachers and Families *continued*

| | Director's rating | Validation procedure |
|---|---|---|

**Criterion**

**C-10a.** Administrators and teachers are familiar with and make appropriate use of community resources, including social services; mental and physical health agencies; and educational programs such as museums, libraries, and neighborhood centers.

Director's rating

| Not met | Partially met | Fully met |
|---|---|---|
| **1** | **2** | **3** |

*Director's comments on rating*

_____

_____

_____

_____

_____

_____

_____

_____

_____

Validation procedure

*Staff Questionnaire C-10a*

**Validation decision**
❑ V    ❑ NV

| | | |
|---|---|---|
| 1 | 2 | 3 |

Interview director.

*For validator* _____

_____

_____

_____

_____

_____

_____

_____

_____

**C-10b.** Program personnel connect families with needed resources and comprehensive services based on the needs and interests observed by staff or expressed by families.

| **1** | **2** | **3** |
|---|---|---|

*Director's comments on rating*

_____

_____

_____

_____

_____

_____

_____

_____

_____

_____

*Staff Questionnaire C-10b*

**Validation decision**
❑ V    ❑ NV

| | | |
|---|---|---|
| 1 | 2 | 3 |

Interview director.

*For validator* _____

_____

_____

_____

_____

_____

_____

_____

_____

_____

Program Description

## C. Relationships among Teachers and Families *continued*

**Director's rating**

**Validation procedure**

**Criterion**

| Not met | Partially met | Fully met |
|---------|---------------|-----------|
| 1 | 2 | 3 |

**C-11.** Policies ensure that staff and parents have an effective way of negotiating difficulties and differences that arise in their interactions. The program has a variety of known and accepted techniques to handle differences, such as a parent policy council, an appeals committee, special conferences, or individual meetings.

*Director's comments on rating*

_____

_____

_____

_____

_____

_____

_____

_____

*Staff Questionnaire C-11*

| | | |
|---|---|---|
| 1 | 2 | 3 |

**Validation decision**

❑ V   ❑ NV

*Family Questionnaire #22*

| | | |
|---|---|---|
| DK | No | Yes |

Interview director; check documents.

*For validator* _____

_____

_____

_____

_____

_____

_____

## D. Staff Qualifications and Development

**Validation decision**

❑ V   ❑ NV

**D-1a.** Staff who work directly with children are 18 years of age or older and demonstrate the appropriate personal characteristics for working with children as exemplified in the criteria for Interactions among Teachers and Children and Curriculum.

| 1 | 2 | 3 |
|---|---|---|

*Director's comments on rating*

_____

_____

_____

_____

_____

_____

_____

_____

Sample documents.

*For validator* _____

_____

_____

_____

_____

_____

_____

_____

# D. Staff Qualifications and Development *continued*

| Criterion | Director's rating | Validation procedure |
|---|---|---|

**Director's rating**

**Validation procedure**

**Criterion**

**D-1b.** Early Childhood Teacher Assistants (staff who implement program activities under direct supervision) are high school graduates or the equivalent, have been trained in early childhood education/child development, and/or participate in ongoing professional development programs.

Not met **1**  Partially met **2**  Fully met **3**

Out of _____ Early Childhood Teacher Assistants, _____ meet these qualifications.

*Director's comments on rating*

_____

_____

_____

_____

**Validation decision**
❑ V  ❑ NV

Sample documents to verify Staff Qualifications reported in Center Profile.

*For validator* _____

_____

_____

_____

_____

_____

**D-1c.** Early Childhood Teachers (staff who are responsible for the care and education of a group of children from birth through age 5) have at least a CDA Credential or an A.A. degree in early childhood/child development or equivalent. Preferably teachers have baccalaureate degrees in early childhood education/child development.

**1**  **2**  **3**

Out of _____ Early Childhood Teachers, _____ meet these qualifications.

*Director's comments on rating*

_____

_____

_____

_____

_____

_____

_____

_____

**Validation decision**
❑ V  ❑ NV

Sample documents to verify Staff Qualifications reported in Center Profile.

*For validator* _____

_____

_____

_____

_____

_____

_____

_____

_____

Program Description

## D.    Staff Qualifications and Development *continued*

| Criterion | Director's rating | Validation procedure |
|---|---|---|

**D-1d.** Staff working with school-age children have professional preparation in child development, early childhood education, elementary education, recreation, or a related field.

Director's rating

| Not met | Partially met | Fully met |
|---|---|---|
| **1** | **2** | **3** |

☐ **Not applicable**

*Director's comments on rating*

_____

_____

_____

_____

**Validation decision**

☐ V      ☐ NV

Sample documents to verify Staff Qualifications reported in Center Profile.

*For validator* _____

_____

_____

_____

_____

---

**D-1e.** Volunteers receive orientation and ongoing professional development and only work with children under supervision of qualified staff members.

| | | |
|---|---|---|
| **1** | **2** | **3** |

*Director's comments on rating*

_____

_____

_____

_____

**Validation decision**

☐ V      ☐ NV

Sample documents.

*For validator* _____

_____

_____

_____

_____

---

**D-2a.** The administrator has expertise (acquired through formal education and experience) in both early childhood education/child development and administration such as human resource and financial management.

| | | |
|---|---|---|
| **1** | **2** | **3** |

*Director's comments on rating*

_____

_____

_____

_____

**Validation decision**

☐ V      ☐ NV

Check documents.

*For validator* _____

_____

_____

_____

_____

# D. Staff Qualifications and Development *continued*

**Criterion**

**Director's rating**

**Validation procedure**

## D-2b.
In programs serving infants, toddlers, preschoolers, and/or kindergartners, an Early Childhood Specialist (an individual with a bachelor's degree in early childhood education/child development and at least three years of full-time teaching experience with young children and/or a graduate degree in ECE/CD) is employed to direct the educational program (may be the director or other appropriate person). In public schools, the individual who provides support to prekindergarten and kindergarten teachers and/or who is responsible for program development is a qualified Early Childhood Specialist.

| Not met | Partially met | Fully met |
|---|---|---|
| 1 | 2 | 3 |

*Director's comments on rating*

_____

_____

_____

_____

_____

_____

_____

**Validation decision**

☐ V  ☐ NV

Check documents to verify Staff Qualifications reported in Center Profile.

*For validator* _____

_____

_____

_____

_____

_____

_____

## D-2c.
In programs serving only school-age children, the educational program is directed by a school-age specialist with a bachelor's degree in elementary education, recreation, or related field and at least three years of experience working with school-age children.

| 1 | 2 | 3 |
|---|---|---|

☐ **Not applicable**

*Director's comments on rating*

_____

_____

_____

_____

_____

_____

_____

_____

**Validation decision**

☐ V  ☐ NV

Check documents.

*For validator* _____

_____

_____

_____

_____

_____

_____

_____

Program Description

## D. Staff Qualifications and Development *continued*

**Director's rating**

**Validation procedure**

**Criterion**

**D-3.** New staff, volunteers, and substitutes are adequately oriented about the goals and philosophy of the program, emergency health and safety procedures, individual needs of children assigned to the staff member's care, guidance and classroom management techniques, child abuse and neglect reporting procedures, planned daily activities of the program, and expectations for ethical conduct.

Not met | Partially met | Fully met
[1] [2] [3]

*Director's comments on rating*

*Staff Questionnaire D-3*
[ ] [ ] [ ]
1 2 3

Interview director.

**Validation decision**
☐ V   ☐ NV

*For validator*

**D-4a.** The program provides regular opportunities for staff to participate in ongoing professional development to improve skills in working with children and families or to prepare them to assume more responsible positions.

[1] [2] [3]

*Director's comments on rating*

*Staff Questionnaire D-4a*
[ ] [ ] [ ]
1 2 3

Sample documents.

**Validation decision**
☐ V   ☐ NV

*For validator*

**D-4b.** Ongoing professional development provides continuing education and other opportunities for staff to keep abreast of the latest developments in the field, including new programs and practices and pending policy, legislation, or regulatory changes. The amount and kind of continuing education provided varies, depending on the needs of the program, the preservice qualifications of the staff, and the number of staff pursuing higher education while employed.

[1] [2] [3]

*Director's comments on rating*

*Staff Questionnaire D-4b*
[ ] [ ] [ ]
1 2 3

Sample documents.

**Validation decision**
☐ V   ☐ NV

*For validator*

# E. Administration

| Criterion | Director's rating | | | Validation procedure |
|---|---|---|---|---|

**E-1a.** At least annually, the director and staff conduct an assessment to identify strengths and weaknesses of the program and to set program goals for the year.

Director's rating

| Not met | Partially met | Fully met |
|---|---|---|
| 1 | 2 | 3 |

*Director's comments on rating*

_____

_____

_____

_____

_____

*Staff Questionnaire E-1a*

| | | |
|---|---|---|
| 1 | 2 | 3 |

Check document.

*For validator* _____

_____

_____

_____

_____

**Validation decision**

❑ V ❑ NV

---

**E-1b.** The annual program evaluation examines the adequacy of staff compensation and benefits and rate of staff turnover, and a plan is developed to increase salaries and benefits to ensure recruitment and retention of qualified staff and continuity of relationships.

| 1 | 2 | 3 |
|---|---|---|

*Director's comments on rating*

_____

_____

_____

_____

*Staff Questionnaire E-1b*

| | | |
|---|---|---|
| 1 | 2 | 3 |

Interview director. Verify rate of turnover information in Center Profile. Sample documents.

*For validator* _____

_____

_____

_____

**Validation decision**

❑ V ❑ NV

---

**E-2a.** The program has written policies and procedures for operating, including hours, fees, illness, holidays, refund information, and termination of enrollment. Child enrollment and termination policies protect children's rights as outlined in the Americans with Disabilities Act.

| 1 | 2 | 3 |
|---|---|---|

*Director's comments on rating*

_____

_____

_____

_____

*Staff Questionnaire E-2a*

| | | |
|---|---|---|
| 1 | 2 | 3 |

Check documents.

*For validator* _____

_____

_____

_____

**Validation decision**

❑ V ❑ NV

Program Description

# E.   Administration *continued*

| | Director's rating | | | Validation procedure | | |
|---|---|---|---|---|---|---|

**Criterion**

**E-2b.** The program has a child abuse and neglect policy that includes reporting requirements for staff as well as procedures to be followed should a staff member be accused of abuse or neglect.

Director's rating: Not met **1**  Partially met **2**  Fully met **3**

*Director's comments on rating*

_____

_____

_____

_____

_____

Validation procedure:

*Staff Questionnaire E-2b*

☐ 1   ☐ 2   ☐ 3

**Validation decision**   ❑ V   ❑ NV

Check documents.

*For validator* _____

_____

_____

_____

_____

---

**E-3a.** The program has written personnel policies, including job descriptions; salary scales with increments based on professional qualification, length of employment, and performance; benefits; resignation and termination; and grievance procedures.

**1**   **2**   **3**

*Director's comments on rating*

_____

_____

_____

_____

*Staff Questionnaire E-3a*

☐ 1   ☐ 2   ☐ 3

**Validation decision**   ❑ V   ❑ NV

Check documents.

*For validator* _____

_____

_____

_____

---

**E-3b.** Hiring practices are nondiscriminatory. *(Present copy of advertised position or other evidence of equal opportunity employment.)*

**1**   **2**   **3**

*Director's comments on rating*

_____

_____

_____

_____

_____

**Validation decision**   ❑ V   ❑ NV

Check documents.

*For validator* _____

_____

_____

_____

_____

# E.   Administration *continued*

**Criterion**

| | **Director's rating** | | **Validation procedure** |
|---|---|---|---|

**E-3c.** Every effort is made to hire staff who reflect diverse cultural, racial, and linguistic characteristics as needed to communicate with the children and families served.

**Director's rating**

| Not met | Partially met | Fully met |
|---|---|---|
| 1 | 2 | 3 |

*Director's comments on rating*

_____

_____

_____

_____

*Staff Questionnaire E-3c*

| 1 | 2 | 3 |
|---|---|---|

**Validation decision**
❏ V    ❏ NV

*For validator* _____

_____

_____

_____


**E-4.** Benefits packages for full-time staff include paid leave (annual, sick, and personal), medical insurance, and retirement. Other benefits such as subsidized child care or continued education may be negotiated as unique to the situation. Benefits for part-time staff who are employed at least half-time are available on a prorated basis.

| 1 | 2 | 3 |
|---|---|---|

*Director's comments on rating*

_____

_____

_____

_____

*Staff Questionnaire E-4*

| 1 | 2 | 3 |
|---|---|---|

**Validation decision**
❏ V    ❏ NV

*For validator* _____

_____

_____

_____


**E-5a.** Attendance records of staff and children are kept.

| 1 | 2 | 3 |
|---|---|---|

*Director's comments on rating*

_____

_____

_____

_____

_____

**Validation decision**
❏ V    ❏ NV

Check documents.

*For validator* _____

_____

_____

_____

_____

Program Description

# E. Administration *continued*

| | Director's rating | Validation procedure |

**Criterion**

**Director's rating**

| Not met | Partially met | Fully met |

**Validation procedure**

**E-5b.** Confidential personnel files are kept including

- ❏ résumés with record of experience,
- ❏ transcripts of education,
- ❏ documentation of ongoing professional development, and
- ❏ results of performance evaluation.

| 1 | 2 | 3 |

*Director's comments on rating*

**Validation decision**

❏ V ❏ NV

Sample documents.

*For validator* _____

_____

_____

_____

_____

**E-6a.** In cases where the program is governed by a board of directors, the program has written policies defining roles and responsibilities of board members and staff.

| 1 | 2 | 3 |

❏ **Not applicable**

*Director's comments on rating*

**Validation decision**

❏ V ❏ NV

Check documents.

*For validator* _____

_____

_____

_____

_____

**E-6b.** Board members and other administrators such as school principals are informed about the elements and methods involved in implementing a high-quality, developmentally appropriate program.

| 1 | 2 | 3 |

❏ **Not applicable**

*Director's comments on rating*

**Validation decision**

❏ V ❏ NV

Interview director.

*For validator* _____

_____

_____

_____

_____

# E. Administration *continued*

**Criterion**

**Director's rating**

**Validation procedure**

| Not met | Partially met | Fully met |
| --- | --- | --- |
| 1 | 2 | 3 |

**Validation decision**

☐ V   ☐ NV

**E-6c.** Records of board meetings (minutes) are kept.

☐ **Not applicable**

Check documents.

*For validator* _____

*Director's comments on rating*

_____   _____

_____   _____

_____   _____

_____   _____

---

**Validation decision**

☐ V   ☐ NV

**E-7.** Fiscal records are kept with evidence of long-range budgeting and sound financial planning (projections of at least one year are needed). Operating budgets are prepared annually, and there is a quarterly reconciliation of expenses to budget.

| 1 | 2 | 3 |
| --- | --- | --- |

Check documents.

*Director's comments on rating*

*For validator* _____

_____   _____

_____   _____

_____   _____

_____   _____

---

**Validation decision**

☐ V   ☐ NV

**E-8a.** Accident protection and liability insurance coverage is maintained for children and adults. *(Present policy and/or most recent canceled check or receipt for payment.)*

| 1 | 2 | 3 |
| --- | --- | --- |

Check documents.

*Director's comments on rating*

*For validator* _____

_____   _____

_____   _____

_____   _____

_____   _____

# E. Administration *continued*

| Criterion | Director's rating | Validation procedure |
|---|---|---|

**Director's rating**

**Validation procedure**

**Criterion**

**E-8b.** Vehicle insurance is maintained on any vehicle owned or leased by the facility and used to transport children.

Not met **1**  Partially met **2**  Fully met **3**

❑ Not applicable

*Director's comments on rating*

**Validation decision**
❑ V  ❑ NV

Check documents.

*For validator* _____

_____

_____

_____

_____

_____

**E-9a.** Staff interactions reflect mutual trust, respect, and support for each other.

**1**  **2**  **3**

*Director's comments on rating*

*Staff Questionnaire E-9a*
☐ ☐ ☐
1  2  3

**Validation decision**
❑ V  ❑ NV

*For validator* _____

_____

_____

_____

_____

_____

**E-9b.** Staff members seek out and acknowledge each other's ideas and opinions. Staff give positive recognition to each other's skills and accomplishments.

**1**  **2**  **3**

*Director's comments on rating*

*Staff Questionnaire E-9b*
☐ ☐ ☐
1  2  3

**Validation decision**
❑ V  ❑ NV

*For validator* _____

_____

_____

_____

_____

_____

# E. Administration *continued*

| Criterion | Director's rating | | | Validation procedure | | | |
|---|---|---|---|---|---|---|---|
| | Not met | Partially met | Fully met | *Staff Questionnaire E-9c* | | | Validation decision |

**E-9c.** Staff provide appropriate supports for each other when dealing with stress.

Director's rating: 1 2 3

*Staff Questionnaire E-9c*: 1 2 3

**Validation decision** ☐ V ☐ NV

*Director's comments on rating*

*For validator* _____

_____  _____

_____  _____

_____  _____

_____  _____

**E-9d.** Staff respect each other's rights to confidentiality.

Director's rating: 1 2 3

*Staff Questionnaire E-9d*: 1 2 3

**Validation decision** ☐ V ☐ NV

*Director's comments on rating*

*For validator* _____

_____  _____

_____  _____

_____  _____

_____  _____

**E-9e.** Staff communicate with each other to ensure smooth operations.

Director's rating: 1 2 3

*Staff Questionnaire E-9e*: 1 2 3

**Validation decision** ☐ V ☐ NV

*Director's comments on rating*

*For validator* _____

_____  _____

_____  _____

_____  _____

_____  _____

_____  _____

Program Description

# E.   Administration *continued*

| | Director's rating | Validation procedure |
|---|---|---|

**Criterion**

**E-10a.** Staff and administrators plan and consult together frequently about the program, children, and families.

Director's rating

| Not met | Partially met | Fully met |
|---|---|---|
| 1 | 2 | 3 |

**Validation procedure**

*Staff Questionnaire E-10a*

| | | |
|---|---|---|
| 1 | 2 | 3 |

**Validation decision**

❑ V        ❑ NV

*Director's comments on rating*

*For validator* _____

_____    _____

_____    _____

_____    _____

_____    _____

**E-10b.** Staff plan and consult together.

| 1 | 2 | 3 |
|---|---|---|

*Staff Questionnaire E-10b*

| | | |
|---|---|---|
| 1 | 2 | 3 |

**Validation decision**

❑ V        ❑ NV

*Director's comments on rating*

*For validator* _____

_____    _____

_____    _____

_____    _____

_____    _____

**E-10c.** Regular staff meetings are held for staff to consult on program planning, to plan for implementing and attaining goals, to plan for individual children, and to discuss program and working conditions (may be meetings of small group of or full staff).

| 1 | 2 | 3 |
|---|---|---|

*Staff Questionnaire E-10c*

| | | |
|---|---|---|
| 1 | 2 | 3 |

**Validation decision**

❑ V        ❑ NV

*Director's comments on rating*

*For validator* _____

_____    _____

_____    _____

_____    _____

_____    _____

_____    _____

# E. Administration *continued*

**Director's rating**

**Validation procedure**

**Criterion**

|  | Not met | Partially met | Fully met |
|---|---|---|---|
|  | 1 | 2 | 3 |

**E-10d.** Teachers are provided weekly paid planning time, away from responsibility for children.

*Staff Questionnaire E-10d*

| | | |
|---|---|---|
| 1 | 2 | 3 |

**Validation decision**

❑ V    ❑ NV

*Director's comments on rating*

*For validator* _____

_____     _____

_____     _____

_____     _____

_____     _____

_____     _____

_____     _____

_____     _____

_____     _____

|  | | | |
|---|---|---|---|
|  | 1 | 2 | 3 |

**E-11.** Staff are provided space and time away from children during the day. (When staff work directly with children for more than four hours, staff are provided breaks of at least 15 minutes in each four-hour period.)

*Staff Questionnaire E-11*

| | | |
|---|---|---|
| 1 | 2 | 3 |

**Validation decision**

❑ V    ❑ NV

*Director's comments on rating*

*For validator* _____

_____     _____

_____     _____

_____     _____

_____     _____

_____     _____

_____     _____

_____     _____

_____     _____

_____     _____

Program Description

# E.   Administration *continued*

**Criterion**

|  | **Director's rating** | | | **Validation procedure** | |
|---|---|---|---|---|---|

**Director's rating**

Not met   Partially met   Fully met

**Validation procedure**

**E-12.** Staff keep information about children, families, and associates confidential. Staff refrain from commenting about children or families in the presence of other adults or children.

Director's rating: 1  2  3

*Staff Questionnaire E-12*

□ □ □
1  2  3

**Validation decision**

❏ V    ❏ NV

*Director's comments on rating*

*For validator* _____

_____   _____

_____   _____

_____   _____

_____   _____

_____   _____

_____   _____

_____   _____

_____   _____

**E-13.** An appropriate person on-site is designated to assume authority and to take action in an emergency, in the event of the director's absence.

Director's rating: 1  2  3

*Staff Questionnaire E-13*

□ □ □
1  2  3

**Validation decision**

❏ V    ❏ NV

*Director's comments on rating*

*For validator* _____

_____   _____

_____   _____

_____   _____

_____   _____

_____   _____

_____   _____

_____   _____

_____   _____

_____   _____

# F. Staffing

**F-1 and F-2. Recommended staff-child ratios within group size***

| | | | | | | Group size | | | | | |
|---|---|---|---|---|---|---|---|---|---|---|---|
| Age of children | 6 | 8 | 10 | 12 | 14 | 16 | 18 | 20 | 22 | 24 | 30 |
| Infants (birth to 12 months) | 1:3 | 1:4 | | | | | | | | | |
| Toddlers (12 to 24 months) | 1:3 | 1:4 | 1:5 | 1:4 | | | | | | | |
| 2-year-olds (24 to 30 months) | | 1:4 | 1:5 | 1:6 | | | | | | | |
| 2½-year-olds (30 to 36 months) | | | 1:5 | 1:6 | 1:7 | | | | | | |
| 3-year-olds | | | | | 1:7 | 1:8 | 1:9 | 1:10 | | | |
| 4-year-olds | | | | | | 1:8 | 1:9 | 1:10 | | | |
| 5-year-olds | | | | | | 1:8 | 1:9 | 1:10 | | | |
| Kindergartners | | | | | | | | 1:10 | 1:11 | 1:12 | |
| 6- to 8-year-olds | | | | | | | | 1:10 | 1:11 | 1:12 | 1:15 |
| 9- to 12-year-olds | | | | | | | | | 1:12 | 1:15 | |

*Smaller group sizes and lower staff-child rations have been found to be strong predictors of compliance with indiciators of quality such as positive interactions among staff and children and developmentally appropriate curriculum. Variations in group sizes and ratios are acceptable in cases where the program demonstrates a very high level of compliance with criteria for interactions (A), curriculum (B), staff qualifications (D), health and safety (H), and physical environment (G).

**Criterion**

**F-1.** The number of children in a group is limited in accordance with NAEYC Criteria to facilitate adult-child interaction and constructive activity among children. Groups of children may be age-determined or multiage. (A group is the number of children assigned to a staff member or a team of staff members occupying an individual classroom or well-defined space, with clear physical boundaries that prevent intermingling of children, within a larger room.)

*(Using the chart on this page, determine which groups meet or exceed the required group sizes.)*

**Director's rating**

| Not met | Partially met | Fully met |
|---|---|---|
| 1 | 2 | 3 |

Out of _____ groups,
(total number of)

_____ groups meet NAEYC's group-size requirements.

*Director's comments on rating*

_____

_____

_____

_____

_____

**Validation procedure**

*Staff Questionnaire F-1*

| | | |
|---|---|---|
| 1 | 2 | 3 |

**Validation decision**

❑ V   ❑ NV

Verify group sizes reported in Center Profile; observe sample of classrooms/groups.

*For validator* _____

_____

_____

_____

# F.  Staffing *continued*

**Criterion**

**Director's rating**

**Validation procedure**

---

**F-2a.** Sufficient staff with primary responsibility for working with children are available to provide frequent personal contact, meaningful learning activities, and supervision and to offer immediate care as needed.

*(Using the chart on the previous page, determine which groups meet or exceed the required staff-child ratios.)*

| Not met | Partially met | Fully met |
|:---:|:---:|:---:|
| 1 | 2 | 3 |

Out of _____ groups,
(total number of)

_____ groups meet NAEYC's staff-child ratio requirements.

*Director's comments on rating*

_____

_____

_____

_____

*Staff Questionnaire F-2a*

| | | |
|:---:|:---:|:---:|
| 1 | 2 | 3 |

**Validation decision**
❑ V    ❑ NV

Verify staff-child ratios reported in Center Profile; observe sample of classrooms/groups.

*For validator* _____

_____

_____

_____

_____

---

**F-2b.** Substitutes are provided to maintain staff-child ratios when regular staff are absent. Substitutes for infants and toddlers are familiar with the children and oriented to children's schedules and individual differences in a systematic way before assignment. Volunteers who work with children complete a pre-assignment orientation and participate in ongoing training.

| 1 | 2 | 3 |
|:---:|:---:|:---:|

*Director's comments on rating*

_____

_____

_____

_____

*Staff Questionnaire F-2b*

| | | |
|:---:|:---:|:---:|
| 1 | 2 | 3 |

**Validation decision**
❑ V    ❑ NV

*For validator* _____

_____

_____

_____

---

**F-3a.** Each staff member has primary responsibility for and develops a deeper attachment to an identified group of children.

| 1 | 2 | 3 |
|:---:|:---:|:---:|

*Director's comments on rating*

_____

_____

_____

_____

*Staff Questionnaire F-3a*

| | | |
|:---:|:---:|:---:|
| 1 | 2 | 3 |

**Validation decision**
❑ V    ❑ NV

Check Staffing Pattern.

*For validator* _____

_____

_____

_____

# F. Staffing *continued*

**Director's rating**

**Validation procedure**

**Criterion**

|  | Not met | Partially met | Fully met |
|--|--|--|--|

**F-3b.** Every attempt is made to have continuity of adults who work with children within each day and over extended periods of time (several years of the child's enrollment), particularly infants and toddlers.

| 1 | 2 | 3 |
|--|--|--|

*Director's comments on rating*

_____

_____

_____

*Staff Questionnaire F-3b*

| | | |
|--|--|--|
| 1 | 2 | 3 |

*Family Questionnaire #23*

| | | |
|--|--|--|
| DK | No | Yes |

Check Staffing Pattern.

*For validator* _____

**Validation decision**
❑ V ❑ NV

_____

_____

_____

_____

_____

_____

**F-3c.** Infants and toddlers spend the majority of the time interacting with the same person each day.

| 1 | 2 | 3 |
|--|--|--|

❑ **Not applicable**

*Director's comments on rating*

_____

_____

_____

_____

_____

_____

_____

*Staff Questionnaire F-3c*

| | | |
|--|--|--|
| 1 | 2 | 3 |

**Validation decision**
❑ V ❑ NV

Check Staffing Pattern.

*For validator* _____

_____

_____

_____

_____

_____

_____

Program Description

## F.   Staffing *continued*

**Criterion**

Director's rating

Not met    Partially met    Fully met

**Validation procedure**

**F-3d.** The program is organized and staffed to minimize the number of group transitions an individual child experiences during the time the child is enrolled in the program. Every attempt is made to maintain continuity of relationships between teachers and children and among groups of children.

| 1 | 2 | 3 |

*Director's comments on rating*

_____

_____

_____

_____

*Staff Questionnaire F-3d*

| | | |
| 1 | 2 | 3 |

**Validation decision**
❑ V    ❑ NV

Check Staffing Pattern.

*For validator* _____

_____

_____

_____

**Validation procedure**

*Staff Questionnaire F-4*

| | | |
| 1 | 2 | 3 |

**Validation decision**
❑ V    ❑ NV

**F-4.** A majority of the child's day is spent in activities utilizing recommended staff-child ratios and group-size limitations while minimizing the number of transitions or regroupings children experience and maintaining relationships among groups of children as much as possible.

| 1 | 2 | 3 |

*Director's comments on rating*

_____

_____

_____

_____

Check Staffing Pattern; observe classrooms/ groups.

*For validator* _____

_____

_____

_____

## G.   Physical Environment

**Validation decision**
❑ V    ❑ NV

**G-1a.** There is a minimum of 35 square feet (preferably 50 square feet) of usable playroom floor space per child indoors.

| 1 | 2 | 3 |

Provide actual square feet if less than 35 square feet _____.

*Director's comments on rating*

_____

_____

_____

Observe facility.

*For validator* _____

_____

_____

_____

# G. Physical Environment *continued*

| | Director's rating | Validation procedure |
|---|---|---|

**Criterion**

**Director's rating**

| Not met | Partially met | Fully met |
|---|---|---|
| 1 | 2 | 3 |

**Validation procedure**

**G-1b.** There is a minimum of 75 square feet (preferably 100 square feet) of play space outdoors per child (when space is in use).

Provide actual square feet if less than 75 square feet _____.

*Director's comments on rating*

_____

_____

_____

_____

**Validation decision**

❏ V   ❏ NV

Observe facility.

*For validator* _____

_____

_____

_____

_____

---

**G-10a.** The work environment for staff, including classrooms and staff rooms, is comfortable, well-organized, and in good repair.

| 1 | 2 | 3 |
|---|---|---|

*Director's comments on rating*

_____

_____

_____

_____

*Staff Questionnaire G-10a*

| | | |
|---|---|---|
| 1 | 2 | 3 |

Observe facility.

*For validator* _____

**Validation decision**

❏ V   ❏ NV

_____

_____

_____

---

**G-10b.** The environment includes a place for adults to take a break or work away from children, an adult-sized bathroom, a secure place for staff to store their personal belongings, and an administrative area that is separated from the children's areas for planning or preparing materials.

| 1 | 2 | 3 |
|---|---|---|

*Director's comments on rating*

_____

_____

_____

_____

*Staff Questionnaire G-10b*

| | | |
|---|---|---|
| 1 | 2 | 3 |

Observe facility.

*For validator* _____

**Validation decision**

❏ V   ❏ NV

_____

_____

_____

Program Description

# H.  Health and Safety

**Director's rating**

**Validation procedure**

**Criterion**

**H-1.** The program presents valid certification that it is in compliance with all legal requirements for protection of the health and safety of children in group settings, such as building codes, sanitation, water quality, and fire protection. The program is licensed or accredited to operate by the appropriate state/local agencies. The program maintains a high level of compliance with licensing standards, free of a record of repeated serious violations. If exempt from licensing, the program demonstrates compliance with its own state or local community's regulations (building, sanitation, and licensing codes) for early childhood programs/child care centers subject to licensing.

| Not met | Partially met | Fully met |
|---------|---------------|-----------|
| **1** | **2** | **3** |

**Validation decision**
❑ V   ❑ NV

Check license; verify results of recent inspections.

*Director's comments on rating*

*For validator* _____

_____  _____

_____  _____

_____  _____

_____  _____

_____  _____

_____  _____

_____  _____

_____  _____

**Validation decision**
❑ V   ❑ NV

**H-2a.** Staff health records include results of pre-employment tuberculosis test and evaluation of any infection and evidence of tuberculosis test every two years thereafter and emergency contact information.

| **1** | **2** | **3** |
|-------|-------|-------|

Sample documents.

*Director's comments on rating*

*For validator* _____

_____  _____

_____  _____

_____  _____

_____  _____

_____  _____

_____  _____

_____  _____

# H. Health and Safety *continued*

| Criterion | Director's rating | Validation procedure |
|---|---|---|

**Criterion**

**Director's rating**

**Validation procedure**

|   | Not met | Partially met | Fully met |
|---|---|---|---|

**H-2b.** Hiring practices include careful checking of personal references of all potential employees and volunteers.

| 1 | 2 | 3 |
|---|---|---|

*Director's comments on rating*

**Validation decision**

❑ V   ❑ NV

Interview director.

*For validator* _____

_____   _____

_____   _____

_____   _____

_____   _____

**Validation decision**

❑ V   ❑ NV

**H-2c.** New staff members serve a probationary employment period during which the director or other qualified person makes a professional judgment as to their physical and psychological competence for working with children.

| 1 | 2 | 3 |
|---|---|---|

Interview director.

*Director's comments on rating*

*For validator* _____

_____   _____

_____   _____

_____   _____

_____   _____

**Validation decision**

❑ V   ❑ NV

**H-3.** Child health records include
- ❑ results of recent health examination,
- ❑ up-to-date record of immunizations,
- ❑ emergency contact information,
- ❑ names of people authorized to call for the child, and
- ❑ important health history (such as allergies, chronic illness).

| 1 | 2 | 3 |
|---|---|---|

Sample documents.

*Director's comments on rating*

*For validator* _____

_____   _____

_____   _____

_____   _____

_____   _____

_____   _____

Program Description

# H. Health and Safety *continued*

| | **Director's rating** | | **Validation procedure** |
|---|---|---|---|

**Criterion**

| | Not met | Partially met | Fully met |
|---|---|---|---|

**H-4a.** The program has a written policy given to all families specifying the conditions under which sick children are excluded, included but isolated, or included in the regular classroom, in accordance with local licensing and public health regulations.

Director's rating: [ 1 ] [ 2 ] [ 3 ]

*Director's comments on rating*

_____

_____

_____

_____

_____

_____

_____

_____

**Validation procedure**

*Staff Questionnaire H-4a*

[  ] [  ] [  ]
 1    2    3

*Family Questionnaire #1d*

[  ] [  ] [  ]
DK   No   Yes

Check documents.

*For validator* _____

_____

_____

_____

_____

_____

_____

**Validation decision**
☐ V    ☐ NV

---

**Validation decision**
☐ V    ☐ NV

**H-4b.** When sick children are permitted to attend, the decision is based on the comfort of ill children, the protection of well children and staff, the resources available to the program to meet any special care that is required, and the needs of families.

Director's rating: [ 1 ] [ 2 ] [ 3 ]

*Director's comments on rating*

_____

_____

_____

_____

_____

_____

_____

_____

_____

Interview director.

*For validator* _____

_____

_____

_____

_____

_____

_____

_____

_____

# H. Health and Safety *continued*

**Criterion**

**Director's rating**

| Not met | Partially met | Fully met |
|---------|---------------|-----------|
| 1 | 2 | 3 |

**Validation procedure**

**Validation decision**
❑ V    ❑ NV

**H-5.** Provisions are made for safe arrival and departure of all children that also allow for parent-staff interaction. A system exists for ensuring that children are released only to authorized people. A procedure for accountability when a child fails to show for the program is in place and followed. A system exists to ensure the safety of older school-age children whose parents have agreed to allow their children to leave the program on their own. The system includes written agreements between parents and the program and consistent sign-out procedures for released children.

Observe arrival/departure; check documents.

*Director's comments on rating*     For validator _____

_____     _____

_____     _____

_____     _____

_____     _____

_____     _____

_____     _____

_____     _____

**H-6.** If transportation is provided for children by the program, vehicles are equipped with age-appropriate restraint devices, and appropriate safety precautions are taken. The program presents certification that vehicles used in transporting children are appropriately licensed, inspected, and maintained.

| 1 | 2 | 3 |
|---|---|---|

❑ **Not applicable**

*Director's comments on rating*

**Validation decision**
❑ V    ❑ NV

Interview director; observe vehicles; check documents.

For validator _____

_____     _____

_____     _____

_____     _____

_____     _____

_____     _____

_____     _____

_____     _____

_____     _____

Program Description

# H. Health and Safety *continued*

| Criterion | Director's rating | Validation procedure |
|---|---|---|

**H-7b.** There is specific accountability for each child by one staff member. Systems are in place for accounting for children's whereabouts at regular intervals, especially during periods of transition.

**Director's rating**

| Not met | Partially met | Fully met |
|---|---|---|
| **1** | **2** | **3** |

*Director's comments on rating*

_____

_____

_____

**Validation procedure**

*Staff Questionnaire H-7b*

| | | |
|---|---|---|
| 1 | 2 | 3 |

**Validation decision**

❑ **V**   ❑ **NV**

*For validator* _____

_____

_____

**H-7c.** Families are informed about procedures and policies for field trips. Families are notified of all activities outside the center. Field trips are accompanied by parents and other volunteers to ensure adequate supervision. Field trips are preplanned and emergency procedures are prepared. Transportation meets requirements (see **H-6**).

| **1** | **2** | **3** |
|---|---|---|

*Director's comments on rating*

_____

_____

_____

_____

_____

*Family Questionnaire #9*

| | | |
|---|---|---|
| DK | No | Yes |

Interview director.

*For validator* _____

_____

_____

_____

**Validation decision**

❑ **V**   ❑ **NV**

**H-8.** Staff are alert to the health of each child. Individual medical problems and accidents are recorded and reported to staff and families, and a written record is kept of such incidents.

| **1** | **2** | **3** |
|---|---|---|

*Director's comments on rating*

_____

_____

_____

_____

_____

*Staff Questionnaire H-8*

| | | |
|---|---|---|
| 1 | 2 | 3 |

*Family Questionnaire #10*

| | | |
|---|---|---|
| DK | No | Yes |

Check documents.

*For validator* _____

_____

_____

**Validation decision**

❑ **V**   ❑ **NV**

# H. Health and Safety *continued*

| | Director's rating | Validation procedure |
|---|---|---|

**Criterion**

**H-9a.** Staff know procedures for reporting suspected incidents of child abuse and/or neglect.

Director's rating

| Not met | Partially met | Fully met |
|---|---|---|
| 1 | 2 | 3 |

*Director's comments on rating*

Validation procedure

*Staff Questionnaire H-9a*

| | | |
|---|---|---|
| 1 | 2 | 3 |

**Validation decision**
❑ V ❑ NV

*For validator* _____

_____

_____

_____

_____

**H-9b.** Suspected incidents of child abuse and/or neglect by families, staff, volunteers, or others are reported to the appropriate local agencies.

| 1 | 2 | 3 |
|---|---|---|

*Director's comments on rating*

*Staff Questionnaire H-9b*

| | | |
|---|---|---|
| 1 | 2 | 3 |

**Validation decision**
❑ V ❑ NV

*For validator* _____

_____

_____

_____

_____

**H-10.** At least one staff member who has certification in emergency pediatric first-aid treatment, including CPR for infants and children and emergency management of choking, from a licensed health professional is always present. Current certificates are kept on file.

| 1 | 2 | 3 |
|---|---|---|

*Director's comments on rating*

**Validation decision**
❑ V ❑ NV

Check documents.

*For validator* _____

_____

_____

_____

_____

Program Description

## H.    Health and Safety *continued*

| | Director's rating | | | Validation procedure | |
|---|---|---|---|---|---|

**Criterion**

**H-11a.** Adequate first-aid supplies are readily available.

For example, bandages, ice packs, sterile gauze, adhesive tape, medicated soap, cotton, and tweezers.

Director's rating

| Not met | Partially met | Fully met |
|---|---|---|
| **1** | **2** | **3** |

*Director's comments on rating*

_____

_____

_____

_____

_____

*Staff Questionnaire H-11a*

| | | |
|---|---|---|
| 1 | 2 | 3 |

**Validation decision**

❏ V    ❏ NV

Observe facility.

*For validator* _____

_____

_____

_____

_____

---

**H-11b.** A plan exists for dealing with medical emergencies that includes

❏ a source of emergency care,
❏ written parental consent forms, and
❏ transportation arrangements.

| **1** | **2** | **3** |
|---|---|---|

*Director's comments on rating*

_____

_____

_____

_____

_____

*Staff Questionnaire H-11b*

| | | |
|---|---|---|
| 1 | 2 | 3 |

**Validation decision**

❏ V    ❏ NV

Sample documents.

*For validator* _____

_____

_____

_____

_____

---

**H-13a.** The facility is cleaned daily, including disinfecting bathroom fixtures and removing trash.

| **1** | **2** | **3** |
|---|---|---|

*Director's comments on rating*

_____

_____

_____

_____

**Validation decision**

❏ V    ❏ NV

Observe facility; interview director.

*For validator* _____

_____

_____

_____

# H. Health and Safety *continued*

**Criterion**

**Director's rating**

**Validation procedure**

**H-13b.** Infants' equipment is washed and disinfected at least twice a week. Toys that are mouthed are washed daily.

| Not met | Partially met | Fully met |
|---|---|---|
| 1 | 2 | 3 |

❑ **Not applicable**

*Director's comments on rating*

**Validation decision**
❑ V    ❑ NV

Interview director.

*For validator* _____

_____

_____

_____

_____

**H-14b.** Staff and volunteers know and follow proper procedures during handwashing, including washing with soap and warm, running water for at least 10 seconds; using single use or disposable towels; and avoiding recontamination from faucets by turning off faucets with towel.

| 1 | 2 | 3 |
|---|---|---|

*Director's comments on rating*

_____

_____

_____

_____

*Staff Questionnaire H-14b*

| | | |
|---|---|---|
| 1 | 2 | 3 |

**Validation decision**
❑ V    ❑ NV

Observe facility and signs.

*For validator* _____

_____

_____

_____

**H-14d.** Staff and volunteers follow universal precautions to prevent transmission of blood-borne diseases.

| 1 | 2 | 3 |
|---|---|---|

*Director's comments on rating*

_____

_____

_____

*Staff Questionnaire H-14d*

| | | |
|---|---|---|
| 1 | 2 | 3 |

**Validation decision**
❑ V    ❑ NV

Observe facility.

*For validator* _____

_____

_____

_____

Program Description

# H.  Health and Safety *continued*

**Director's rating**

**Validation procedure**

**Criterion**

| Not met | Partially met | Fully met |
|---------|---------------|-----------|

*Staff Questionnaire H-16a*    **Validation decision**

**H-16a.** Individual bedding is washed at least once a week and used by only one child between washings. Individual cribs, cots, and mats are washed if soiled.

| 1 | 2 | 3 |
|---|---|---|

| | | | |
|---|---|---|---|
| 1 | 2 | 3 | NA |

❑ V    ❑ NV

❑ **Not applicable**

Observe facility.

*Director's comments on rating*

*For validator* _____

_____        _____

_____        _____

_____        _____

_____        _____

**Validation decision**
❑ V    ❑ NV

**H-17.** Hot water does not exceed 120°F (43°C) at faucets used by children.

| 1 | 2 | 3 |
|---|---|---|

Feel water temperature.

*Director's comments on rating*

*For validator* _____

_____        _____

_____        _____

_____        _____

_____        _____

**Validation decision**
❑ V    ❑ NV

**H-18d.** Program provides certification that nontoxic building materials, no lead paint or asbestos, are used in the facility (or lead abatement procedures are in place for older facilities).

| 1 | 2 | 3 |
|---|---|---|

Interview director or check documents.

*Director's comments on rating*

*For validator* _____

_____        _____

_____        _____

_____        _____

_____        _____

# H. Health and Safety *continued*

| Criterion | Director's rating | Validation procedure |

**Director's rating**

| Not met | Partially met | Fully met |
|---|---|---|
| 1 | 2 | 3 |

**Validation procedure**

**Validation decision**
❏ V   ❏ NV

**H-18e.** Stairways are well-lighted and equipped with handrails.

❏ **Not applicable**

*Director's comments on rating*

Observe facility.

*For validator* _____

_____

_____

_____

_____

_____

---

**Validation decision**
❏ V   ❏ NV

**H-20b.** Medication is administered to children only when a written order is submitted by a parent and the medication is administered by a consistently designated staff member. Written records are kept of medication given to children.

| 1 | 2 | 3 |

*Director's comments on rating*

Check records and/or written policy.

*For validator* _____

_____

_____

_____

_____

_____

---

*Staff Questionnaire H-21a*   **Validation decision**
❏ V   ❏ NV

**H-21a.** Staff and volunteers are familiar with primary and secondary evacuation routes and practice evacuation procedures monthly with children.

| 1 | 2 | 3 |

| | | |
|---|---|---|
| 1 | 2 | 3 |

*Director's comments on rating*

Check documents.

*For validator* _____

_____

_____

_____

_____

_____

Program Description

# H.  Health and Safety *continued*

**Criterion**

| | Director's rating | | | Validation procedure | | |

**H-22a.** Staff and volunteers are familiar with emergency procedures and procedures for severe storm warnings.

Director's rating
Not met [ 1 ]  Partially met [ 2 ]  Fully met [ 3 ]

*Director's comments on rating*

_____
_____
_____
_____

Validation procedure

*Staff Questionnaire H-22a*
[ ] [ ] [ ]
 1   2   3

**Validation decision**
❏ V    ❏ NV

*For validator* _____
_____
_____
_____

**H-22b.** Smoke detectors and fire extinguishers are provided and periodically checked.

[ 1 ]  [ 2 ]  [ 3 ]

*Director's comments on rating*

_____
_____
_____
_____

**Validation decision**
❏ V    ❏ NV

Observe facility; interview director.

*For validator* _____
_____
_____
_____

**H-22c.** Emergency telephone numbers including police, fire, rescue, and poison control services are posted by telephones.

[ 1 ]  [ 2 ]  [ 3 ]

*Director's comments on rating*

_____
_____
_____
_____
_____

**Validation decision**
❏ V    ❏ NV

Observe facility.

*For validator* _____
_____
_____
_____
_____

## I. Nutrition and Food Service

**Criterion**

**Director's rating**

**Validation procedure**

**I-1.** Meals and/or snacks are planned to meet the child's nutritional requirements in proportion to the amount of time the child is in the program each day, as recommended by the Child Care Food Program of the U.S. Department of Agriculture. Amount of food served is adjusted according to the age of the children because infants and toddlers require smaller amounts of food served more frequently and school-age children require much more food than preschoolers.

Not met **1**   Partially met **2**   Fully met **3**

**Validation decision**
☐ V   ☐ NV

Check meal plans.

*Director's comments on rating*

*For validator* _____

_____

_____

_____

_____

_____

_____

_____

_____

**I-2a.** Written menus are provided for families.

**1**   **2**   **3**

*Family Questionnaire #1e*

☐ DK   ☐ No   ☐ Yes

**Validation decision**
☐ V   ☐ NV

*Director's comments on rating*

Check documents.

*For validator* _____

_____

_____

_____

_____

_____

_____

_____

_____

_____

_____

_____

## I.  Nutrition and Food Service *continued*

**Criterion**

**Director's rating**

| Not met | Partially met | Fully met |
|---------|---------------|-----------|

**Validation procedure**

**I-2b.** Feeding times and food consumption information is provided to families of infants and toddlers at the end of each day.

| **1** | **2** | **3** |

❑ **Not applicable**

*Director's comments on rating*

_____

_____

_____

_____

*Family Questionnaire #1f*

| | | | |

DK    No    Yes    NA

**Validation decision**

❑ V       ❑ NV

Check documents.

*For validator* _____

_____

_____

_____

**I-3.** Foods indicative of children's cultural backgrounds are served periodically.

| **1** | **2** | **3** |

*Director's comments on rating*

_____

_____

_____

_____

**Validation decision**

❑ V       ❑ NV

Check meal plans.

*For validator* _____

_____

_____

_____

**I-4.** If the program does not provide food, families are educated regarding well-balanced meals that may be brought from home. Food brought from home is stored appropriately until consumed.

| **1** | **2** | **3** |

❑ **Not applicable**

*Director's comments on rating*

_____

_____

_____

_____

**Validation decision**

❑ V       ❑ NV

Check documents; observe facility.

*For validator* _____

_____

_____

_____

## I. Nutrition and Food Service *continued*

| | Director's rating | Validation procedure |

**Criterion**

**Director's rating**

| Not met | Partially met | Fully met |
|---|---|---|
| 1 | 2 | 3 |

**Validation procedure**

**Validation decision**

☐ V    ☐ NV

**I-5.** Where food is prepared on the premises, the program is in compliance with legal requirements for food preparation and service. Food may be prepared at an approved facility and transported to the program in appropriate sanitary containers and at appropriate temperatures.

Check current food inspection certificate.

*Director's comments on rating*

*For validator* _____

_____    _____

_____    _____

_____    _____

_____    _____

## J. Evaluation

**J-1a.** All staff, including the program administrator, are evaluated at least annually by the director or other appropriate supervisor.

*Staff Questionnaire J-1a*

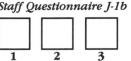

**Validation decision**

☐ V    ☐ NV

Sample documents.

*Director's comments on rating*

*For validator* _____

_____    _____

_____    _____

_____    _____

**J-1b.** Results of staff evaluation are written and confidential. They are discussed privately with the staff member.

| 1 | 2 | 3 |

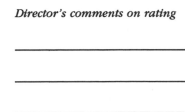

*Staff Questionnaire J-1b*

**Validation decision**

☐ V    ☐ NV

Sample documents.

*Director's comments on rating*

*For validator* _____

_____    _____

_____    _____

_____    _____

_____    _____

Program Description

## J. Evaluation *continued*

**Criterion**

|  | **Director's rating** | **Validation procedure** |
| --- | --- | --- |

**Director's rating**

**Validation procedure**

**J-1c.** Staff evaluations include classroom observation. Evaluation is based on the employees's job description and previously established goals for improvement.

Director's rating

| Not met | Partially met | Fully met |
| --- | --- | --- |
| **1** | **2** | **3** |

*Director's comments on rating*

_____

_____

_____

_____

_____

*Staff Questionnaire J-1c*

| | | |
| --- | --- | --- |
| 1 | 2 | 3 |

**Validation decision**

❑ V    ❑ NV

Sample documents.

*For validator* _____

_____

_____

_____

_____

**J-1d.** Staff are informed of evaluation criteria in advance.

| **1** | **2** | **3** |
| --- | --- | --- |

*Director's comments on rating*

_____

_____

_____

_____

_____

*Staff Questionnaire J-1d*

| | | |
| --- | --- | --- |
| 1 | 2 | 3 |

**Validation decision**

❑ V    ❑ NV

Sample documents.

*For validator* _____

_____

_____

_____

_____

**J-1e.** Staff have an opportunity to evaluate their own performance.

| **1** | **2** | **3** |
| --- | --- | --- |

*Director's comments on rating*

_____

_____

_____

_____

*Staff Questionnaire J-1e*

| | | |
| --- | --- | --- |
| 1 | 2 | 3 |

**Validation decision**

❑ V    ❑ NV

Sample documents.

*For validator* _____

_____

_____

_____

# J. Evaluation *continued*

| | Director's rating | Validation procedure |
|---|---|---|

**Criterion**

| | | Not met | Partially met | Fully met | | Validation decision |
|---|---|---|---|---|---|---|

**J-1f.** A plan for staff training is generated from the staff-evaluation process.

Director's rating: **1** **2** **3**

Validation procedure — *Staff Questionnaire J-1f*

☐ 1  ☐ 2  ☐ 3

**Validation decision**  ☐ V  ☐ NV

*Director's comments on rating*

Sample documents.

_____

*For validator* _____

_____    _____

_____    _____

_____    _____

_____    _____

_____    _____

_____    _____

**J-2a.** At least annually, administrators, families, staff, school-age children, and other routinely participating adults are involved in evaluating the program's effectiveness in meeting the needs of children and families.

Director's rating: **1** **2** **3**

*Staff Questionnaire J-2a*

☐ 1  ☐ 2  ☐ 3

**Validation decision**  ☐ V  ☐ NV

*Family Questionnaire #24*

☐ DK  ☐ No  ☐ Yes

*Director's comments on rating*

Check documents.

_____

*For validator* _____

_____    _____

_____    _____

_____    _____

_____    _____

_____    _____

_____    _____

_____    _____

_____    _____

_____    _____

Program Description

# J.  Evaluation *continued*

**Criterion**

| | **Director's rating** | | | **Validation procedure** | | |
|---|---|---|---|---|---|---|

**J-2b.** The program regularly establishes goals for continuous improvement and innovation.

**Director's rating**

Not met [ 1 ]   Partially met [ 2 ]   Fully met [ 3 ]

*Director's comments on rating*

_____

_____

_____

_____

_____

_____

_____

*Staff Questionnaire J-2b*

[ ] [ ] [ ]
1   2   3

Check documents.

*For validator* _____

_____

_____

_____

_____

_____

_____

**Validation decision**

❑ V    ❑ NV

---

**J-3.** Individual descriptions of children's development and learning are written and compiled as a basis for planning appropriate learning activities, as a means of facilitating optimal development of each child, as a means of identifying children who may be in need of more systematic diagnosis of a learning or developmental problem, and as records for use in communications with families.

[ 1 ]   [ 2 ]   [ 3 ]

*Director's comments on rating*

_____

_____

_____

_____

_____

_____

*Staff Questionnaire J-3*

[ ] [ ] [ ]
1   2   3

Sample documents.

*For validator* _____

_____

_____

_____

_____

_____

**Validation decision**

❑ V    ❑ NV

# Section 8

## How to Prepare for the Validation Visit

### Validation Visit Tasks and Sample Timelines
### Validation Process Verification Form

# Section 8

## How to Prepare for the Validation Visit

**What is the purpose of the validation visit?**

After the self-study is completed, the next step is the validation visit. Qualified early childhood professionals, called validators, visit your program to verify the results of your self-study that are reported in the Program Description. The purpose of the validation visit is to verify that the Program Description is an accurate description of the program's daily operations.

Before validators are assigned, Academy staff examine the Program Description to determine that it is complete. Academy staff may conduct phone interviews to obtain additional information for incomplete or unclear areas of the Program Description. Academy staff may advise the director to record additional information or to delay seeking accreditation until program improvements have been made.

**What is the role of the validator?**

The validator's role is to verify the accuracy of the Program Description that will be reviewed by the Commission. The validators do *not* make the accreditation decision. The accreditation decision is made by a Commission that is compiled of early childhood experts who consider the validated Program Description and use their professional judgment to determine if the overall quality of the program merits accreditation.

The validation process looks for consistency between different sources of information. For example, if the program reports that it does or does not meet a criterion and the validator agrees, then the item is validated (whether or not the criterion is met). Similarly, if the program reports that it does or does not meet a criterion and the validators disagrees, then the item is not validated. For example, the program might report that it does not have adequate materials because that is an area it would like to improve. However, the validator finds evidence that the program does have adequate materials. In this case, the criterion is not validated because the validator's rating is not consistent with the director's, but the validator reports the reason for the item not being validated and records the director's comments about the item in the Program Description. The purpose of making a validation decision on the criteria is to ensure that the Commission receives an accurate reflection of the program. All nonvalidated criteria will be discussed by the validator(s) and director(s) during the exit interview. The discussion of nonvalidated criteria is an opportunity to present both interpretations on the criteria and record the interpretations in the Program Description. It is crucial that director's view the exit interview as an opportunity to present additional information to the Commission.

**Who are the validators?**

Validators are early childhood professionals who usually live within driving distance (within 100 miles) of the program. Validators are selected and trained by the Academy. They meet the Academy's qualifications which include having a college degree in early childhood education or child development or the equivalent, knowledge of the accreditation process, experience working with young children in accredited programs, administering programs for young children, and personal characteristics including good observation and communication skills and high standards of professional and ethical conduct. Validators volunteer their time and are reimbursed only for their expenses.

Validators are assigned by the Academy. Validators are required to report any conflicts of interest that might make it impossible for them to fairly validate a program. Potential conflicts of interest include situation such as the validator previously was employed or sought employment by the program, had a child enrolled in the program, serves on an advisory board to the program, operates a program in direct competition, and so forth. If the director perceives a possible conflict of interest, she or he should make the Academy aware of the potential conflict and request a different validator.

**How many validators come and how long do they stay?**

The number of validators and the length of the validation visit depends on the number of children present on a given day and the number of groups to be observed. The number of validator(s) and length of visit may differ to fit the individual needs of your early childhood program.

**Program enrollment**

**Level 1**    Fewer than 60 children; One validator—one day

**Level 2**    61 to 120 children; Two validators—one day or one validator—two days

**Level 3**    121 to 240 children; Two validators—two days
or three validators—one day

**Level 4**    More than 240 children; Three validators—two days

**What are the validation tasks?**

Validation involves three major tasks:

(1) Validators verify the accuracy of the ratings reported on the Classroom Observation Summary Sheet by observing a sample of classrooms and comparing their rating to the program's rating. Validators randomly select classrooms to be observed with an attempt to see all the different age groups. **Validators need to observe at least 50% of the groups. Approximately two-thirds of the children enrolled should be present for the visit to be conducted.** For example, inclement weather or sickness may prevent two-thirds of the children to be in attendance. If this occurs, contact the Academy to reschedule your validation visit.

(2) Validators verify the accuracy of the administrative criteria by comparing evidence, checking documents, and sampling the Family and Teaching-Staff

Questionnaires. The validation procedure varies depending upon the evidence that is needed for each criterion.

(3) Validators discuss all nonvalidated criteria with the director and record the director's and validator's comments about the Criteria on the Program Description.

## How are the observed criteria validated?

To validate Part 2 of the Program Description—Results of Classroom Observations, the validator compares her or his ratings to the ratings reported by the program (on the Early Childhood Classroom Observation Summary Sheet) for those classrooms she or he observed.

To make the validation decision, the following rules are applied:

- When one or two classrooms are observed, the ratings reported by the program and the validator must be consistent in order for a criterion to be validated.

- When three or more classrooms are observed, there can be no more than one case of a one-point difference and no cases of a two-point difference in order for a criterion to be considered validated.

- When seven or more groups are observed, there can be no more than two cases of a one-point difference and no cases of a two-point difference in order for a criterion to be considered validated.

Below is an example of a validation decision for an observed criterion.

## G.  Physical Environment

**Criterion**

**Ratings of Center and Validator**

| | Average rating | Inf. | | Tod. | | PS | | SA | | | | | | | | | | | |
|---|---|---|---|---|---|---|---|---|---|---|---|---|---|---|---|---|---|---|---|
| | | C | V | C | V | C | V | C | V | C | V | C | V | C | V | C | V | C | V |
| G-7. The environment includes soft elements. | 2.5 | 2 | 3 | 2 | 3 | 3 | 3 | 3 | 2 | | | | | | | | | | |

*For example,*
Rugs, cushions, soft furniture, soft toys, comfortable chairs for adults to hold children in their laps

*Director's comments on rating*

Younger children's classes have fewer elements because they're hard to keep clean.

**Validation decision**   ☐ V   ☑ NV

*For validator* _____

In this case the decision would be to validate because out of more than three groups observed there was only one case of a one-point difference. The Program Description includes space for the director to explain the average rating. In this case, because the rating was below 2.7, the director provided an explanation. If the criterion were not validated, the director and validator would discuss the difference in ratings. The results of the discussion would be reported in the space marked "For validator."

> Reminder:
> - Validated means that there is consistency between what the program personnel reported and what the validator observed. It does not necessarily mean that the criterion is fully met.
> - Nonvalidated means there is a difference between what program personnel reported and what the validator observed. A criterion may be nonvalidated because a validator rates a criterion higher or lower than the program rated itself. In the example on page 257, the program rated the infant and toddler groups partially met [2] for criterion **G-7**, but the validator observed many soft elements and rated the criterion fully met [3]. The criterion would be nonvalidated. However, the Commission would recognize that the criterion was fully met.

**How are the administrative criteria validated?**

The validation process for Part 3 of the Program Description—Results of the Administrator Report varies depending upon the required evidence for the criterion. The evidence will be

- results of Family and Teaching-Staff Questionnaires,
- written documents and records,
- interviews with the director, and
- observation of the physical facility.

To be sure that the results of the questionnaires were reported accurately on the summary sheets, the validator first examines the questionnaires. A few items on each are randomly selected, responses are counted and matched with numbers reported by the program. If the summary sheets are not accurate, the director is asked to redo the summary sheets and the Program Description is corrected.

To validate criteria that require written documents, the validator will need to have access to those documents. To help the validator, the director should collect all the required documents in one place or identify their location for the validator on the List of Documents on pages 94 to 96 of the *Guide*.

> Reminder: Some criteria require documentation to support compliance with the criteria. If the required documents are not available on-site during the validation visit, a written letter of verification must be provided by the program to determine the location and level of compliance with the criteria. The validator then uses this letter to validate.

The "validation procedure" column on the Program Description tells the validator and director what sources of evidence to compare to verify the accuracy of the director's rating of each criterion. If the sources of evidence are consistent, the criterion is validated (V). If the sources of evidence are not consistent (doesn't support the director's rating), the criterion is not validated (NV) and the validator asks the director for more information.

**The possible sources of evidence and the procedures used by the validator are explained below.**

**Family Questionnaire**—Each item on the Family Questionnaire corresponds to a criterion. The validator compares parent responses to the director's rating and other sources of evidence such as a document or Teaching-Staff Questionnaire.

For a director's rating of [3] to be validated, at least 75% of the parents who returned the questionnaire must answer the question "yes." Keep in mind that at least 50% of all the parents should have returned the questionnaire.

For a director's rating of [2] or [1] to be validated, all sources of evidence must be consistent. In other words, the sources of evidence must agree that the criterion is partially met or not fully met.

**Teaching-Staff Questionnaire**—Each item on the Teaching-Staff Questionnaire corresponds to the same criterion. The validator compares staff responses to other sources of evidence such as director's ratings.

For a director's rating of [3] to be validated, at least 75% of the staff must rate the item a [3] (when there are at least four staff members). If there are fewer than four staff members; all staff responses must be in agreement with the director's rating to be validated.

For a director's rating of [2] or [1], see above.

**Observe facility**—Validator observes the facility to see if criterion is met (for example, **G-22b**—Emergency telephone numbers are posted by telephones).

**Interview**—Validator interviews the director to verify compliance with the criterion.

**Check Staffing Pattern**—The validator compares observed staff-child ratio and group sizes with those reported in the Center Profile. The validator verifies whether group sizes and staff-child ratios are in compliance with NAEYC recommendations. The validator verifies that the chart has been filled out correctly.

**Check Staff Qualifications Chart**—The validator compares a sample of staff records to the qualifications reported on the Staff Qualifications chart. The validator verifies the reported leve of compliance and makes the validation decision.

Check documents—Validator verifies that the written documents exist and contain the required information.

Sample documents—Validator carefully examines the *content* of a sample of multiple documents required (staff records or health forms) using the following rules for sampling.

Rules for sampling:
- To sample child records, sample from each age group served in the program—infants, toddlers, preschoolers, kindergartners, and school-agers. Sample from the beginning, middle, and end of each group of documents using a list of enrolled children to verify that forms exist for all of them. **Check at least 10 documents, or if there are more than 100 children enrolled, sample 10%.**
- To sample staff records, check 4 selected at random, or if there are 20 or more staff members, sample 25%.

# E. Administration

| Criterion | Director's rating | | | Validation procedure | |
|---|---|---|---|---|---|
| | Not met | Partially met | Fully met | *Staff Questionnaire E-4* | Validation decision |
| E-4. Benefits packages for full-time staff include paid leave (annual, sick, and personal), medical insurance, and retirement. Other benefits such as subsidized child care or continued education may be negotiated as unique to the situation. Benefits for part-time staff who are employed at least half-time are available on a prorated basis. | 1 | (2) | 3 | 5 (1) 10 (2) 0 (3) | ☑ V  ☐ NV |

Director's comments on rating

No medical insurance provided.

For validator _____

In this case the decision would be to validate the director's rating of partially met because it is consistent with the ratings reported by staff members on the Teaching-Staff Questionnaire. All the staff agree with the director that this criterion is not fully met.

**What happens when criteria are not validated?**

In each case where a criterion is not validated, the validator and director discuss the criterion, and the validator records on the Program Description the results of the discussion. Validators should not change the director's rating or their own.

## How is the validation visit organized?

Samples of the validation tasks and suggested timelines for completing them are provided on pages 263 to 266 of the *Guide*. These are only *samples* to aid the validator and director so that all tasks are completed in the limited time available.

At the end of the visit, the director and validator(s) sign the Validation Process Verification Form, verifying that the validator(s) followed the correct procedures during the visit. A copy of the Validation Process Verification Form appears on pages 267 to 269 of the *Guide*.

## What will the director need to do during the validation visit?

The director should be at the center approximately 30 minutes before the majority of the children arrive to meet the validator(s) and should plan to be there until the visit is completed—approximately 5:30 or 6:00 p.m. Sometimes validation visits may go longer depending on the size of the program and the organization of the materials required for validation. The director should plan to be available to the validator(s) during the entire day, but primarily in the afternoon when the exit interview about nonvalidated criteria is conducted. The director will not be needed during the time the validator is observing in classrooms. However, if the director is also a teacher, it will be necessary to be relieved of teaching duties during the afternoon to be available to work with the validator(s).

## What should the staff know?

Be sure that staff and children are prepared for the validator's visit. Some of the teaching staff will have their classrooms observed by validators. Staff should try to behave as naturally and normally as possible. Remind teachers that validators use the same observation tool that the program used during the self-study. They should also maintain their normal classroom routine. A simple explanation to the children is best, such as "Today we have a visitor who is watching to see what we do in our school. She will write things down on her paper to help her remember what she sees." The validator may need to interview the teacher briefly after the observation to obtain evidence for criteria that could not be observed. This interview should take only 10 to 15 minutes. It should take place during the teachers break or lunch period, and should not interrupt the teacher from her or his responsibilities. The director or other available person may need to relieve the teacher for this brief period of time. It may not be necessary to interview teachers if validators are able to observe enough evidence during their observations.

**What special arrangements are needed for validators?**

Validators will bring the Program Description that was completed by the director. This same form is used for completing all the validation tasks. **Validators will need**

(1) a relatively quiet space with room to work,

(2) copies of the Family Questionnaire that were returned to the program and Family Questionnaire Summary Sheet,

(3) copies of the Teaching-Staff Questionnaire filled out by staff and Teaching-Staff Questionnaire Summary Sheet, and

(4) access to the documents required by the Criteria (see List of Documents, pages 94 to 96).

---

Where documents are not available on-site, the director provides written certification by the authorized agency or individual of the document's existence, location, and level of compliance with the criteria.

---

**Points to remember:**

(1) The validator does not make the accreditation decision.

(2) The validator's job is to make sure the Program Description is accurate. The discussion of nonvalidated criteria is the director's opportunity to supply any additional information that would be helpful to the Commission.

(3) You and your staff have worked hard in preparation for the validation visit. View it as another step in a series of professional development experiences for you and your program.

(4) All directors should take time to complete the Validator Evaluation following the validation visit. The Academy relies on your feedback to protect the integrity of the system.

(5) If you feel that validation procedures were not followed accordingly, contact the Academy staff as soon as possible. Do not wait until your commission decision is made.

---

**What happens after the validation visit?**

The validator mails the completed Program Description, copies of the Early Childhood Classroom Observation, and the Validation Process Verification Form to the Academy. Staff review the results of the visit and prepare the Program Description for the Commission meeting.

Commissions meet at the end of each month. You may contact the Academy to inquire when your program is scheduled for Commission review.

# Validation Visit Tasks and Sample Timelines
## One validator—one day

| Time | Validator task |
|------|----------------|

*At least three days prior to the validation visit the validator contacts the director to make arrangements for the validation visit, establish arrival time and obtain directions.

**8:00** Approximately 8:00 a.m. or 30 minutes before the majority of the children arrive. Validator arrives at program, meets personnel, tours facility, finalizes schedule for completing validation tasks, and observes arrival of children.

**9:00** Conducts two classroom observations, observing at least 1 hour in each classroom. If part-time program; conduct 3 classroom observations in the morning and begin validation tasks of Program Description in the afternoon.

**11:30** Begins validation tasks of Program Description—Parts 1 and 3. Verifies reported results of Teaching-Staff and Family Questionnaires by sampling a few criteria from each. Verifies reported Staff Qualifications by checking the documentation for a sample of the staff.

*Establish a time to interview classroom teacher(s) for approximately 15 minutes to complete ratings for items unable to observe.

**12:00** Lunch break

**12:30** Completes validation tasks of Program Description—Parts 1 and 3. Checks documents. Checks Staffing Pattern to make sure it is completed correctly and to verify its accuracy compared to observed staff-child ratios and group sizes. Makes a validation decision for each administrative criterion in Part 3. For each nonvalidated criterion, validator records relevant comment.

**2:00** Conducts one classroom observation (if a full-day program; in half-day program observation time would be earlier and validation of Program Description—Parts 1 and 3 would follow).

**3:15** Copies validator's ratings for classrooms observed onto the Program Description—Part 2. Copies center's ratings for classrooms observed from the Classroom Observation Summary Sheet into the Program Description. Makes a validation decision for each observed criterion on Part 2 of the Program Description. For each nonvalidated criterion, validator records comments from the Early Childhood Classroom Observation into Program Description.

**4:00** Conducts exit interview with the director and validator to complete validation of Program Description—Parts 2 and 3. Validator and director discuss all nonvalidated criteria, and validator records director's and validator's comments into Program Description.

**5:30**
**or**
**6:00** Director and validator sign the Validation Process Verification Form after all other tasks are completed.

*Following the validation visit directors should complete the Director's Evaluation to provide feedback to the Academy regarding the visit and the validator's performance.

*Schedule for the day is an approximate. Variations may occur due to size and structure of program. Director's organization of required paperwork can expedite document verification by validators.

# Validation Visit Tasks and Sample Timelines
## Two validator—one day

| Time | Validator A | Validator B |
|------|-------------|-------------|

*At least three days prior the validation visit the validators contact one another and the director to make arrangements for the validation visit, establish arrival time, and obtain directions.

**8:00** Approximately 8:00 a.m. or 30 minutes before the majority of the children arrive. Both validators arrive at program, meet personnel, tour facility, finalize schedule for completing validation tasks, and observe arrival of children.

**9:00** Conducts two classroom observations, observing at least one hour in each classroom.  |  Conducts two classroom observations, observing at least one hour in each classroom.

*Establish a time to interview classroom teacher(s) for approximately 15 minutes to complete ratings for items unable to observe.

**11:30** Lunch break    Lunch break
Brief observation of children's lunch time activity is conducted by one or both validators.

**12:15** Completes validation tasks in Center Profile. Verifies reported Staff Qualifications by checking the documentation for a sample of staff. Checks Staffing Pattern to make sure its is completed correctly and to verify its accuracy compared to ratios and group sizes. Assist Validator B in the sampling of documents to validate Program Description–Part 3.  |  Completes validation tasks on Program Description–Part 3. Verifies reported results of Teaching-Staff and Family Questionnaires by sampling a few criteria from each. Checks documents, samples multiple documents such as health records. Compares evidence to make a validation decision for each administrative criterion in Part 3. For each nonvalidated criterion, validator records relevant comment.

**2:00** Conducts classroom observation.    Conducts classroom observation.

**3:15** Copies validator's ratings for classrooms observed onto the Program Description–Part 2. Copies center's ratings for classrooms observed from the Classroom Observation Summary Sheet onto the Program Description. Makes a validation decision for each observed criterion on Part 2 of the Program Description. For each nonvalidated criterion, validator records comments from the Early Childhood Classroom Observation into the Program Description.  |  Assist Validator A.

**4:00** Conducts exit interview with the director and both validators to complete validation of Program Description–Part 2 and 3. Validators and director discuss all nonvalidated criteria and validator records director's and validator's comments into the Program Description.

**5:30 or 6:00** Director and validators sign the Validation Process Verification Form after all other tasks are completed.

*Following the validation visit directors should complete the Director's Evaluation to provide feedback to the Academy regarding the visit and the validator's performance.

*Schedule for the day is an approximate. Variations may occur due to size and structure of program. Director's organization of required paperwork can expedite document verification by validators.

# Validation Visit Tasks and Sample Timelines
# Two validators—two days

## Day 1

| Time | Validator A | Validator B |
|------|-------------|-------------|
| | *At least three days prior the validation visit the validators contact one another and the director to make arrangements for the validation visit, establish arrival time, and obtain directions. | |
| 8:00 | Approximately 8:00 a.m. or 30 minutes before the majority of the children arrive. Both validators arrive at program, meet personnel, tour facility, finalize schedule for completing validation tasks, and observe arrival of children. | |
| 9:00 | Conducts two classroom observations, observing at least 1 hour in each classroom. | Conducts two classroom observations, observing at least 1 hour in each classroom. |
| | *Establish a time to interview classroom teacher(s) for approximately 15 minutes to complete ratings for items unable to observe. | |
| 11:30 | Lunch break<br>Brief observation of children's lunch time activity is conducted by one or both validators. | Lunch break |
| 12:30 | Completes validation tasks on Program Description–Part 3. Verifies reported results of Teaching-Staff and Family Questionnaires by sampling a few criteria from each. Checks documents, samples multiple documents such as health records. Compares evidence to make a validation decision for each administrative criterion in Part 3. For each nonvalidated criterion, record relevant comments. | Verifies reported Staff Qualifications by checking the documentation for a sample of staff. Assist Validator A in the sampling of documents to validate Program Description–Part 3. |
| 2:00 | Conducts one or two classroom observations. | Conducts one or two classroom observations. |
| | *Establish a time to interview classroom teacher(s) for approximately 15 minutes to complete ratings for items unable to observe. | |
| 3:15<br>or<br>4:30 | Copies validator's ratings for classrooms observed on day 1 into the Program Description–Part 2. Copies center's ratings for classrooms observed from the Classroom Observation Summary Sheet into the Program Description. | Assist Validator A. |
| 4:30<br>or<br>5:30 | End of Day 1 | End of Day 1 |

*Schedule for the day is approximate. Variations may occur due to size and structure of program. Some tasks from Day 1 may be completed on Day 2.

# Validation Visit Tasks and Sample Timelines
## Two validators—two days

**Day 2**

| Time | Validator A | Validator B |
|------|-------------|-------------|
| 8:00 | Approximately 8:00 a.m. or 30 minutes before the majority of the children arrive. Both validators arrive at program and finalize schedule for completing validation tasks. | |
| 8:30 | Conducts one or two classroom observations. | Conducts one or two classroom observations. |
| | *Establish a time to interview classroom teacher(s) for approximately 15 minutes to complete ratings for items unable to observe. | |
| 11:30 | Lunch break | Lunch break |
| 12:30 | Copies ratings from second day observations into Program Description—Part 2. Copies corresponding ratings from Classroom Observation Summary Sheet. Makes validation decision and records comments for each nonvalidated criterion. | Assist Validator A. |
| 2:00 | Conducts exit interview with the director and both validators to complete the validation of Program Description—Parts 2 and 3. Validators and director discuss all nonvalidated criteria and validator records director's and validators' comments. | |
| 4:00 | Director and validators complete Validation Process Verification Form after all other tasks are completed. | |

*Following the validation visit directors should complete the Director's Evaluation to provide feedback to the Academy regarding the visit and the validator's performance.

*Schedule for the day is an approximate. Variations may occur due to size and structure of program. Director's organization of required paperwork can expedite document verification by validators.

# Validation Visit Tasks and Sample Timelines
## Two validators—first day
## Three validators—second day

Follow timelines for two validators—two days; except that on second day, Validator C does same activities as Validator A.

National Association for the Education of Young Children

# Validation Process Verification Form

Name of program _____

Date of visit _____

Directions: During the validation visit, the director and validator(s) initial each procedure listed below, verifying that it was properly followed. At the end of the visit, the director and validator(s) sign the form verifying that all procedures were properly followed.

| **Validation procedure** | **Procedure properly followed** | |
| --- | --- | --- |
| | **Director** | **Validator(s)** |
| Validator(s) meets with director to review validation tasks and plan visit. | _____ | _____ |
| Validator(s) briefly tours facility. | _____ | _____ |
| Groups are randomly selected to be observed by validator(s) with an attempt made to see as many different age groups as possible observing at least 50% of the groups. | _____ | _____ |
| Validator(s) compares ratings of observed groups to ratings reported by program and makes validation decision for each criterion on Part 2 of Program Description applying decision rules. | _____ | _____ |
| Validator(s) verifies accuracy of Family and Teaching-Staff Questionnaire Summary Sheets. (If Summary Sheet(s) are inaccurate, director redoes Summary Sheet(s) and corrects Program Description.) | _____ | _____ |
| Validator(s) provided access to written documents required by the Criteria (where information is not available on site, director provides certification by authorized agency or individual of the documents' existence and location). | _____ | _____ |

| **Validation procedure** | **Procedure properly followed** | |
|---|---|---|
| | **Director** | **Validator(s)** |
| Validator compares evidence and makes validation decision for each criterion on Part 3 of the Program Description. | _____ | _____ |
| Validator and director discuss each nonvalidated criterion, and validator records director's and validator's comments on the Program Description. | _____ | _____ |

**For director:**

As _____
                                    (Title)

of _____,
                          (Name of program)

I affirm that all validation procedures described above were properly completed. I affirm that I have had an opportunity to comment about each nonvalidated criterion, that I have read the comments of myself and the validator(s) recorded on the Program Description, and that the comments accurately represent the results of my discussion with the validator(s) about each nonvalidated criterion.

Signature _____

Date _____

**If one or more of the validation procedures were improperly followed, contact the Academy staff immediately to report the violation(s).**

**For validator:**

I _____ ,
                                    (Name)

as a validator for the National Association for the Education of Young Children, affirm that all validation procedures described above were properly completed during this validation visit. I affirm my commitment to maintaining confidentiality regarding all information obtained about this program through the Program Description and during the validation visit, except as required by law.

Signature _____

Date _____

**For validator:**

I _____ ,
                                    (Name)

as a validator for the National Association for the Education of Young Children, affirm that all validation procedures described above were properly completed during this validation visit. I affirm my commitment to maintaining confidentiality regarding all information obtained about this program through the Program Description and during the validation visit, except as required by law.

Signature _____

Date _____

**For validator:**

I _____ ,
                                    (Name)

as a validator for the National Association for the Education of Young Children, affirm that all validation procedures described above were properly completed during this validation visit. I affirm my commitment to maintaining confidentiality regarding all information obtained about this program through the Program Description and during the validation visit, except as required by law.

Signature _____

Date _____

# Section 9

## The Accreditation Decision

# Section 9

## The Accreditation Decision

**Who makes the accreditation decision?**

Accreditation decisions are made by a combination of internal and external Commission review. Academy staff serve as commissioners by meeting in teams to discuss and review programs being considered. External commissioners, who are appointed by the NAEYC Governing Board, serve as auditors of the staff's preliminary decisions.

**What information do commissioners receive?**

Commissioners consider the validated Program Description. The information on the Program Description includes the director's original report of the program's compliance with the Criteria and an explanation for any criteria that are not met or partially met, the results of validation, and the validator's and director's comments about all nonvalidated criteria. It is crucial that directors ensure that the Program Description presented to the Commission fairly and accurately describes their program.

**How do commissioners decide whether to accredit a program?**

The Commission decision allows for the application of professional judgment within the limits of the Criteria. Accreditation decisions are based on substantial compliance and rely on professional judgment rather than a point system. Commissioners consider

- the unique aspects of the program,
- the context in which the program operates, and
- the overall impact of varying degrees of compliance with the Criteria.

Although there is no explicit weighting system, it is obvious that some criteria are more important than others. For example, providing developmentally appropriate activities is certainly more critical than providing a change of clothing.

Greatest weight is given to the following components of the Criteria:
- interactions among teachers and children
- curriculum
- health and safety
- group size and ratios
- staff qualifications and development

Because the system involves actually observing what happens to children in the program, we give greatest weight to the results of the observations.

The administrative criteria such as the number of adults to children, the qualifications of the staff, the personnel policies, and the operating procedures support the delivery of quality care and education in the classroom. Compliance with these administrative criteria increases the likelihood that positive interactions and appropriate curriculum will occur in classrooms; however, compliance with the administrative criteria does not guarantee that such high quality experiences will occur.

Having had several years of experience making accreditation decisions, the Academy now has a clearer picture of how the early childhood profession defines high quality. What has become clear is that there are important relationships between criteria that can never be clearly communicated through a simple listing of the standards. In early childhood programs, good things tend to happen together. In addition, the way in which programs meet standards may sometimes result in the opposite effect than the intent of the Criteria. Some examples will clarify the complex issues involved. The most obvious example of how Criteria are related concerns staff-child ratios. Ratios and group sizes are important predictors of quality. If a program is in compliance with NAEYC's standards for staffing, it is more likely that the adult-child interactions will be positive and the curriculum will be developmentally appropriate. However, compliance with staffing standards does not guarantee this type of quality for children. Other criteria also have an effect. For example, the amount and kind of training the teachers have had, the administrator's qualifications, the availability of appropriate materials, and the organization of the environment also play a vital role in influencing the nature of the child's experiences.

An attempt to meet the "letter" of the standard may sometimes result in not meeting the "spirit" of the standard. For example, in order to maintain staff-child ratios throughout the day, some programs regroup (or reshuffle) children several times. These transitions can be very difficult, especially for younger children. In fact, in these situations it would be better to exceed the ratios for a short time and require fewer regrouping of children. In short, one criterion cannot be addressed in isolation from others.

From our accreditation experience, we have found that having a well qualified early childhood specialist to direct the educational program and well-trained teachers are more powerful predictors of classroom practice than are staff-child are ratios and group sizes. As a result, programs have been accredited in which criteria for ratios and groups sizes are not fully met in every classroom, while some programs that are in compliance with these standards have been deferred. Because we do not exclude programs that do not meet our staffing standards, we have had a unique research opportunity to collect date about how those standards influence children's experience. Not surprisingly, **we have found that the more out-of-compliance a program is with the staffing criteria, the less likely it is that we will observe positive interactions among adults and children and developmentally appropriate curriculum practice.** Compliance with the staffing criteria not only affects, but actually predicts, compliance with other criteria.

The decision to accredit a program is based on quantitative information as well as qualitative analysis. For instance, the more criteria that are not met, the less likely is a positive accreditation decision. But noncompliance with a few key criteria may result in a negative decision because the children are judged to be at-risk of harm. For example, a program that used physical punishment (Criterion A-6) or did not adequately supervise children (Criterion H-7) could not be accredited until those situations were corrected.

The Commission also considers the unique context of the program. For example, a program may have slightly less indoor space than is required, but it may be located in a warm climate where teachers do many activities outdoors. Similarly, the program may be located in an arctic climate where daily outdoor play is impossible, but the program demonstrates how they provide opportunities for large-muscle activity and fresh air through alternate means.

A high-quality program for young children and families is more than the sum of its parts. The Criteria listed in this book provide the framework from which individual programs will build. As a result, accredited programs will not all look alike. Some are in church basements, others in public school buildings, while others have specially designed model facilities. What they share in common is that they have demonstrated substantial compliance with the profession's Criteria for High-Quality Early Childhood Programs and they have demonstrated a commitment to self-evaluation and improvement.

> The decision to accredit does *not* require 100% compliance with the Criteria. Accreditation requires substantial compliance. Where criteria are not met or partially met, it is important that the director provides the validators and the commissioners with clear information about the program's level of compliance with the Criteria. Also, when a director feels that a criterion is met through alternate means, it is important to provide an explanation.

## What options do the commissioners have?

Academy staff work with the program director to assist in evaluating and improving the program and in preparing the Program Description. **Academy staff are available by telephone to answer questions during the three-step process.** Prior to assigning validators, Academy staff review the Program Description and may communicate with the director to ensure that the Program Description is as accurate and complete as possible.

Two decisions are possible: to accredit the program or to defer accreditation until improvements have been made. When commissioners feel that validation procedures were not followed or they do not have enough information to make a decision, a revisit may be necessary.

**What happens if accreditation is deferred?**

The program receives a detailed Commission Decision Report explaining why accreditation was deferred and what the program must do to achieve accreditation. The program also receives a copy of the Academy's Appeals Procedures that describes the three ways for the deferred decision to be appealed—

1. Accreditation may be pursued by addressing recommendations from the Commission Decision Report and implementing improvements to the program. The program may take up to nine months to make necessary improvements. An additional visit is then necessary to verify program improvements. The program will be charged a fee for the verification visit.

2. The decision may be automatically appealed to another Commission for a second decision. The second Commission is not informed that the case is an appeal. If the second Commission decides to accredit the program, accreditation is awarded for a three-year period. If the decision to defer is upheld by a second Commission and the program disagrees with the decision, the program may pursue accreditation as described above under #1.

3. A program may appeal the deferred decision on the grounds that validation procedures were not properly followed. A program must submit documentation and/or evidence that validation procedures were not properly followed.

A deferred program must notify the Academy of its intent to appeal, and which option, within 30 days after receipt of the Commission Decision Report.

**What happens if the program is accredited?**

The program receives a letter of congratulations. The original validated Program Description is returned along with a copy of the Commission Decision Report that provides recommendations for further improvement and the Annual Report. Receiving accreditation is a recognition that is reserved for early childhood programs that demonstrate compliance with the profession's Criteria for High-Quality Early Childhood Programs.

In order to publicize your achievement the Academy provides materials to promote your accreditation:

- a certificate,
- a full-color poster,
- logo sheets,
- a sample press release,
- ribbons for staff, and
- multiple copies of a parent brochure describing what accreditation means.

Advertising accreditation or affiliation with NAEYC is a privilege given only to those programs that are currently accredited by NAEYC.

# Section 10

## Maintaining Accreditation and Reaccreditation

### Annual Report
### Reaccreditation Application

# Section 10
## Maintaining Accreditation and Reaccreditation

**How is accreditation maintained?**

Accreditation is valid for three years. During that time, accredited programs are required to

- Submit an Annual Report that is used to indicate any changes that have taken place in the program such as staff turnover and any improvements made in response to the Commission's recommendations. When programs experience staff turnover, a revisit may be necessary to verify continued compliance with the Criteria. The Annual Report also requests information regarding the program's compliance with criteria that should be met on an annual basis, such as the annual staff and program evaluation. Failure to submit an Annual Report may be grounds for withdrawal of accreditation. **The Annual Report is due to the Academy on or before the first anniversary of accreditation.**

- Report changes in director or administration to the Academy as soon as the changes occur.

- Report change of ownership and/or location to the Academy as soon as possible and submit to a site visit.

- Respond to complaints submitted to the Academy regarding alleged lack-of-compliance with the Criteria. See *Accreditation Criteria & Procedures of the National Association for the Education of Young Children* for the complaint procedures.

## Reaccreditation

In order to maintain accreditation a program must renew the three-step process. The reaccreditation process is similar to the initial accreditation process because programs seeking reaccreditation will complete the three-step process again. The reaccreditation process will be easier for those programs that continue to comply with the Criteria.

On the second anniversary of accreditation programs should apply for reaccreditation. The results of the reaccreditation self-study should be submitted to the Academy for validation at least 90 days prior to expiration of accreditation. The Academy staff will coordinate the validation visit and the results of the visit will be submitted to the Commission for a reaccreditation decision. If the completed Program Description is not received by the Academy prior to expiration, accreditation will lapse and the program will be removed from the list of accredited programs. Expired programs may not use the signs, seals, certificates, logos, posters, or other indications of accreditation.

**Summary of reaccreditation procedures**

- On the second anniversary of accreditation the program orders self-study materials for reaccreditation.
- Program completes the self-study process and submits the completed Program Description and validation fee to the Academy at least 90 days prior to expiration.
- Academy staff arranges validation visit, visit occurs and results are submitted to Commission.
- Program is notified by mail of Commission decision.

| Program ID Number |
| --- |

Annual Report due _____

National Association for the Education of Young Children

# Annual Report by Accredited Program

## Instructions

Accreditation by the National Association for the Education of Young Children is valid for three years. During that period, accredited programs are required to submit Annual Reports on the first anniversary of accreditation. The purpose of the Annual Report is to

(1) inform the National Academy of Early Childhood Programs of any program improvements made in response to the recommendations of the Commission,

(2) inform the Academy of major changes that have occurred in the program since accreditation was granted, and

(3) report the program's compliance with criteria that require action on an annual basis.

The Academy sends the Annual Report to programs when accreditation is awarded. The Annual Report is due at NAEYC on the first anniversary of accreditation. The Annual Report should be completed by the director or other appropriate person who is responsible for the daily operation of the program. When the Annual Report is completed, the director should identify an individual who is knowledgeable about the program to read the Annual Report and verify its accuracy (see page 290). That person could be an assistant director, lead teacher, board member or chair, parent, or other individual who is familiar with the daily operation of the program.

If you have questions about completing this form, please e-mail the Academy staff at academy@naeyc.org or call 202-232-8777 or 800-424-2460.

Date _____

Name of program _____

Name and title of person completing this form _____

_____

Telephone _____ FAX _____

E-mail _____

❑ Check here is the person listed above was not the program director when accreditation was granted. List new director's qualifications on the chart provided.

❑ Check here if there has been a change of ownership since accreditation was granted.

---

**Please provide the information below ONLY if there has been a change.**

Location of program

Street _____

City _____ State _____ ZIP _____

Number of children enrolled _____

Enrollment is _____ fewer than when the program became accredited.
       (Number of children)

Enrollement is _____ greater than when the program became accredited.
       (Number of children)

Number of children enrolled by developmental level

_____ Infants (birth through 12 months)        _____ School-agers (6-year-olds and older)

_____ Toddlers (13 through 35 months)           _____ Kindergartners (usually 5-year-olds)

_____ Preschoolers (3- through 5-year-olds)

---

# Part 1—Reporting program improvements

Please refer to the Recommendations for Further Improvement in your program's Commission Decision Report to complete this part of the form. Fill in the appropriate criterion number, circle your rating of the program's compliance with the criterion currently, and add any brief comments you want to make about improvements made in response to the Commission's recommendations. For example, report ongoing professional development obtained by staff during the last year.

|  | **Director's rating** |  |  | **Director's comment on rating** |
|---|---|---|---|---|
| **Criterion number** | Not met | Partially met | Fully met | |
| | 1 | 2 | 3 | |
| | | | | |
| **Criterion number** | 1 | 2 | 3 | |
| | | | | |
| **Criterion number** | 1 | 2 | 3 | |
| | | | | |
| **Criterion number** | 1 | 2 | 3 | |
| | | | | |
| **Criterion number** | 1 | 2 | 3 | |
| | | | | |
| **Criterion number** | 1 | 2 | 3 | |
| | | | | |
| **Criterion number** | 1 | 2 | 3 | |
| | | | | |
| **Criterion number** | 1 | 2 | 3 | |

# Reporting program improvements *continued*

| | Director's rating | | | Director's comment on rating |
|---|---|---|---|---|
| | Not met | Partially met | Fully met | |

**Criterion number**

_____

[1] [2] [3]

_____
_____
_____

**Criterion number**

_____

[1] [2] [3]

_____
_____
_____

**Criterion number**

_____

[1] [2] [3]

_____
_____
_____

**Criterion number**

_____

[1] [2] [3]

_____
_____
_____

**Criterion number**

_____

[1] [2] [3]

_____
_____
_____

**Criterion number**

_____

[1] [2] [3]

_____
_____
_____

**Criterion number**

_____

[1] [2] [3]

_____
_____
_____

**Criterion number**

_____

[1] [2] [3]

_____
_____
_____

**Criterion number**

_____

[1] [2] [3]

_____
_____

## Part 2—Reporting changes

Please report any major changes in your program. For example, criteria that were previously fully met (rated [3]), that are currently partially met (rate a [2]) or not met (rate a [1]). Use the separate pages that follow to report changes in Staff Qualifications and Staffing Pattern for staff members who have been employed since accreditation was granted.

|  | Director's rating | | | Director's comment on rating |
|---|---|---|---|---|

**Criterion number**

Not met [1]   Partially met [2]   Fully met [3]

_____

**Criterion number**

[1]   [2]   [3]

_____

**Criterion number**

[1]   [2]   [3]

_____

**Criterion number**

[1]   [2]   [3]

_____

**Report staff changes**—We need to know the percentage of staff turnover that has occurred since accreditation was granted and the qualifications of the current staff. Compare your *current* staff who were employed at the time accreditation was granted, and answer the questions below:

There are _____ lead teachers; _____ of the leads were employed here 12 months ago.
  (total number of)        (number of)

There are _____ Assistant Teachers; _____ of the Assistant Teachers were employed here 12 months ago.
  (total number of)           (number of)

Comment on the turnover data. (Add additional pages if necessary.)

Use the chart below to report the Teaching-Staff Qualifications for each administrator and teaching-staff member working directly with children who was not employed when accreditation was granted.

Check the highest level achieved in formal education and early childhood/child development training. Check all credentials completed. An ECE/CD unit = 16 classroom hours or 1 credit hour of study in early childhood education or child development. ECE/CD units may be earned through college level courses, vocational-technical courses, or other forms of professional development. Be sure to identify all staff members in this chart and on the Staffing Pattern using the same first name and last initials.

| | Teaching staff members | | | | | |
|---|---|---|---|---|---|---|
| Staff member (use first name and last initial only) | | | | | | |
| Job title | | | | | | |
| Years of relevant experience | | | | | | |
| Date of employment in this program | | | | | | |
| Formal education completed Some high school | | | | | | |
| High school graduate | | | | | | |
| Some college | | | | | | |
| College graduate (specify major) | | | | | | |
| Early childhood training completed 1–6 units in ECE/CD | | | | | | |
| 7–12 units in ECE/CD | | | | | | |
| 13 or more units in ECE/CD (specify number) | | | | | | |
| A.A. degree in ECE/CD | | | | | | |
| B.A./B.S. degree in ECE/CD | | | | | | |
| Graduate work in ECE/CD (specify units) | | | | | | |
| Master's degree in ECE/CD | | | | | | |
| Doctorate degree in ECE/CD | | | | | | |
| Credentials/certificates CDA (year received) | | | | | | |
| State certificate in early childhood education | | | | | | |
| State certificate in elementary education | | | | | | |
| Other (specify the credential or comprehensive training program and the number of ECE/CD units required) | | | | | | |

| | Teaching staff members | | | | | |
|---|---|---|---|---|---|---|
| Staff member (use first name and last initial only) | | | | | | |
| Job title | | | | | | |
| Years of relevant experience | | | | | | |
| Date of employment in this program | | | | | | |
| Formal education completed<br>    Some high school | | | | | | |
|     High school graduate | | | | | | |
|     Some college | | | | | | |
| College graduate (specify major) | | | | | | |
| Early childhood training completed<br>    1–6 units in ECE/CD | | | | | | |
|     7–12 units in ECE/CD | | | | | | |
|     13 or more units in ECE/CD (specify number) | | | | | | |
|     A.A. degree in ECE/CD | | | | | | |
|     B.A./B.S. degree in ECE/CD | | | | | | |
|     Graduate work in ECE/CD (specify units) | | | | | | |
|     Master's degree in ECE/CD | | | | | | |
|     Doctorate degree in ECE/CD | | | | | | |
| Credentials/certificates<br>    CDA (year received) | | | | | | |
|     State certificate in early childhood education | | | | | | |
|     State certificate in elementary education | | | | | | |
| Other (specify the credential or comprehensive training program and the number of ECE/CD units required) | | | | | | |

**Staffing Pattern**—use the following chart to report major changes in your staffing pattern. Report groups of children that have been added. Only report grouping changes if they affect your program's compliance with the criteria for group size and staff-child ratio (**F-1** and **F-2**).

For each hour of the day indicate the number of children enrolled in the group, the staff members assigned to the group (use first names and last initial only), and the hours worked by the staff members. A *group* is the number of children assigned to a staff member or team of staff members occupying an individual classroom or well-defined space within a larger room. (See the examples under Section 4 of the *Guide.*)

## New-Staffing Pattern

| Group of children | Staffing Pattern | | | | | | | | | | | | | |
|---|---|---|---|---|---|---|---|---|---|---|---|---|---|---|
| **Group name** | **AM** | | | | | **Number of children enrolled each hour** | | | | | | | | **PM** |
| | 6:00 | 7:00 | 8:00 | 9:00 | 10:00 | 11:00 | 12:00 | 1:00 | 2:00 | 3:00 | 4:00 | 5:00 | 6:00 | 7:00 |
| | | | | | | | | | | | | | | |
| | | | **Number of staff in attendance each hour** | | | | | | | | | | | |
| **Age range    Number** | | | | | | | | | | | | | | |
| Infants _____ | Hours of each staff member | | | | | | | | | | | | | |
| Toddlers _____ | | | | | | | | | | | | | | |
| Preschoolers _____ | | | | | | | | | | | | | | |
| Kindergartners _____ | | | | | | | | | | | | | | |
| School-agers _____ | | | | | | | | | | | | | | |
| **Group name** | **AM** | | | | | **Number of children enrolled each hour** | | | | | | | | **PM** |
| | 6:00 | 7:00 | 8:00 | 9:00 | 10:00 | 11:00 | 12:00 | 1:00 | 2:00 | 3:00 | 4:00 | 5:00 | 6:00 | 7:00 |
| | | | | | | | | | | | | | | |
| | | | **Number of staff in attendance each hour** | | | | | | | | | | | |
| **Age range    Number** | | | | | | | | | | | | | | |
| Infants _____ | Hours of each staff member | | | | | | | | | | | | | |
| Toddlers _____ | | | | | | | | | | | | | | |
| Preschoolers _____ | | | | | | | | | | | | | | |
| Kindergartners _____ | | | | | | | | | | | | | | |
| School-agers _____ | | | | | | | | | | | | | | |
| **Group name** | **AM** | | | | | **Number of children enrolled each hour** | | | | | | | | **PM** |
| | 6:00 | 7:00 | 8:00 | 9:00 | 10:00 | 11:00 | 12:00 | 1:00 | 2:00 | 3:00 | 4:00 | 5:00 | 6:00 | 7:00 |
| | | | | | | | | | | | | | | |
| | | | **Number of staff in attendance each hour** | | | | | | | | | | | |
| **Age range    Number** | | | | | | | | | | | | | | |
| Infants _____ | Hours of each staff member | | | | | | | | | | | | | |
| Toddlers _____ | | | | | | | | | | | | | | |
| Preschoolers _____ | | | | | | | | | | | | | | |
| Kindergartners _____ | | | | | | | | | | | | | | |
| School-agers _____ | | | | | | | | | | | | | | |

## Staffing Pattern *continued*

| Group of children | Staffing Pattern | | | | | | | | | | | | | |
|---|---|---|---|---|---|---|---|---|---|---|---|---|---|---|

**Group name**

| AM | Number of children enrolled each hour | | | | | | | | | | | | PM |
|---|---|---|---|---|---|---|---|---|---|---|---|---|---|
| 6:00 | 7:00 | 8:00 | 9:00 | 10:00 | 11:00 | 12:00 | 1:00 | 2:00 | 3:00 | 4:00 | 5:00 | 6:00 | 7:00 |
|  |  |  |  |  |  |  |  |  |  |  |  |  |  |

Number of staff in attendance each hour

|  |  |  |  |  |  |  |  |  |  |  |  |  |  |
|---|---|---|---|---|---|---|---|---|---|---|---|---|---|

**Age range      Number**

Hours of each staff member

Infants _____

Toddlers _____

Preschoolers _____

Kindergartners _____

School-agers _____

**Group name**

| AM | Number of children enrolled each hour | | | | | | | | | | | | PM |
|---|---|---|---|---|---|---|---|---|---|---|---|---|---|
| 6:00 | 7:00 | 8:00 | 9:00 | 10:00 | 11:00 | 12:00 | 1:00 | 2:00 | 3:00 | 4:00 | 5:00 | 6:00 | 7:00 |
|  |  |  |  |  |  |  |  |  |  |  |  |  |  |

Number of staff in attendance each hour

|  |  |  |  |  |  |  |  |  |  |  |  |  |  |
|---|---|---|---|---|---|---|---|---|---|---|---|---|---|

**Age range      Number**

Hours of each staff member

Infants _____

Toddlers _____

Preschoolers _____

Kindergartners _____

School-agers _____

**Group name**

| AM | Number of children enrolled each hour | | | | | | | | | | | | PM |
|---|---|---|---|---|---|---|---|---|---|---|---|---|---|
| 6:00 | 7:00 | 8:00 | 9:00 | 10:00 | 11:00 | 12:00 | 1:00 | 2:00 | 3:00 | 4:00 | 5:00 | 6:00 | 7:00 |
|  |  |  |  |  |  |  |  |  |  |  |  |  |  |

Number of staff in attendance each hour

|  |  |  |  |  |  |  |  |  |  |  |  |  |  |
|---|---|---|---|---|---|---|---|---|---|---|---|---|---|

**Age range      Number**

Hours of each staff member

Infants _____

Toddlers _____

Preschoolers _____

Kindergartners _____

School-agers _____

**Group name**

| AM | Number of children enrolled each hour | | | | | | | | | | | | PM |
|---|---|---|---|---|---|---|---|---|---|---|---|---|---|
| 6:00 | 7:00 | 8:00 | 9:00 | 10:00 | 11:00 | 12:00 | 1:00 | 2:00 | 3:00 | 4:00 | 5:00 | 6:00 | 7:00 |
|  |  |  |  |  |  |  |  |  |  |  |  |  |  |

Number of staff in attendance each hour

|  |  |  |  |  |  |  |  |  |  |  |  |  |  |
|---|---|---|---|---|---|---|---|---|---|---|---|---|---|

**Age range      Number**

Hours of each staff member

Infants _____

Toddlers _____

Preschoolers _____

Kindergartners _____

School-agers _____

# Part 3—Reporting compliance with criteria requiring annual action

Please rate your program for each of the following criteria:

**Criterion** | **Rating** | **Comments**

| | Not met | Partially met | Fully met |
|---|---|---|---|

**C-6b.** Conferences are held at least once a year and at other times, as needed, to discuss children's progress, accomplishments, and difficulties at home and in the program.
[1] [2] [3]

**E-8a.** Accident protection and liability insurance coverage is maintained for children and adults. (*Present policy and/or most recent canceled check or receipt for payment.*)
[1] [2] [3]

**E-8b.** Vehicle insurance is maintained on any vehicle owned or leased by the facility and used to transport children.
[1] [2] [3]

☐ **Not applicable**

**H-1.** The program presents valid certification that it is in compliance with all legal requirements for protection of the health and safety of children in group settings, such as building codes, sanitation, water quality, and fire protection. The program is licensed to operate by the appropriate state/local agencies. The program maintains a high level of compliance with licensing standards, free of a record of repeated serious violations. If exempt from licensing, the program demonstrates compliance with its own state or local community's regulations (building, sanitation, and licensing codes) for early childhood programs/child care centers subject to licensing.
[1] [2] [3]

**J-1a.** All staff, including the program administrator, are evaluated at least annually by the director or other appropriate supervisor.
[1] [2] [3]

**J-1b.** Results of staff evaluation are written and confidential. They are discussed privately with the staff member.
[1] [2] [3]

# Reporting compliance with criteria requiring annual action *continued*

| Criterion | Rating | | | Comments |
|---|---|---|---|---|
| | Not met | Partially met | Fully met | |
| **J-1c.** Staff evaluations include classroom observation. Evaluation is based on the employees's job description and previously established goals for improvement. | 1 | 2 | 3 | |
| **J-1d.** Staff are informed of evaluation criteria in advance. | 1 | 2 | 3 | |
| **J-1e.** Staff have an opportunity to evaluate their own performance. | 1 | 2 | 3 | |
| **J-1f.** A plan for staff training is generated from the evaluation process. | 1 | 2 | 3 | |
| **J-2a.** At least annually, administrators, families, staff, school-age children, and other routinely participating adults are involved in evaluating the programs effectiveness in meeting the needs of children and families. | 1 | 2 | 3 | |
| **J-2b.** The program regularly establishes goals for continuous improvement and innovation. | 1 | 2 | 3 | |

# Verification

Please read and sign.

I certify that the attached Annual Report is true and accurate to the best of my knowledge. I understand that accreditation is null and void if false information is knowingly submitted to the Academy at any time. I understand that failure to submit an Annual Report may be grounds for withdrawal of accreditation. I understand that on the basis of information reported herein, the Academy may initiate a review of the program's compliance with the accreditation Criteria, that the program may be required to respond in writing or submit to a site visit. I understand that accreditation may be revoked if the Academy determines that the program is no longer in substantial compliance with the Criteria or if the program fails to comply with Academy procedures.

_____

Signature of program director or authorized administrator

_____

Name (please print)

_____

Date

Please identify an appropriate person within your program to verify that the attached Annul Report is true and accurate. That individual should read the Annual Report and certify its accuracy by signing below:

I have read the attached Annual Report and verify that it is true and accurate to the best of my knowledge.

_____

Signature of person verifying accuracy

_____

Name and title of person verifying accuracy (please print)

Return to
National Association for the Education of Young Children
1509 16th Street, N.W., Washington, DC 20036-1426

---

FOR OFFICE USE ONLY

Date Annual Report received _____

# National Academy of Early Childhood Programs
## *Order form for accreditation self-study materials*

**Mail to**
National Academy of Early Childhood Programs
NAEYC
1509 16th Street, N.W., Washington, DC 20036-1846
202-328-2601   800-424-2460

Name of program _____

Director _____

Address of program _____

_____

_____
| City | State | ZIP + 4 |

County _____ Telephone _____
(Area Code)

Name and address of administrative agency (if different from above)
☐ Check here if materials should be sent to *this* address.

_____

_____

_____

## Program information

Hours of operation _____

Total number of children enrolled in the program _____

Number of classrooms (or clearly defined groups of children, such as a.m. and p.m. groups) _____

Number of staff members working directly with children _____

Do you need the Parent Questionnaire in Spanish? If so, how many copies? _____

Payment of the application fee must accompany this order (see Accreditation fee structure on page 294). Please make check payable to "NAEYC." This order and accompanying application fee entitle the designated program to receive self-study materials from the National Academy of Early Childhood Programs. This fee does *not* entitle the program to an on-site visit or accreditation. If the program wishes to pursue accreditation, the completed Program Description form must be submitted to the Academy with payment of the validation fee.

**For NAEYC use**

Date _____ Ck. # _____ Amt. $ _____

Program Code _____ Level _____

# Accreditation fee structure

The National Academy of Early Childhood Programs sponsors a national, voluntary accreditation system for early childhood centers and schools. The accreditation system is a non-profit, self-supporting, and permanent project. Its purpose is to improve the quality of early childhood programs in the United States. The ongoing operation of the system is sustained by fees paid by participating programs.

The cost of accreditation varies depending upon the number of children enrolled in the program. Programs occupying different locations, even if administered by a central agency, must apply and be considered separately. A program that has one administrator and that occupies more than one adjacent building is considered one program.

## Accreditation Fees
### (effective January 1998)

|  | Application | Validation | TOTAL |
|---|---|---|---|
| **Level 1** <br> (60 or fewer children) | $125 | $300 | $425 |
| **Level 2** <br> (61–120) | $200 | $450 | $650 |
| **Level 3** <br> (121–240) | $250 | $575 | $825 |
| **Level 4** <br> (241–360) | $300 | $700 | $1,000 |

**For each additional 120 children, each fee increases $50.**

Accreditation fees are paid at two points in the process.

1. The **application fee** is paid to initiate the process and to receive self-study materials. This fee is determined by the total number of children enrolled regardless of whether they attend on a half-day or full-day basis.

The program receives these self-study materials:
- *Accreditation Criteria & Procedures of the National Academy of Early Childhood Programs*
- *Guide to Accreditation*
- Multiple copies of forms and questionnaires
- Program Description form
- Consultation by telephone
- Subscription to *The Academy Update* newsletter (published three times each year)

2. The **validation fee** is paid if based on the results of the self-study a program decides to pursue accreditation. This fee is determined by the largest number of children attending on a given day. For this fee, the program receives an on-site validation visit and the accreditation decision.

Accreditation is valid for three years. No additional fees are paid during that time.

# Section 11

## Bibliography

# Section 11

# Bibliography

*NAEYC gratefully acknowledges the numerous, specific 1998 Criteria revisions provided by*

City of Madison Child Care Unit, Office of Community Services. 1990. Madison, WI: City Certification Standards for Centers.

*The Criteria were developed from a thorough review of the research, theoretical, and practical literature on the effects of various components of an early childhood program on children. The following is a selected bibliography of those sources that were most applicable in developing and revising the Criteria:*

American Public Health Association & American Academy of Pediatrics. 1992. *Caring for our children: National health and safety performance—Guidelines for out-of-home child care programs.* Washington, DC: American Public Health Association.

Arnett, J. 1989. Caregivers in day care centers: Does training matter? *Journal of Applied Developmental Psychology* 10: 541–552.

Barnett, W.S. 1995. Long-term effects of early childhood programs on cognitive and social outcomes. Center for the Future of Children, Long-term outcomes of early childhood programs. *The Future of Children* 5 (3):25–50.

Bloom, P. J. 1996. *Improving the quality of work life in the early childhood setting: Resource guide and technical manual for the Early Childhood Work Environment Survey.* Rev. ed. Wheeling, IL: Early Childhood Professional Development Project, National-Louis University.

Bloom, P.J. 1996. The quality of work life in early childhood programs: Does accreditation make a difference? In *NAEYC accreditation: A decade of learning and the years ahead,* eds. S. Bredekamp & B.A. Willer. Washington, DC: National Association for the Education of Young Children.

Bloom, P.J., & M. Sheerer. 1992. The effect of leadership training on child care program quality. *Early Childhood Research Quarterly* 7 (4): 579–594.

Bredekamp, S. 1986. The reliability and validity of the Early Childhood Classroom Observation scale for accrediting early childhood programs. *Early Childhood Research Quarterly,* 1 (2): 103–118.

Bredekamp, S., ed. 1987. *Developmentally appropriate practice in early childhood programs serving children birth through age 8.* Washington, DC: National Association for the Education of Young Children.

Bredekamp, S. 1990. Setting and maintaining professional standards. In *Early childhood teacher preparation: Yearbook of early childhood education: Vol. 1,* eds. B. Spodek & O.N. Saracho. New York: Teachers College Press.

Bredekamp, S. 1996. Early childhood education. In *Handbook of research on teacher education,* eds. J. Sikula, T.J. Buttery, & E. Guyton, 323–347. New York: Macmillan.

Bredekamp, V.S. 1985. *The reliability of the instruments and procedures of a national accreditation system for early childhood programs.* Unpublished doctoral dissertation, University of Maryland, College Park, MD.

Bredekamp, S., & P. Apple. 1986. How early childhood programs get accredited: An analysis of accreditation decisions. *Young Children,* 42 (1): 34–38.

Bredekamp, S., & C. Copple, eds. 1997. *Developmentally appropriate practice in early childhood programs.* Rev. ed. Washington, DC: National Association for the Education of Young Children.

Bredekamp, S., & B. Willer, eds. 1996. *NAEYC accreditation: A decade of learning and the years ahead.* Washington, DC: National Association for the Education of Young Children.

Bronfenbrenner, U. 1979. *The ecology of human development.* Cambridge, MA: Harvard University Press.

Bryant, D., R. Clifford, & E. Peisner. 1989. *Best practices for beginners: Quality programs for kindergartners.* Chapel Hill, NC: Frank Porter Graham Child Development Center.

Burchinal, M., M.W. Lee, & C.T. Ramey. 1989. Type of day care and preschool intellectual development in disadvantaged children. *Child Development,* 60: 128–137.

Caldwell, B.M., & Freyer, M. 1982. Day care and early education. In B. Spodek (Ed.), *Handbook of research on early childhood education.* New York: Free Press.

Carew, J. 1980. Experience and development of intelligence in young children at home and in day care. Monographs of the Society for Research in Child Development, 45(6-7): Serial No. 187.

Center for Career Development in Early Care and Education at Wheelock College. 1995. Regulation and the prevention of harm. Boston, MA: Author.

Center for the Future on Children. 1995. Long-term outcomes of early childhood programs. The Future of Children, 5 (3). Los Altos, CA: The David and Lucile Packard Foundation.

Chandler, P. A. 1994. A place for me: Inbcluding children with special needs in early care and education settings. Washington, DC: NAEYC.

Children's Foundation. 1997. 1997 Child care licensing study. Washington, DC: Author.

Clarke-Stewart, K.A., & C. Gruber. 1984. Daycare forms and features. In Quality variations in daycare, ed. R.C. Ainslie, 35-62. New York: Praeger.

Clarke-Stewart, K.A. 1987. Predicting child development from child care forms and features: The Chicago Study. In Quality in child care: What does research tell us? ed. D.A. Phillips. Washington, DC: NAEYC.

Cost, Quality, and Child Outcomes Study Team. 1995. Cost, quality, and child outcomes in child care centers, public report. 2nd ed. Denver: Economics Department, University of Colorado at Denver.

DEC Task Force on Recommended Practices. 1993. DEC recommended practices: Indicators of quality in program for infants and young children with special needs and their families. Reston, VA: Author.

Derman-Sparks, L., & the A.B.C. Task Force. 1989. *Anti-bias curriculum.* Washington, DC: National Association for the Education of Young Children.

Epstein, A. 1993. Training for quality: Improving early childhood programs through systematic inservice training. Ypsilanti, MI:High/Scope Press.

Ethiel, N., ed. 1996. Reflections on NAEYC accreditation: Lessons learned and goals for the future. Washington, DC: NAEYC.Falender, C.A., & Mehrabian, A. 1979. The effects of day care on young children: An environmental psychology approach. *Journal of Psychology, 101*(2), 241-255.

Fiene, R. 1978. *Child development program evaluation: Weighing consensus of individual items: What are the major risks to children in day care centers?* Harrisburg, PA: Office of Children and Youth.

Francis, P., & P. Self. 1982. Imitative responsiveness of young children in day care and home settings: The importance of the child to caregiver ratio. Child Study Journal, 12: 119-126.Galinsky, E. 1990. The costs of not providing quality early childhood programs. In B. Willer (Ed.), *Reaching the full cost of quality.* Washington, DC: National Association for the Education of Young Children.

General Accounting Office. 1990, January. *Early childhood education: What are the costs of high-quality programs?* Briefing report to the Chairman, Committee on Labor and Human Resources, U.S. Senate.

Goelman, H. & A. Pence. 1987. Effects of child care, family and individual characteristics on children's language development: The Victoria day care research project. In Quality in child care: What does research tell us? ed. D.A. Phillips. Washington, DC: NAEYC.

Golden, M., & Rosenbluth, L. 1978. *The New York City Infant Day Care Study.* New York: Medical and Health Research Association of New York City.

Gormley, W.T., Jr. 1997. Regulatory enforcement: Accommodation and conflict in four states. *Public Administration Review,* 57 (4): 285-293.

Hadler, S., Erben, J., Francis, D., Webster, H., & Maynard, J. 1982. Risk factors for Hepatitis A in day care centers. *The Journal of Infectious Diseases, 145,* 255-261.

Hart, B., & T. Risley. 1995. *Meaningful differences in the everyday experiences of young American children.* Baltimore: Paul H. Brookes.

Hayes, C. D., J.L. Palmer, & M. J. Zaslow, eds. 1990. *Who cares for America's children? Child care policy in the 1990s.* Washington, DC: National Academy Press.

Helburn, S., ed. *Cost, quality and child outcomes in child care centers.* Technical report. Denver: University of Colorado at Denver.

Hofferth, S. 1989. The demand for and supply of child care in the United States. *Young Children, 44*(5), 28-33.

Holloway, S., & Reichhart-Erickson, M. 1988. The relationship of day care quality to children's free play behavior and social problem-solving skills. *Early Childhood Research Quarterly,* (1), 39-54.

Holloway, S., & Reichhart-Erickson, M. 1991. Child care quality, family structure, and maternal expectations: Relationship to preschool children's peer relations. *Journal of Applied Developmental Psychology.*

Howes, C. 1983. Caregiver behavior in center and family day care. *Journal of Applied Developmental Psychology, 4,* 99-107.

Howes, C. 1988. Relations between early child care and schooling. Developmental Psychology, 24:53-57.

Howes, C. 1990. Can the age of entry into child care and the quality of child care predict adjustment in kindergarten? *Developmental Psychology,* 26 (2): 292-303.

Howes, C., & Rubenstein, J. 1985. Determinants of toddlers' experience in day care: Age of entry and quality of setting. *Child Care Quarterly, 14,* 140-151.

Howes, C., E. Smith & E. Galinsky. 1995. *The Florida child care quality improvement study.* New York: Families and Work Institute.

Kagan, S.L. & N. Cohen. 1997. Not by chance: Creating an early care and education system. New Haven, CT: Yale Bush Center for Child Development and Social Policy.

Jorde-Bloom, P. 1989. *The Illinois directors study: A report to the Illinois Department of Children and Family Services.* Evanston, IL: Illinois Department of Children and Family Services.

Lazar, I., R. Darlington, H. Murray, J. Royce, & A. Snipper. 1982. Lasting effects of early education: A report from the Consortium for Longitudinal Studies. *Monographs of the Society for Research in Child Development,* 47: Serial No. 201.

Kaiser, B. & J.S. Rasminsky. 1995. *HIV/AIDS and child care: Fact book.* Ottawa, Canada: Canadian Child Care Federation and Health Canada.

Kendall, E.D. 1983. Child care and disease: What is the link? *Young Children,* 38(5), 68–77.

Kendrick, A.S., Kaufmann, R., & Messenger, K.P. 1995. *Healthy young children: A manual for programs.* Washington, DC: National Association for the Education of Young Children.

Kilmer, S. 1979. Infant-toddler group day care: A review of research. In L. Katz (Ed.), *Current topics in early childhood education: Vol. 2.* Norwood, NJ: Ablex.

McCartney, K. 1984. Effect of quality of day care environment on children's language development. *Developmental Psychology,* 20, 244–260.

McCartney, K., Scarr, S., Phillips, D., Grajek, S., & Schwarz, C. 1982. Environmental differences among day care centers and their effects on children's development. In E.F. Zigler & E.W. Gordon (Eds.), *Day care: Scientific and social policy issues.* Boston: Auburn House Publishing.

McCracken, J.B. 1993. Valuing diversity: The primary years. Washington, DC: NAEYC.

Meyers, W.J. 1977. *Staffing characteristics and child outcomes.* Washington, DC.: U.S. Department of Health, Education and Welfare. (ERIC Document Reproduction Service No. 156 341)

Morgan, G. 1996. Licensing and accreditation: How much quality is quality? In NAEYC accreditation: A decade of learning and the years ahead, eds. S. Bredekamp and B.A. Willer. Washington, DC: NAEYC.

NAEYC. 1996a. Guidelines for preparation of early childhood professionals. Washington, DC: Author.

NAEYC. 1996b. NAEYC Position statement: Responding to linguistic and cultural diversity–Recommendations for effective early childhood education. *Young Children,* 51(2), 4-12.

NAEYC. 1996c. NAEYC Position statement: Technology and young children–Ages three through eight. *Young Children,* 51(6), 11-16.

NAEYC. 1997. Position statement on public regulation of early childhood programs in centers and family child care homes.

National Resource Center for Health and Safety in Child Care. 1997. *Stepping stones to using Caring for ourchildren: National health and safety performance standards guidelines for out-of-home child care programs.* Denver: Author.

Newberger, J.J. 1997. New brain development research–A wonderful window of opportunity to build public support for early childhood education. *Young Children,* 52 (4): 4–9.

NICHD Early Child Care Research Network. 1997. Mother-Child interaction and cognitive outcomes associated with early child care: Results of the NICHD study. Paper presented at the 1997 Biennial Conference of the Society for Research in Child Development, Washington, DC.

Peisner, E.S., & M.R. Burchinal. 1997. Relations between preschool children's child-care experiences and concurrent development: The Cost, Quality, and Outcomes Study. *Merrill-Palmer Quarterly,* 43 (3):451–477.

Phillips, D. Ed.. 1987. *Quality in child care: What does research tell us?* Washington, DC: National Association for the Education of Young Children.

Phillips, D., C. Howes & M. Whitebook. 1992. The social policy context of child care: Effects on quality. American *Journal of Community Psychology,* 20 (1): 25–51.

Phillips, D., Scarr, S., & McCartney, K. 1987. Child care quality and children's social development. *Developmental Psychology, 23,* 537–543.

Phyfe-Perkins, E. 1980. Children's behavior in preschool settings–A review of research concerning the influence of the physical environment. In L. Katz (Ed.), *Current topics in early childhood education: Vol. III.* Norwood, NJ: Ablex.

Phyfe-Perkins, E. 1981. *Effects of teacher behavior on preschool children: A review of research.* Washington, DC.: National Institute of Education. (ERIC Document Reproduction Service No. 211 176)

Pickering, L., & Woodward, W. 1982. Diarrhea in day care centers. *Pediatric Infectious Disease, 1,* 47–52.

Prescott, E. 1981. Relations between physical setting and adult/child behavior in day care. In *Advances in early education and day care,* vol. 2, ed. S. Kilmer. Greenwich, CT: JAI Press.

Prescott, E., E. Jones, & S. Kritchevsky. 1972. *Day care as a child-rearing environment.* Washington, DC: National Association for the Education of Young Children.

Ruopp, R., J. Travers, F. Glantz, & C. Coelen. 1979. *Children at the center. Final report of the National Day Care Study,* vol. 1. Cambridge, MA: Abt Associates.

Schweinhart, L.J., H.V. Barnes, & D.P. Weikart with W.S. Barnett, & A.S. Epstein. 1993. Significant benefits: The High/Scope Perry Preschool study through age 27. High/Scope Educational Research Foundation Monograph No. 10. Ypsilanti, MI: High/Scope.

Shore, R. 1997. *Rethinking the brain: New insights into early development.* New York: Families and Work Institute.

Sibley, A., M. Abbott-Shim, & E. Galinsky. 1994. *Child care licensing: Georgia impact study.* Atlanta: Quality Assist, Inc.

Smith, P.K., & K.J. Connolly. 1980. *The ecology of preschool behaviour.* Cambridge, England: Cambridge University Press.

Snow, C.W., J.K. Teleki, & J.T. Reguero-de-Atiles. Child care center licensing standards in the United States: 1981 to 1995. *Young Children,* 51 (6): 36–41.

Teaching Tolerance. 1997. *Starting small: Teaching tolerance in preschool and the early grades.* Atlanta: Southern Poverty Law Center.

U.S. Department of Health, Education and Welfare. 1978. *Appropriateness of the federal interagency day care requirements.* Washington, DC.

U.S. Department of Health and Human Services. Maternal and Child Health Bureau. 1997. *Stepping stones to using Caring for Our Children.* Denver, CO: National Resource Center for Health and Safety in Child Care.

United States General Accounting Office. 1992. *Child care: States face difficulties enforcing standards and promoting quality.* GAO/HRD-93-13. Washington, DC: U.S. Government Printing Office.

Vandell, D., V. Henderson, & K. Wilson. 1988. A longitudinal study of children with day care experiences of varying quality. *Child Development,* 59, 1286–1292.

Vandell, D., & C. Powers. 1983. Day care quality and children's free play activities. *American Journal of Orthopsychiatry,* 53, 493–500.

Whitebook, M., C. Howes, & D.A. Phillips. 1989. *Who cares? Child care teachers and the quality of care in America. The National Child Care Staffing Study.* Oakland, CA: Child Care Employee Project.

Whitebook, M., L. Sakai, & C. Howes. 1997. *NAEYC accreditation as a strategy for improving child care quality, executive summary.* Washington, DC: National Center for the Early Childhood Workforce.

Willer, B., ed. 1994. A conceptual framework for early childhood professional development. In *The early childhood career lattice: perspectives on professional development,* eds. J. Johnson & J.B. McCracken. Washington, DC: National Association for the Education of Young Children.

Willer, B., ed. 1990. *Reaching the full cost of quality in early childhood programs.* Washington, DC: National Association for the Education of Young Children.

Willer, B., S.L. Hofferth, E.E. Kisker, P. Divine-Hawkins, E. Farquhar, & F.B. Glantz. 1991. *The demand and supply of child care in 1990.* Washington, DC: National Association for the Education of Young Children.

Wolery, M., & J. Wilbers, eds. 1994. *Including children with special needs in early childhood programs.* Washington, DC: National Association for the Education of Young Children.

Wright, J.L., & D.D. Shade, eds. 1994. *Young children: Active learners in a technological age.* Washington, DC: National Association for the Education of Young Children.

*Specified Criteria (in 1984 and 1991 editions) were reprinted with permission from the following sources (specific wording may be slightly changed in the 1998 edition):*

Auerbach, S. 1981. *Choosing child care: A guide for parents.* New York: Dutton. (Criterion A-8)

Community Coordinated Child Care in Dane County. 1975. *Dane County early childhood program standards.* Madison, WI. (Criteria A-11, B-20, C-4b, C-5, F-3b, G-2, G-9, H-10, H-21, H-22, I-3, and I-5)

Comprehensive Community Child Care of Cincinnati. n.d. *Child care performance standards.* Cincinnati, OH. (Criteria A-2, E-10, and I-3)

Missouri Department of Elementary and Secondary Education. 1983. *Standards and procedures for voluntary accreditation of early childhood programs: State of Missouri.* Jefferson City, MO. (Criteria A-1, A-3, A-5, A-6, B-2, C-1, E-5, E-7, and J-2)

Pizzo, P., & S. Aronson. 1976. *Concept paper on health and safety issues in day care.* Mimeo. Washington, DC.: U.S. Department of Health, Education and Welfare. (Criteria H-21, I-4, and I-5)

Texas Department of Human Resources. 1981. *Day care quality evaluation/validation criteria.* Austin, TX. (Criteria B-7, D-3, and D-4)

*The following instruments and sets of standards were also used as resources in the development of the 1984 and 1991 Criteria (upon which the 1998 Criteria are based):*

Action for Children. n.d. *Quality child care: What it is . . . and how to recognize it.* Columbus, OH.

American Academy of Pediatrics. 1980. *Standards for day care centers for infants and children.* Evanston, IL: Author.

American Home Economics Association. 1990. *Project home safe; children in self-care.* Alexandria, VA.

American Public Health Association, & American Academy of Pediatrics. 1991. *Caring for our children—National health and safety performance standards: Guidelines for out-of-home child care programs.* Washington, DC: Author.

Aronson, S., R. Fiene, & E. Douglas. 1978. *Child development program evaluation: Child care centers—Center instrument.* Harrisburg, PA: Bureau of Child Development Programs of the Pennsylvania Department of Public Welfare.

Bergstrom, J.M., & L. Joy. 1981. *Going to work? Choosing care for infants and toddlers.* Washington, DC: Day Care Council of America.

California State Department of Education. 1982. *Child development program quality review.* Sacramento, CA.

Child Care Coordinating and Referral Service. n.d. *How to choose a good child care center.* Ann Arbor, MI.

Child Day Care Association of St. Louis. 1982. *Standards for day care service.* St. Louis, MO.

Child Welfare League of America. 1973. *Standards for day care service.* New York.

Children's Home Society of Minnesota. n.d. *Day care programs quality control checklist.* Mimeo. St. Paul, MN.

Children's World. 1978. *Quality control checklist.* Evergreen, CO.

City of Madison Day Care Unit, Department of Human Resources. 1981. *Guidelines for certification/recertification.* Madison, WI.

Community Coordinated Child Care for Central Florida. n.d. *Program audit assessment tool.* Orlando, FL.

Comprehensive Community Child Care. 1979. *Selecting quality child care for parents of young children.* Cincinnati, OH.

Council for Early Childhood Professional Development. 1983. *CDA competency standards and assessment system.* Washington, DC: Author.

Council for Early Childhood Professional Recognition. 1984. *CDA competency standards for infant/toddler caregivers.* Washington, DC: Author.

Day Care Evaluation Task Force of the United Way of Greater Rochester. 1982. *Day care center evaluation process.* Rochester, NY.

Day Nursery Association of Cleveland Consultation Service. 1963. *Preschool center evaluation scale.* Cleveland, OH.

Endsley, R.C., & M.R. Bradbard. 1981. *Quality day care: A handbook of choices for parents and caregivers.* Englewood Cliffs, NJ: Prentice-Hall.

Familiae, Inc. 1981. *Standards for accreditation by Familiae, Inc.* Columbus, OH.

Fiene, R., E. Douglas, & K. Kroh. 1980. *Child development program evaluation: Center licensing instrument.* Harrisburg, PA: Pennsylvania Department of Public Welfare.

Gold, J.R., & J.M. Bergstrom. n.d. *Checking out child care: A parent guide.* Washington, DC: Day Care and Child Development Council of America.

Harms, T., & R.M. Clifford. 1980. *Early childhood environment rating scale.* New York: Teachers College Press.

Hartman, B. n.d. *The Hartman assessment.* Mimeo. Santa Ana, CA.

KCMC Child Development Corporation. n.d. *Agency assessment/self-assessment.* Mimeo. Kansas City, MO.

Kendrick, R., E. Williamson, & J. Yorck. n.d. *Finding quality child care.* Eugene, OR: Lane County 4-C Council.

Mattick, I., & F. Perkins. 1980. *Guidelines for observation and assessment: An approach to evaluating the learning environment of a day care center.* Mt. Ranier, MD: Gryphon House.

Missouri Department of Elementary and Secondary Education. n.d. *Choosing the right early education program for your child: A checklist for parents.* Jefferson City, MO.

National Association for the Education of Young Children. 1984. "How to plan and start a good early childhood program." Washington, DC: Author.

New Jersey State Department of Education. 1980. *Self-study process for preschool programs.* Trenton, NJ.

Oregon Association for the Education of Young Children. 1979. *Criteria for assessing early childhood programs.* Portland, OR.

Oregon Association for the Education of Young Children. 1981. *Assessment criteria checklist for criteria for assessing early childhood programs.* Portland, OR.

U.S. Department of Health, Education and Welfare. 1968. *Federal interagency day care requirements.* Washington, DC. (DHEW Publication No. 68-31-081)

U.S. Department of Health, Education and Welfare. 1973. *Guides for day care licensing.* Washington, DC. (DHEW Publication No. 73-1053)

U.S. Department of Health, Education and Welfare. March 19, 1980. *HEW day care regulations. Federal Register* 45 (55).

U.S. Department of Health and Human Services. 1981. *Comparative licensing study: Profiles of state day care licensing requirements,* Rev. ed., vols. 1–6. Washington, DC.

U.S. Department of Health and Human Services. 1981. *Head Start performance standards self-assessment/validation instrument.* Washington, DC. (DHHS Publication No. 81-31132)

U.S. Department of Health and Human Services. 1981. *Head Start program performance standards.* Washington, DC. (DHHS Publication No. 81-31131)

Upgrading Preschool Programs. n.d. *The book of UPP.* Mimeo. Phoenix, AZ.

Washington Child Development Council. 1980. *Child development center self-assessment.* Washington, DC.

# Index

# Information about NAEYC

## NAEYC is . . .

. . . a membership-supported organization of people committed to fostering the growth and development of children from birth through age 8. Membership is open to all who share a desire to serve and act on behalf of the needs and rights of young children.

## NAEYC provides . . .

. . . educational services and resources to adults who work with and for children, including

- *Young Children,* the journal for early childhood educators
- books, posters, brochures, and videos to expand your knowledge and commitment to young children, with topics including infants, curriculum, research, discipline, teacher education, and parent involvement
- an Annual Conference that brings people together from all over the country to share their expertise and advocate on behalf of children and families
- Week of the Young Child celebrations sponsored by NAEYC Affiliate Groups
- insurance plans for individuals and programs
- public affairs information and access to information available through NAEYC resources and communication systems for knowledgeable advocacy efforts at all levels of government and through the media
- the National Academy of Early Childhood Programs, a voluntary accreditation system for high-quality programs for children
- the National Institute for Early Childhood Professional Development, which offers resources and services to improve professional preparation and development of early childhood educators
- Young Children International to promote international communication and information exchanges

For free information about membership, publications, or other NAEYC services, visit NAEYC's Web site at http://www.naeyc.org

National Association for the Education of Young Children
1509 16th Street, N.W., Washington, DC 20036-1426
202-232-8777   800-424-2460   FAX 202-328-1846